EXPOSING SEVENTH-DAY ADVENTISM

D1595819

EXPOSING SEVENTH-DAY ADVENTISM

Russell Earl Kelly, Ph. D.

Author of
Should the Church Teach Tithing?
A Theologian's Conclusions about a Taboo Doctrine

iUniverse, Inc.
New York Lincoln Shanghai

Exposing Seventh-day Adventism

iUniverse books may be ordered through booksellers or by contacting:

iUniverse
2021 Pine Lake Road, Suite 100
Lincoln, NE 68512
www.iuniverse.com
1-800-Authors (1-800-288-4677)

ISBN-13: 978-0-595-36342-1 (pbk)
ISBN-13: 978-0-595-80779-6 (ebk)
ISBN-10: 0-595-36342-3 (pbk)
ISBN-10: 0-595-80779-8 (ebk)

Printed in the United States of America

SEP   2008

*This book is dedicated to
Robert K. Sanders
whose web site,
Truth or Fables.com,
is a beacon of truth for
present and former SDAs.*

*This book is also dedicated to
Jerry Gladson, Ph. D., my former
professor and pastor
and my eternal brother
in Christ.*

CONTENTS

CHAPTER ONE

MY TESTIMONY AND INTRODUCTION

I was born and grew up in a Southern Baptist family. As a small child, I accepted Christ as my Savior. Thanks to a devout Sunday School teacher, I early learned to love the Bible and study it daily.

With an insatiable curiosity to know what others believed, when I was 27 years old, in 1972, I began visiting other churches, studying their doctrines and listening to various radio programs in order to learn more about God's Word.

Southern Baptists are strong in promoting the Ten Commandments in schools and courthouses. They teach that the Ten Commandments are the eternal unchangeable moral law of God. When I encountered the Seventh-day Adventist's emphasis on the Ten Commandment Sabbath, I felt unable to remain a Baptist and still strive to obey all of God's commandments.

Seventh-day Adventism's strong presentation of the Ten Commandments drew me into a closer look. After (wrongly) convincing me that only the Old Covenant ceremonial sabbaths had been abolished, primarily for that reason I felt compelled to become a Seventh-day Adventist. I learned later that their best evangelistic strategy was to get one "hooked" on the Sabbath first and teach the other "testing truths" later. This strategy worked as well with me as it has with millions of others.

At that time, it seemed to me that the logic of Seventh-day Adventism outweighed that of Southern Baptists. This was my reasoning:

One: Since the Ten Commandments are supposedly the unchangeable eternal moral Law of God, as both churches claimed, then they must be observed!

Two: Since the Sabbath was part of the Ten Commandments, then it must not have been changed, because God does not change His own character.

Three: The Sabbath that was abolished in Colossians 2:16 must have only been the ceremonial Sabbath and not the seventh day of the Ten Commandments.

Four: If this were true, then I must become a Sabbath-keeper at all costs.

Five: If this were true, then all churches who insist that the Ten Commandments are still in force, should also become Sabbath-keepers.

Although convinced about the Sabbath, I felt quite uneasy about a lot of their other doctrines. There were several important questions I insisted on having a positive answer to before joining the Seventh-day Adventist church. I asked the evangelist the following questions:

One: Do Seventh-day Adventists believe that "the Bible only" was their standard for determining doctrine?

Two: Do they believe that salvation was "by grace through faith alone"?

Three: Do they believe that believers observed the Sabbath "because" they have been saved and not "in order to be saved"?

Four: Do they believe that sincere believers of other Christian faiths would also be saved even though they did not know or keep the Sabbath?

Five: Do Adventists think that Ellen G. White is not as equally inspired as the Bible?

I later realized that I had been deliberately lied to and betrayed by the evangelist whom I had grown to trust and respect. The way that my questions were answered satisfied me, but the "answers" did not really mean what I thought they meant. The evangelist assured me that the answers to all of my questions were definitely "yes." As I look back at that time I am still disturbed that a church that emphasizes the Ten Commandments so strongly, can so deliberately and consistently break one of them and lie to honest seekers in order to obtain converts.

Evangelists present themselves as "Bible only" advocates. The evangelist even showed me the statement on the back of the baptismal certificate that confirmed the "yes" answers.

As previously stated, I joined the Seventh-Day Adventist Church primarily in order to observe the Saturday-Sabbath. Concerning the other doctrines, I thought, if mainline Christianity were so wrong about the Sabbath, then, perhaps, they were also wrong about a lot of other doctrines.

My early studies revealed that the book, *Kingdom of the Cults*, by Martin and Barnhouse, did not call Seventh-day Adventism a false cult. The Adventist reply to Martin's book, *Questions on Doctrine*, seemed conservative and evangelical. It even de-emphasized Ellen G. White's influence in determining doctrine. By the time I realized that I had been deceived, I was supporting an evangelistic reform movement within the church which was eventually harshly suppressed. Many leading theologians and teachers were disciplined for their attempts to become more evangelical and more accepted by other denominations. A non-Adventist Australian, Geoffrey Paxton, published *The Shaking of Adventism*, which hopefully predicted that the "righteousness by faith" doctrine would reform Seventh-day Adventism. It did not.

Their honest answers to my questions should have been:

One: "The Bible only" means "the Bible and Ellen G. White" because the Bible teaches that the true church has a guiding prophet who is just as inspired as Bible prophets.

Two: "Salvation by grace through faith" does not mean salvation by grace through faith "alone." In actual practice, salvation is by grace, but retaining salvation is through obedience to such things as Sabbath-keeping and avoiding unclean foods. They go far beyond their early Methodist influence in denying the perseverance of the saints. Absolute assurance of salvation is not possible until Jesus "closes the books" on each person usually long after they die. When Jesus comes, active Sunday worshipers will not be saved. For an Adventist, EGW's statement settles the argument and further scholarly research cannot proceed. Other doctrines such as soul-sleep and no continuing hell-fire are stressed, but these lack the importance of Saturday worship and unclean foods.

Three: Sabbath-keeping is just as important as conversion. *The Great Controversy,* Ellen White's most promoted book (under many titles), repeatedly stresses that Saturday worship is THE SUBJECT around which all church history revolves. The book teaches that all other Christians will eventually hunt them down and try to kill SDAs because they refuse to worship on Sunday. They are told to stockpile food and be prepared to flee at a moment's notice when the U.S. government issues a death decree on all those who do not worship on Sunday. Such paranoia makes Sabbath-keeping a "work" and a "necessity" of salvation. The convoluted explanations of their theologians cannot explain away such clear teaching from Ellen White. Instead of defending the Bible, they spend much time discussing her inspiration and defending her interpretation.

Four: Non-Adventist churches are "Babylon the great, the harlot church." The "fall" of these churches began shortly after the spring of 1844 and they are still "falling" from truth. SDAs view other Christians as ignorant and deceived. Sunday-worshipers will receive the mark of the beast and be lost. SDAs are the only true church. Many Adventists teach that Christ will not return until the SDA Church produces 144,000 perfect sinless members who prove to the world that God's Law can be perfectly kept.

Five: Within the church family Ellen G. White is quoted as much as, if not more than, the Bible to prove their points. When pressed extremely hard for a straight answer, SDA leaders will often admit that their doctrines cannot disagree with the "inspired" interpretation of the Bible by Ellen G. White, their prophetess. They cannot move away from what she has plainly written about a subject. When their theologians do "bend," they do so over her often-contradictory statements, and not over her plain teachings. Regardless of what the Hebrew, Greek or their own Bible research might indicate, if it does not agree with Ellen G. White, then it is not truth and must be rejected. Real scholarship is severely limited.

Personally, I have concluded that Seventh-day Adventism is a false Christian cult. Two major things make them into a cult. First is their doctrine of inspiration. In Ellen G. White's writings, they have added other writings to the Bible and treat them with equal reverence and inspiration. Second is their exclusiveness. They teach that they are the only true church and totally disdain other Christians who do not observe the Sabbath and who will be lost if Jesus comes and finds them worshiping on Sunday. Their appointed committee that provided Martin and Barnhouse answers in the early 1960s was later ridiculed as not representing true Adventism. *Questions on Doctrine* is not recommended. The church is controlled by those who elevate Ellen G. White to the Bible level.

SDA basic doctrine has not changed and will not change because of the stagnating effect of Ellen G. White. Recent visits to the Adventist college from which I graduated were very discouraging because of how Ellen White's writings reign even in Bible classes. Their own Bible version, Sabbath School literature and in-house literature still support almost every paragraph with EGW quotations. To me at least, they have retreated farther into a cultic shell and away from true Christianity.

Yet today they are sharing church buildings and hospitals with their archenemies, the "false Babylonians." Their ministers are joining more and more ministerial associations and are pretending to be just another part of the evangelical group. They are sitting on both sides of the fence in order to proselytize other churches.

It is my hope and prayer that this book will rescue many of my sincere God-fearing friends from the fear and uncertainty of the Seventh-day Adventist Church and lead them to the assurance of resting in God's true Sabbath, the righteousness of Jesus Christ.

I also hope that Protestant evangelical ministers and Roman Catholic priests will begin questioning Adventist ministers who pretend to be so "normal," yet inwardly fear and despise other clergy at ministerial meetings.

CHAPTER TWO

SEVENTH-DAY ADVENTISM IN A NUTSHELL
A Summary of What Seventh-day Adventists Teach

The Disappointment: It is October 23, 1844 and Jesus had not returned yesterday as William Miller and the other Adventists had predicted. These Sunday-worshiping, pork-eating, immortal-soul believing Adventists had suffered their second wrong guess in a year. Most churches had laughed at them for date-setting and Miller had called the other churches "fallen Babylon." Now most of the Adventists, including William Miller, had given up trying to guess the date of Jesus' return and had decided to go back to their former churches.

The Insistent: A small group refused to admit that they had been wrong about October 22, 1844. They asked themselves, "What about Daniel 8:14? 'Unto two thousand and three hundred days, then shall the sanctuary be cleansed'? Something must have been wrong with Miller's interpretation." They re-affirmed that the 2300 "days" were 2300 prophetic "years" and that Miller's calculations ending in 1844 were absolutely correct. Next they re-affirmed that Miller's connection of 'cleansed' to the Day of Atonement on October 22 that year was also certainly correct.

The Heavenly Sanctuary: "Where did we go wrong?," they asked themselves. To their great delight, a fellow believer told the group that Christ was not coming back yet but had only moved from the Holy Place in the heavenly sanctuary into the Most Holy Place in the heavenly sanctuary just as the high priest had done in Leviticus 16 on the Day of Atonement. This small group then decided that Miller had been wrong about the 'sanctuary' in Daniel 8:14—it was not the earth itself, but God's dwelling place in heaven!

The Investigative Judgment and Annihilationism: God soon began sending the "truth" and one doctrine after another changed. If Christ had only begun to "investigate" the records of professed believers in 1844, then the doctrine of the "immortality of the soul" must be wrong because nobody could be in heaven yet! Therefore, they decided that, at death, the soul ceases to exist until the resurrection. Thus, the doctrine of the immortality of the soul must be wrong.

The Sabbath: When a Seventh-day Baptist told them about the Sabbath, a young Adventist named Ellen (White) confirmed the new "truth" with visions. They concluded that God had given all mankind every seventh day, every Saturday, as a memorial that He was the Creator and that the creation seventh-day had not been lost on the calendar since Adam. They had become Seventh-day Adventists.

The Spirit of Prophecy: They eventually interpreted Revelation 12:17 and 19:10 as descriptions of themselves as the only true last-day remnant church which kept all ten of the commandments and also had the Spirit of Prophecy through Ellen White. This meant that all other churches which did not agree with them were now "fallen Babylon." Ellen White guided the church as a prophetess until her death in 1915. She wrote many books and also taught SDAs to observe the old covenant food laws and strict dress codes.

Prophecy: Roman Catholicism was blamed for changing the Sabbath to Sunday and was described as the "little horn" of Daniel and the Babylonian "beast" of Revelation. Other Sunday-worshiping churches were declared to be the "daughters of fallen Babylon." The "1260 years," "42 months," and "3 ½ times" of Daniel and Revelation were limited to A. D. 538 to 1798 which ended when Roman Catholicism was wounded to death in France after it had killed the "two witnesses", the Old and New Testaments.

The United States of America: All three will be revived just before Christ returns. The Seventh-day Adventist church will be God's instrument in the revival of the Old and New Testaments by teaching the truth in the last days. The United States government will restore the Roman Catholic Church in the last days when its Sunday-worshiping Protestants will enforce national Sunday-observance laws.

The Great Controversy: God and Satan are locked in a "great controversy." Satan has charged God with unrighteousness because His Law cannot be obeyed. God will prove that He is righteous by demonstrating that 144,000 Seventh-day Adventists will stand before Him without a mediator immediately before Jesus returns.

The Last Days: As the second coming approaches, Jesus will finish investigating the records of all those who professed faith since Adam and will make His final decision to determine who is qualified to be resurrected. He will close the books in the Most Holy Place, will stop mediating as a priest and will be in the process of returning. In the meantime, the United States government, in alliance with the Roman Catholic Church and apostate Protestants, will set a date for Seventh-day Adventists to be put to death because the last day devastation is blamed on them. At the last moment, Jesus will return, destroy all non-Seventh-day Adventists who have the mark of the beast (Sunday worshipers) and take his remnant church to heaven.

The Millennium: For 1000 years the earth will lay desolate during its Sabbath millennial rest. At the end of the 1000 years, all of the wicked dead will be re-created for resurrection and then judged before finally being cast into the lake of fire to be soon burned out of existence.

And the Seventh-day Adventists will live happily ever after.

CHAPTER THREE

BIBLICAL INSPIRATION AND ELLEN G. WHITE

1976: "That the Holy Scriptures of the Old and New Testament were given by inspiration of God, and contain *an all-sufficient* revelation of His will to men, *and are the only unerring rule of faith and practice." Seventh-day Adventist Church Manual*, 1976, page 32.

—compare with—

1980: "The Holy Scriptures, Old and New Testaments, are the written Word of God, given by *divine inspiration through holy men* of God who spoke and wrote as they were moved by the Holy Spirit. In this Word God has committed *to man the knowledge necessary for salvation. The Holy Scriptures are the* infallible revelation of His will. They are the standard of character, the test of experience, the authoritative revelator of doctrines, and the trustworthy record of God's acts in history." From the *27 Fundamental Beliefs of Seventh-day Adventists.*

1989: "Seventh-day Adventists recognize in Ellen G. White an authority in doctrine and life that is *second only to that of the Scriptures....*The Seventh-day Adventist church holds the writings of Ellen G. White in the *highest regard as a source of doctrinal understanding....*Some Adventists have inferred that in Dr. [Desmond] Ford's view Ellen White's authority does not extend to doctrinal issues. On this point the Seventh-day Adventist position is that a prophet's authority cannot justifiably be limited in that way." *Doctrine of the Sanctuary*, Biblical Research Committee, 1989, 223-224.

The first two statements above would be accepted in almost any conservative Christian church. They read very well. They appear to place Seventh-day Adventism securely within the boundary of orthodox Christianity and away from false Christian cultism.

However, when comparing the two statements, an obvious, not-even-very-subtle, change has taken place. SDAs have *deleted* their older statement that the

Scriptures are the *"all-sufficient"* revelation of God's will. They have also *deleted* their older statement that the Scriptures are *"the only unerring rule of faith and practice."* Next, they have *added* the statement that the Scriptures are given by *"divine inspiration through holy men."*

There is a subtle, yet obvious, reason for these changes! And that reason is Ellen G. White, the prophetess of the Seventh-day Adventist Church who died in 1915. When SDAs state that the Scriptures were **"given by** *divine inspiration through holy men* **of God"** and are *"the* **infallible revelation of His will"** (1980 statement), they include Ellen G. White because they hold her writings in the *"highest regard as a source of doctrinal understanding"* and because **"a prophet's authority cannot justifiably be limited"** to exclude doctrine (1989 statement). They regard her as a full-fledged prophet on equal standing with biblical prophets. The Biblical Research Committee represents the unofficial highest level of leadership within the church. When it rebutted Dr. Ford, it was forced to admit that Ellen White's prophetic authority extended to doctrinal correctness.

"One of the gifts of the Holy spirit is prophecy. This gift is an identifying mark of the remnant church and was manifested in the ministry of Ellen G. White. As the Lord's messenger, her writings are *a continuing and authoritative source of truth which provide for the church comfort, guidance, instruction and correction.* **They also make clear that the Bible is the standard by which all teaching and experience must be tested"** [#17 of the *27 Fundamental Beliefs of Seventh-day Adventists*].

The above statement sounds like First Timothy 3:15-17. SDAs try to have it both ways as is clear from the last sentence of the statement. When Ellen White is quoted, she has a rubber nose and this helps Adventist leaders who take a Roman Catholic approach which discourages personal interpretation. They often seem to convey the idea that they are the only ones qualified to properly interpret her writings. When non-Adventists and ex-Adventists quote Ellen White, their quotations are usually passed off as "out of context."

Ellen G. White has a rubber nose inside and outside of Seventh-day Adventism. She has written so much that statements can be found from her that can be made to either support or oppose many positions. This is especially true about her level of inspiration. Read her following quotations and decide for yourself whether or not she considered herself on the same level with the prophets of God's Word.

The following quotations are from Ellen White's own words from the *Introduction* to her book, *The Great Controversy*, the most prolific book distributed for free at evangelistic meetings.

GC v "God has communicated with men by his Spirit, and divine light has been imparted to the world by revelations to His chosen servants." (Quotes 2 Peter 1:21)
GC vii "Yet the fact that God has revealed His will to men through His word, has not rendered needless the continued presence and guiding of the Holy Spirit."
GC vii "Great reproach has been cast on the work of the Holy Spirit by the errors of a class that, claiming its enlightenment, profess to have no further need of guidance from the Word of God."
GC viii "In harmony with the word of God, His Spirit was to continue its work throughout the period of the gospel dispensation....And mention is made of prophets in different ages of whose utterances nothing is recorded. *In like manner*, after the close of the canon of the Scripture, the Holy Spirit was still to continue its work to enlighten, warn and comfort the children of God."
GC ix [quotes prophets Paul, Peter and Joel] "In all ages the wrath of Satan has been manifested against the church of Christ; and God has bestowed His grace and Spirit upon His people to strengthen them to stand against the power of the evil one."
***GC x *"At this time the special endowment of divine grace and power is not less needful to the church than in apostolic days."*
***GC x "Through the *illumination* of the Holy Spirit, the scenes of the long-continued conflict between good and evil have been *opened to the writer of these pages*. From time to time I have been permitted to behold...."
***GC xi "As the Spirit of God has *opened to my mind the great truths of His word, and the scenes* of the past and the future, *I have been bidden to make known to others that which has been revealed*—to trace the history of the controversy in past ages, and especially so to present it as to shed a light on the fast-approaching struggle of the future."
GC xi "Regarding them [her collection of history] in the light of God's word, and by the illumination of His Spirit, we may see unveiled....."

In this introduction Ellen G. White carefully and slowly eased into her declaration that she is an essential last-day prophet. She wrote that God had illuminated her and opened her eyes with scenes of the past and future. God has instructed her to present the content of this book, *The Great Controversy* (with scores of quotations from non-SDA church historians).

Seventh-day Adventists believe that Ellen G. White was inspired by God in exactly the same way that the biblical prophets were inspired, and, as such, her writings are exactly as authoritative and unerring as those of God's Word. In their reasoning, since the Bible authorizes the continuing prophetic gift, especially in the last-day, or "remnant" church, then that is why they added that the Word was given by *"divine inspiration through holy men."* However, they do not normally admit this to new converts, such as myself or to the inquisitive.

Isa. 8:20 To the law and to the testimony: if they speak not according to this word, it is because there is no light in them.

Rev. 12:17 And the dragon was wroth with the woman, and went to make war with the remnant of her seed, which keep the commandments of God and have *the testimony of Jesus Christ.*

Rev 19:10 And I fell at his feet to worship him. And he said unto me, See thou do it not: I am your fellow servant, and of your brethren that have the testimony of Jesus: worship God: for the testimony of Jesus is the *spirit of prophecy.*

SDAs call Ellen G. White's writings "the Spirit of Prophecy." The three texts, Revelation 12:17; 19:10 and Isaiah 8:20 are quoted by SDAs to prove that the last-day remnant church must also have last-day prophetic guidance. However, there are several problems caused by using these texts.

First: Isaiah 8:20 is only a test for Old Covenant prophets because it refers to all of the Mosaic Law, or Old Covenant. However, like most Christians, even SDAs teach that the ceremonial worship statutes (ordinances) and civil legal judgments are no longer valid for their church. Therefore, they disqualify themselves by rejecting two thirds of the entire Law. Yet SDAs use this as a proof text to demonstrate that EGW is a true prophet—and her writings are strongly defended as being essentially without error. However, they will not give audience to those who desire to point out her many errors!

Second: "Keep the commandments" in Revelation 12:17 does not refer to the Ten Commandments, but to love and obedience to what Jesus taught specifically for His New Covenant church. The Apostle John did not use "commandments" in the narrow sense of "Ten Commandments" (Compare John 14:21-23; 15:10-12; 1 Jn. 2:3-10; 3:22-24; 2 Jn. 6:5-6.)

Third: Many believe that 12:17 refers, not to the church, but to the believing Israelites of chapters 7 and 14. The "remnant" is the remnant of restored national Israel.

Fourth: The phrase "testimony of Jesus" is also applied by SDAs as an unofficial title for Ellen G. White. Many of her writings are called "Testimonies." However, it merely refers to the fact that the biblical prophets "testified," or "gave witness," to Jesus Christ.

Fifth: If it is essential for the last-day remnant church to have (to quote their own article #17) "*a continuing and authoritative source of truth,*" then why has there not been a successor to Ellen G. White? She died in 1915 and has not been replaced. In fact, the infamous late David Koresh of the *Branch Davidian, Seventh-day Adventists* (an unrecognized offshoot) claimed to be the legitimate successor to Ellen G. White. Will future claimants be tested for authenticity?

Rev. 13:18 Here is wisdom. Let him that has understanding count the number of the beast: for it is the number of a man; and his number is six hundred threescore and six.

Finally, Seventh-day Adventists point out that the Latin inscription on the pope's tiara (vicar of the son of God) totals 666 when added vertically in Latin (although it does not if correctly added horizontally). Yet, to their shock, the name, Ellen Gould White, also totals 666 when added vertically! See Revelation 13:18. Note that in Roman Numerals: "I" is 1; "U" or "V" is 5; "X" is 10; "L" is 50; "C" is 100; "D" is 500; "W" is "double-U," or "V V" which is 10.

V	5	E		
I	1	L	50	
C	100	L	50	
A		E		
R		N		
I	1			
V	5	G		
S		O		
		V	5 (In Latin)	
F		L	50	
I	1	D	500	
L	50			
L	50	VV	10 (double V)	
I	1	H		
I	1	I	1	
		T		
D	500	E		
E		TOTAL 666		
I	1			
TOTAL 666				

A key element in false Christian cults is additional writings on the same level with God's Word. Either the Bible contains everything necessary for salvation, sanctification and the growth of God's church, or it does not. By their treatment of Ellen G. White, Seventh-day Adventists declare to the entire world that God's Word is not enough. Their in-house literature usually makes a statement, follows it by a Bible text, and then follows that with a confirmation by EGW.

CHAPTER FOUR

DANIEL 8:8-14; LAUNCHING SEVENTH-DAY ADVENTISM

Seventh-day Adventists teach that, on October 22, 1844, at the end of the 2300 "prophetic" year-days of Daniel 8:14 (which began in 457 B. C.), Jesus moved from the Holy Place into the Most Holy Place of the heavenly sanctuary to begin the final phase of His ministry of Investigative Judgment prefigured by the cleansing of the sanctuary on the Day of Atonement from Leviticus 16. This final ministry involves researching the books of heaven, beginning at Adam, in order to determine who among professed believers will qualify to be re-created by resurrection at Christ's return. When this Investigative Judgment is complete, Jesus will return to earth.

The Investigative Judgment is the only Seventh-day Adventist doctrine which cannot be found elsewhere. It is the foundational doctrine of Seventh-day Adventism which gives meaning to its very existence. This doctrine preceded all of its other distinct doctrines such as the Sabbath and health reform. It also forced SDAs to adopt their doctrine of conditional immortality. Otherwise, Seventh-day Adventists would merely be a mixture of Methodists (Arminian), Seventh-day (Sabbath-keeping) Baptists (adult immersion) and health reformers with a Jehovah Witness-like approach to the non-immortality of the soul.

HOW SEVENTH-DAY ADVENTISM BEGAN

Dan. 8:14 "Unto two thousand and three hundred days; then shall the sanctuary be cleansed." KJV

Dan. 8:14 "In 164 B. C., after 2300 evening-mornings, the Hebrew sanctuary will be restored after being defiled in 171 B. C. (or 167 B. C.)." Interpretation accepted today by most denominations.

Dan. 8:14 "In 1843, 1810 years from A. D. 33, Jesus will return and destroy [cleanse] the earth [the sanctuary] by fire." William Miller's and early Adventists' most prominent interpretation.

Dan. 8:14 "In 1844, 2300 years from 457 B. C., Jesus entered the Most Holy Place in the heavenly sanctuary and began investigating the records of all professed believers to determine who will be recreated—a ministry which removes [cleanses] the defilement which their sins caused to the heavenly sanctuary." SDA Investigative Judgment.

S. D. A. PRESUPPOSITIONS OF DANIEL 8:14

Seventh-day Adventists have chosen the most controversial verse in the most controversial book of the entire Old Testament to find a reason for their existence. The book of Daniel is listed among the *Writings* and is not even among the *Minor Prophets* in the Hebrew canon. The author and date of Daniel are among the most challenged by liberal scholars who attempt to disprove that Daniel is even prophecy at all instead of only being recent history. There is disagreement even among conservative scholars about the fourth beast of Daniel 7 and the little horn of Daniel 8. Theories range from Persia, the Maccabeans, pagan Rome, papal Rome and a future Antichrist. Daniel 8:14 has been infamous for radical interpretation throughout history.

In order for the Seventh-day Adventist explanation of Daniel 8:14 to be correct, **all** of the following presuppositions must be correct. If any of these presuppositions are wrong, then the entire argument must be discarded as false.

One: The SDA explanation of 8:8-12 correctly leads up to 8:14.
Two: The SDA explanation of 8:14 correctly answers the question of 8:13.
Three: The correct sanctuary of 8:14 can only be the one in heaven.
Four: The 2300 days of 8:14 could only be prophetic years.
Five: The 2300 days of 8:14 could only began in 457 B. C.
Six: The 2300 days of 8:14 could only end in 1844.
Seven: The "cleansing" of 8:14 only refers to the Day of Atonement.
Eight: The earthly sanctuary was defiled by forgiven sins of worshipers.
Nine: The Day of Atonement pattern was not fulfilled at Calvary.
Ten: The 1844 Day of Atonement is an exact pattern-fulfillment event.
Eleven: The heavenly sanctuary is still being defiled by forgiven sins of worshipers.
Twelve: The Day of Atonement is an investigation of professed believers to determine who will be re-created from the annihilation of death.

DANIEL 8:8-12

Seventh-day Adventists gradually built their Investigative Judgment doctrine upon their unique interpretation of Daniel 8:14. Although 8:8-13 are never quoted by Ellen G. White in *The Great Controversy*, the S. D. A. *Bible*

Commentary and the *S. D. A. Bible Dictionary* attempt to place their interpretation of Daniel 8:14 upon the essential contextual link of Daniel 8:8-13. This makes 8:8 to 8:13 extremely important foundational texts which absolutely must be interpreted correctly. Again, it is important to realize that these links leading to 8:14 must all be correct in order for SDAs to even offer their interpretation of 8:14. Therefore, if 8:8 to 8:13 fail to withstand historical, contextual and theological challenges, then the SDA use of 8:14 should be rendered incorrect.

Dan. 8:8 Therefore the *he goat waxed very great;* and when he was strong, the *great horn* was broken; and for it came up *four notable ones* toward the four winds of heaven.

> **Dan. 8:21 And the rough goat is the king of Greece; and the great horn that is between his eyes is the first king.**
>
> **Dan. 8:22 Now that being broken, whereas four stood up for it, four kingdoms shall stand up out of the nation, but not in his power.**
>
> **Dan. 11:3 And a mighty king shall stand up, that shall rule with great dominion, and do according to his will.**
>
> **Dan. 11:4 And when he shall stand up, his kingdom shall be broken and shall be divided toward the four winds of heaven...**

8:8—SDAs teach that Daniel 8:8 does not refer to the *four Greek kingdoms* that replaced Alexander the Great's empire. It only refers to the *four directions of the wind,* thus allowing 8:9 to refer to pagan Rome.

Historically, the great horn of 8:8 was replaced by four other Greek horns. Most commentaries, including SDAs, agree (1) that the "he goat" was Greece, (2) that the leopard in 7:6 with four heads and four wings was also Greece and (3) that the "great horn" of 8:8 was Alexander the Great. The disagreement is over "for it," "four notable ones" and "four winds."

Most commentaries teach that the emphasis is (comparable to 7:6) to the "four horns" into which the Greek empire was split. These four horns of 8:8 and 8:22, like the four heads of 7:6, were "in place of" the broken horn. When Alexander died, his Greek kingdom was split into the four Greek-ruled kingdoms of Greece, Macedonia, Syria and Egypt.

The Greek third kingdom of brass in 2:39 is the leopard of 7:6 with four wings and four heads and the he-goat of 8:8 with four notable horns towards the four winds—out of which came forth the little Greek horn. This division is also seen in Daniel 8:22 and 11:4. The Roman fourth kingdom of iron in 2:40 is the "dreadful and exceedingly strong" beast of 7:7-8 with iron teeth and ten horns—out of which came forth a different little Roman horn.

Although all conquerors have many similar characteristics, the little horn from 7:7-8 is not the same as the little horn of 8:9-12. Since Greece did not conquer Rome or the Italian peninsula, it is evident that Rome did not come "out of one of the four horns." The little horn of chapter 8 is connected to the third kingdom of chapters 2 and 7 by "four"—compare the "four wings and four heads" of the leopard in 7:6 with the "four horns" and "four winds" of the he-goat in 8:8 and 11:4. However, on the other hand, the little horn of 7:24 is connected to the fourth kingdom of both 2:40-44 and 7:19-20 by "iron" and "ten."

SDAs disagree! They interpret the little horn as an entirely different kingdom (Rome) when the text does not introduce another animal to replace the "he goat"! Their interpretation is inconsistent with the new-animal-to-new-kingdom pattern followed in chapters seven and eight. By ignoring the connection between 8:8 and 11:4, they also deny the greatly detailed struggle between Greek-ruled Egypt and Greek-ruled Syria in Daniel 11. However, if SDAs were to admit error at this first foundation text of 8:8, then they would have to admit that everything else they built upon 8:8 (including 8:14) is also wrong!

Dan. 8:9 And out of one of them came forth *a little horn* **which** *waxed exceeding great* **toward the south, and toward the east, and toward the pleasant land.**

8:9—SDAs teach that the little horn of 8:9 is pagan Rome which came "out of one of the four *winds*" (or directions) rather than "out of one of the four *horns.*" Again, this is because pagan Rome did not emerge from any of the four Greek kingdoms which replaced Alexander.

Historically, the little horn of 8:9 was Antiochus IV (Epiphanes) who emerged from the Seleucid Greeks of Syria. Most commentaries say that "out of one of *them*" means "out of one of the four *horns.*" Although 11:4 equates "4 horns" with the "4 winds," it is not in the context of the little horn.

The SDA argument is that pagan Rome was "exceeding great" in all directions of the compass while Antiochus IV eventually failed. However, *the biblical perspective is from the viewpoint of the Jews.* Although Alexander was historically "greater" than the Seleucids, the Seleucids were "exceeding great" in imposing Greek religion and thought on the Jews. Antiochus IV was also "exceeding great" in causing Temple worship to cease for the first time since 515 B. C. when he erected an altar to Zeus inside it in 167 B.C. Again, if the SDA interpretation is wrong at this second foundational text of 8:9, then everything else that follows is also wrong.

Dan. 8:10 And it waxed great even to the *host* of heaven and it cast down some of the host and of the stars to the ground and stamped upon them.

8:10—SDAs teach that the "host" of 8:10 are Christians.

Historically, the "host" of 8:10 were Jews. "Host" is found in 8:10, 11, 12 and 13. Most commentaries interpret "host" and "stars" to refer to the Jewish people and their leaders who were persecuted by Antiochus IV between 171-164 B. C. However, SDAs interpret "host" as Christians persecuted by, first, the Roman Empire, and, second, by the Roman Catholic Church.

Dan. 8:11 Yea, he magnified himself even to *the prince of the host*, and by him the *daily sacrifice* was taken away, and the place of his sanctuary was cast down.

8:11—SDAs teach that the "prince" of 8:11 is Jesus Christ. Therefore, from 8:8 to 8:11, the little horn is pagan Rome who crucified Christ, "the prince," and pagan Rome who caused the "daily sacrifice" to cease when the Jerusalem Temple was destroyed in A. D. 70.

Historically, the "prince" of 8:11 was the high priest, Onias III. Antiochus IV removed this Jewish high priest and caused the literal daily sacrifices of the Jewish Temple in Jerusalem to cease when he defiled the Temple by offering a pig on its great altar on December 25, 167 B.C.—thus inciting a successful war of independence.

The Seventh-Day Adventist Bible Dictionary, 1960, "little horn," p 656. "The little horn of chapter eight 'takes away the daily sacrifice' and casts down the 'place of his sanctuary' (v11), but after a period called 'two thousand and three hundred days' (v14) the sanctuary is 'cleansed' (KJV), or 'restored to its rightful state' (RSV)."

The above statement is really confusing. SDAs teach that both the "daily sacrifice" and the "sanctuary" in verse 11 refer to the Jerusalem Temple which was defiled by pagan Rome in A. D. 70. They then *switch* to teaching that a restoration of the "daily" in 8:14 refers to Christ's ministry in the heavenly Temple since 1844 to cleanse it from defilement made by Christians (and not the little horn). Actually, the "daily sacrifice" in Daniel always refers to the Jerusalem Temple in Daniel.

SDAs conclude that the "daily sacrifice" in 8:11 must be associated with its restoration on the Day of Atonement. This interpretation is forced from working backwards from their peculiar interpretation of 8:14. Otherwise, there is absolutely no connection between the SDA "daily" implications of 8:11, 13 and 14. (See the discussion on "daily.") While SDAs disqualify Antiochus IV because he did not literally "cast down the sanctuary," neither is there a literal casting down in their own extended explanations either by the papal confessional or by the sins of believers.

Dan. 8:12 And an host was given him against the *daily sacrifice* by reason of transgression, and it cast down the truth to the ground; and it practiced, and prospered.

> Dan. 8:23 And in the latter time of their kingdom, when the transgressors are come to the full, a king of fierce countenance, and understanding dark sentences, shall stand up.

The Seventh-day Adventist Bible Dictionary, Review and Herald, 1960, "*abomination,*" p7. "The two systems are mutually exclusive, since the setting up of the abomination of desolation is accompanied by the trampling down of the sanctuary (8:13) and by the taking away of the 'daily' (11:31; 12:11). This substitute system of worship is abominable, or detestable, because it stands in implacable opposition to that of the true God. *It desolates the sanctuary by replacing its services with its own.* This turn of events naturally appalls worshipers of the true God. In the symbolic prophecy of Daniel 8, it is the power represented by the "little horn" that terminates the worship of the true God in His sanctuary and institutes a false system of worship in its place (vs 9-12). At the end of "two thousand and three hundred days" the sanctuary was to be cleansed (v 14) by the restoration of the worship of the true God." [SDAs Referring to Roman Catholicism]

8:12—In a giant leap SDAs teach that Daniel 8:12 describes the Roman Catholic Church which defiled the heavenly sanctuary by replacing its ministry with their confessional and other doctrines. The above statement from their *Dictionary* makes no sense. In verse 12 the **little horn** of the papacy sets up the abomination of desolation, tramples down the sanctuary and takes away the daily. But in verse 14 the desolation of the heavenly sanctuary is caused by the confessed, forgiven and atoned sins of the *saints*. It is clearly contradictory to teach that *both* **the little horn** *and* **the saints** desolated the heavenly sanctuary. Also, in other places SDAs teach that the "daily" ministry of Christ in the Holy Place of the heavenly sanctuary has *never* ceased.

Historically, Daniel 8:12 describes the desolation of the Jerusalem Temple by Antiochus IV of the Greek Syrian Seleucids. Its cleansing is recorded in Maccabees and was not a Day of Atonement-type cleansing.

Dan. 8:13 *How long* shall be the vision concerning the *daily sacrifice*, and the *transgression of desolation*, to give both the *sanctuary* and the *host* to be trodden under foot? KJV

Dan. 8:13 "How long will it take for the vision to be fulfilled—the vision concerning the daily sacrifice, the rebellion that causes desolation, and the surrender of the sanctuary and of the host that will be trampled underfoot?" NIV

Dan. 8:13 "How long will the vision about the regular sacrifice apply, while the transgression causes horror, so as to allow both the holy place and the host to be trampled?" NASU

8:13—It will be demonstrated that SDAs teach that the questions asked in 8:13 and answered in 8:14 have no relevance to the immediate context of 8:8 to 8:12.

SDAs teach that the "answer" given in 8:14 to the "question" of 8:13 is that, "In 1844, Jesus opened the books of heaven which contain the names and deeds of all who professed faith and *began* judging, or investigating, only professed believers to determine who is worthy of being re-created from annihilation."

First: Instead of answering *how long* until the *"vision"* of 8:8-12 would *end,* the SDA answer tells *when* Christ would only *begin* to cleanse the heavenly sanctuary in 1844.

Second: Instead of answering *when* the *"daily sacrifice"* from 8:11 would *be restored,* the SDA answer tells when the final phase of Christ's ministry will *begin* in heaven (although He has continued a daily ministry in heaven since His ascension). It has still not been restored.

Third: Instead of answering *when* the *"little horn"* of 8:10-12 will stop persecuting the saints, the SDA answer tells us when Christ will *begin* blotting out the sins of the *saints* which have caused the desolation of the heavenly sanctuary since Adam's first sin. Instead of being a judgment of the little horn, the Investigative Judgment is a judgment of professed believers.

Fourth: Instead of answering *when* the *"sanctuary"* will finally be cleansed from defilement by the little horn in 8:10-12, the SDA answer tells us when Christ will move from one room into another in the heavenly sanctuary and finally *begin* cleansing the Most Holy Place. Again, instead of cleansing the sanctuary from its desolation by the little horn, it requires cleansing from the sins of God's own people.

Fifth: Instead of answering *when* the *"host,"* believers, will stop being persecuted by the little horn, the SDA answer blames the desolation of the heavenly sanctuary on the host.

Therefore, incredible as it sounds, one must conclude that the SDA "answer" given in 8:14 to the "question" asked in 8:13 has absolutely nothing to do with its context in 8:8-12!! Even more incredible, the *S. D. A. Bible Dictionary,* "abomination" (see above), does not even mention the investigation of the sins of the saints in its explanation.

Historically, the answer to the question asked in 8:13 provided in most commentaries is very simply that, "After 2300 literal sacrificial days, in 164 B. C., the Jews won their civil war against Antiochus IV, restored the sanctuary and gained their independence for the first time since 586 B. C." What a tremendously important historical event! The Jewish Temple in Jerusalem was "cleansed," "restored," or "rededicated" to resume offering the "daily sacrifices." Today this restoration is still celebrated by the Jewish holy day of *Hanukkah,* meaning "dedication." Also, this was a normal cleansing and not a special Day of Atonement-type cleansing!

CHAPTER FIVE

THE SANCTUARY IN DANIEL

Dan. 8:14 Unto two thousand and three hundred days; then shall the sanctuary be cleansed. KJV

Dan. 8:14 "For 2,300 evenings and mornings; then the holy place will be properly restored." NASU

Dan. 8:14 "For two thousand and three hundred evenings and mornings; then the sanctuary shall be restored to its rightful state." RSV

Dan. 8:14 "It will take 2,300 evenings and mornings; then the sanctuary will be reconsecrated." NIV

Dan. 8:14 *'Ad* (until) *'ereb-boqer* (evening morning) *al-pa-yim* (2000) *u-shlosh* (and 3) *mee-ot* (hundred) *wa-ni-tsa-daq* (then shall be made righteous) *qo-desh* (sanctuary; holy place). Hebrew transliteration.

SDAs teach that the sanctuary of 8:14 is in heaven. This conclusion is forced onto (at least) Daniel 8:14 by their assumption that the 2300 days were prophetic years that ended in 1844. Since there was no Jerusalem Temple in 1844, and, since the previous Adventist assumption that the earth itself was the sanctuary had proven wrong, then the heavenly sanctuary became the alternative explanation of 8:14.

The English word, "sanctuary," occurs six times in the book of Daniel:

One: "And the place of his sanctuary [*miq-dash*] was cast down" (8:11). Most scholars, *including SDAs*, agree that this is a reference to the Jerusalem Temple. However, while most point to Antiochus IV in 171 B. C. or 167 B. C., SDAs teach that it is the Jerusalem Temple which was cast down by pagan Rome in A. D. 70.

Two: "How long....to give both the sanctuary [*qo-desh*] and the host to be trodden under foot?" (8:13). Since its antecedent in 8:11 (SDAs agree) refers to the Jerusalem Temple, then one would expect no disagreement. However, because SDAs change the little horn of 8:10-11 from pagan Rome to papal Rome in 8:12, they ignore their own contextual meaning from 8:11, skip the papacy here, and interpret 8:13 to be the heavenly sanctuary which (they say) has been trodden under by the sins of believers.

Three: "Then shall the sanctuary [*qo-desh*] be cleansed" (8:14). SDAs are the only group which has ever said that this refers to the heavenly sanctuary. During the height of the historical school of biblical interpretation, there were many different speculations about the meaning of Daniel 8:14. Some predicted the re-building of the Jerusalem Temple at the end of the 2300 prophetic days, while others taught that the sanctuary was the earth.

Four: "Shine upon your sanctuary [*miq-dash*] that is desolate" (9:7). Even SDAs concede that this is a reference to the Jerusalem Temple which had been destroyed in 586 B. C. by the Babylonians. In chapter 9, while trying to understand the vision of chapter 8, Daniel was in deep remorse over the continuing ruins of the Jerusalem Temple and was praying for its restoration. Notice that Daniel was not praying for the restoration of a defiled heavenly sanctuary.

Since chapter 8 ends with Daniel saying "I was astonished at the vision, but none understood it," and chapter 9 begins with Daniel praying for the restoration of the Jerusalem sanctuary, then it is difficult to miss the continuity between the sanctuary texts of Daniel 8 and 9.

Five: "Destroy the city and the sanctuary [*qo-desh*]" (9:26). God's answer to Daniel's prayer about the vision of 8:27 and the sanctuary in 9:7 was not what he had expected—yet another desolation! Since chapter 9 is (at the very least) a partial answer to Daniel's question about the vision of chapter 8 (and even if the SDA doctrine were correct), then one would expect to discover some mention of their defiled heavenly sanctuary in the answer given in chapter 9.

Six: "Shall pollute the sanctuary [*miq-desh*]" (11:31), is probably another reference to Antiochus IV which the SDAs attribute to pagan and papal Rome.

Conclusion: Most commentaries, historians and common sense leads even the average reader of Daniel to conclude that the Jerusalem sanctuary was being discussed in all six of the above texts. Both the end of chapter 8 and Daniel's anguishing prayer at the beginning of chapter 9 focus on restoration of the earthly sanctuary for national Israel.

The SDA teaching that 3 of the 6 sanctuary texts in Daniel refer to the heavenly sanctuary comes from their interpretation of the 2300 days and their false interpretation of "cleansed" and not from the context, history and theology of chapter 8.

CHAPTER SIX

THE 2300 DAYS OF DANIEL 8:14 AND THE YEAR-DAY PRINCIPLE

Dan. 8:14 Unto two thousand and three hundred days (KJV); "For 2,300 evenings and mornings" (NASU); "For two thousand and three hundred evenings and mornings" (RSV); "It will take 2,300 evenings and mornings" (NIV); *'ereb-boqer* (Hebrew)

Dan. 8:26 And the vision of the evening and the morning (*'ereb-boqer*) which was told is true: wherefore shut up the vision; for it shall be for many days.

One: The odd Hebrew word for "days" in Daniel 8:14 is not the usual Hebrew word, *yom*, for "day." Instead, it is the Hebrew words, *'ereb-boqer*, meaning "evenings-mornings" which are correctly translated in Daniel 8:26 (even in the KJV). When comparing the KJV, NASU, NIV, and RSV, only the King James Version incorrectly reads "days." It is important to know that *'ereb* (evening) and *boqer* (morning) occur 48 times in the KJV as "evening and morning" and *only once* as "days"—in Daniel 8:14!

Since the common Hebrew word for "day," *yom*, does not appear in 8:14, this is probably a fundamental flaw in SDA calculations. Why? Because when the sanctuary is being discussed, the couplet, *'ereb-boqer* refers to the two daily sacrifices of the evening and the morning and the total count of days could very easily be calculated as half of 2300, or 1150 actual days.

Numb. 14:34 After the number of the days in which you searched the land, even forty days, *each day for a year*, shall you bear your iniquities, even forty years…[40 days became 40 years]

Ezek. 4:5 For I have laid upon you *the years* of their iniquity, according to the number of the days, *three hundred and ninety days*: so shall you bear the iniquity of the house of Israel.

Ezek. 4:6 And when you have accomplished them, lie again on your right side, and you shall bear the iniquity of the house of Judah *forty days*: I have appointed you *each day for a year.* [390 years became 390 days; 40 years became 40 days]

Two: SDAs teach that "day-for-a-year" is an implied prophetic principle given in Numbers 14:34 and Ezekiel 4:4-6 which applies to Daniel 8:14. However, neither text is total prophecy! (1) While both texts use the same Hebrew formula, "day-for-year day-for-year," *yom la-shaanaah yom la-shaanaah,* their applications are *opposite!* While in Numbers 14:34 *each day becomes one year* (40 days to 40 years), in Ezekiel 4 *each year becomes one day* (390 years to 390 days and 40 years to 40 days). (2) These are not future prophetic times at all! Numbers 14:34 is a *judicial sentence* which began immediately. God was not giving a prophecy; He was telling Moses what to do! Moses was not allowed to let Israel cross into Canaan until 40 years had transpired. Neither is Ezekiel wholly a prophecy because the first period was *already* in progress! If there is a "principle" found in Numbers 14 and Ezekiel 4, then the "principle" is "When 'day-year' or 'year-day' is intended, it will be stated that this principle is being used." (3) Even if Numbers 14:34 were a prophecy, it would be *an exception to the rule and not the rule itself.* For example, in Isaiah 23:15-17; Jeremiah 23:11-12; 29:10; Second Chronicles 36:21 and Daniel 9:2 "seventy years" means "seventy years"—not "seventy years of days (70 x 360 = 25200 years)." See the SDAs' own admission in *Doctrine of the Sanctuary,* Biblical Research Institute, Editor Frank Holbrook, 1989, 231: "The year-day relationship can be biblically supported although *it is not explicitly identified as a prophetic principle of interpretation."*

Dan. 9:24 Seventy weeks are determined upon your people and upon your holy city...[70 x 7 weeks of years]

Three: SDAs also use the 490 years of Daniel 9:24 to prove the "day-year" principle. Yet this text can stand on its own integrity without reverting to Numbers 14:34. The Hebrew *sha-bu-yim shi-bi-yim,* can mean "70 weeks of years," "week of 70 years," "70 sevens" or "490 years" without requiring changing days into years! In other words, there is no principle changing one period of time into another period of time found in Daniel 9:24.

2 Peter 3:8 But, beloved, do not be ignorant of this one thing, that one day is with the Lord as a thousand years, and a thousand years as one day. [1 day to 1000 years; 1000 years to 1 day]

Four: It is a good thing that SDAs did not use Second Peter 3:8 as their guide for Daniel 8:14. That would place the beginning of the Investigative Judgment 2,300,000 years away, or in 2.3 days. However, the text does prove that the logic could extend in either direction.

Five: SDAs teach that the question of 8:13 about the "daily" was asking when the Day of Atonement pattern would be fulfilled by Messiah in the heavenly sanctuary. Actually, the question was asking when the Jerusalem Temple would be rededicated through a typical (non Day of Atonement) restoration. The use of 'ereb-boqer in Daniel 8:14 instead of yom is connected, not with prophetic days, as SDAs insist, but with the "evening and morning" "daily sacrifice" which had been defiled by the little horn in Daniel 8:11. This caused the question in 8:13 asking when would it be restored. When SDA founders used *Cruden's Concordance* instead of Hebrew, they were not aware of the difference between yom and 'ereb boqer.

Six: SDAs teach that the context of Daniel 8:14 provided no beginning point and reasoned that both time periods (8:14 and 9:24) must begin at the same point in history. In reality, they mean that Daniel 8 provided no beginning point that would satisfy "their own theory." Actually there are quite a few "beginning points" which better fit the context of Daniel 8. (1) "In the third year of the reign of king Belshazzar a vision appeared unto me" 8:1; (2) the vision literally began when the Persian ram emerged in 8:2; (3) the emergence of the goat in 8:5-7; (3) the breaking of the great horn in 8:8; (4) the emergence of the little horn in 8:9; (5) the persecution of the host in 8:10 and, especially, (6) the desolation of the sanctuary in 8:11-12 which is definitely the focus of 8:13-14. Therefore, the next desolation of the sanctuary in 167 B. C. should be the most obvious "beginning point." However, almost certainly, if Christ has not returned by 2133, somebody will again subtract Antiochus' desolation in 167 B. C. from 2300 to promote that date.

Seven: SDAs teach that the 2300 years must get their beginning from the vision of Daniel 9:24-27.

This is pure speculation. Any of the starting points previously discussed would better fit the context. There was widespread disagreement even within the historical interpretation community during the early 1800s. (See points #4 above and #8 below.) *Adam Clarke's Commentary* (who followed the "day-year" formula) said it started with the conquests of the great Greek horn (Alexander) of 8:8 in 334 B. C. Cumming began the period with the decline of

Persia in 480 B. C. On the other hand, the historical date of December 25, 167 B. C. for the desolation by Antiochus Epiphanes is predominant.

Eight: Although William Miller had 15 different ways to reach 1843 (not 1844), none of them included Ezra 7 and 457 B. C.! However, SDAs now teach that Ezra 7's decree of 457 B. C. is the only valid beginning date of both Daniel 9:24's chronology and the 2300 "years" of Daniel 8:14. But, by discussing Ezra 7 in the chapter on William Miller, ["In the seventh chapter of Ezra the decree is found"] (GC326), SDAs deceive the reader into thinking that it was discovered by Miller. See #7 of Miller's *Time Proved in Fifteen Different Ways,* found in Arasola's *The End of Historicism* and Ratzlaff's *Cultic Doctrine,* 64-65.

In chapter 9 Daniel was attempting to connect the desolation of 8:10-12 to the prophecy of Jeremiah—not to the heavenly sanctuary. "In the first year of his reign I Daniel understood by books the number of the years, whereof the word of the LORD came to Jeremiah the prophet, that he would accomplish seventy years in the desolations of Jerusalem (Dan. 9:2)."

Yet SDAs stand firm on their conclusions that Ezra 7:21-28's decree of 457 B. C. is the beginning of the 2300 "years" which ended in 1844. But even this date is controversial because Daniel 9:24's "from the going forth of the commandment *to restore and to build Jerusalem*" is about a decree to rebuild the walls and city of Jerusalem. Daniel 9:24 and 25 say nothing about the Temple which was rebuilt and restored in 515 B. C. Daniel 9:25 ends with "the street shall be built again, and the wall, even in troublous times." *Ezra is full of decrees about the Temple, but none about the walls of the city itself.* This is extremely damaging to the SDA foundation! "Decree" occurs in Ezra 5:13, 17; 6:1, 3, 8, 11, 12; 7:13, 21. There is an obsession with the "house" of God in Ezra; the word, "house," occurs over 65 times in the short book!

Jeremiah had prophesied in 605 B. C. that there would be 70 years of captivity. When the Persians under Cyrus defeated Babylon in 538 B. C., a decree was issued in that year to authorize the rebuilding of the Temple in Jerusalem—*not the city and its walls* (Ezra 1:1-2). There was a re-issuance of the first decree by Artaxerxes in 457 B. C., but it also only affected the Temple and *not the city and its walls* (Ezra 7).

Nehemiah 2's decree better fits the description of Daniel 9:24. It was not until 446-444 B. C., that a decree was issued which authorized the rebuilding of the city and its walls in fulfillment of the exact wording of Daniel 9:24 and 25 (Nehemiah 2). The book of Nehemiah reflects an obsession with rebuilding the walls of the city. Therefore the SDA use of Ezra 7 instead of Nehemiah 2 for the fulfillment of Daniel 9:24-25 is very questionable and would change their 1844 date.

Nine: SDAs do not teach that the sanctuary of 8:14 become defiled at the *beginning* of the 2300 "years" in 457 B. C. Yet this failure is inconsistent with their 2300 time period

However, since the question of 8:13 was "how long" should the "vision," and the "transgression" and the "trampling under foot" of the "host" continue, then it should be logically deduced that the *beginning* of the 2300 time period was also the *beginning* of the "vision concerning the daily sacrifice." Yet SDAs ignore this conclusion.

When do SDAs teach that the heavenly sanctuary first became defiled? Follow this trail. Since SDAs teach that, in 1844, Christ began investigating the list of professed believers, beginning with Adam, then their logic demands that the heavenly sanctuary first became defiled with the very first sin forgiven by God in Genesis 3:21. (See GC480, 483, 644.) When the LORD (Yahweh) forgave Adam, He must have begun His ministry as mediator inside the heavenly sanctuary and, therefore (as SDAs claim) defiled it. Ellen White states in *The Great Controversy*, page 421, "**In the New Covenant the sins of the repentant are by faith placed upon Christ and** *transferred, in fact, to the heavenly sanctuary.*" Therefore Christ's blood (SDAs teach) causes the greatest defilement of the sanctuary!

SDAs also teach that the Roman Catholic confessional (made mandatory by the Lateran Council in 1215) is the defilement of Daniel 8:12. If this were true, then they should also conclude that the 2300 years began in 1215! As Protestants, they should also agree that the Protestant Reformation (three centuries before 1844) was the beginning of this doctrinal cleansing. Yet they teach neither!

Finally, when SDAs do not include God's own defilement of the Jerusalem Temple when He ripped the veil, they miss the end of its usefulness and the end of its law-pattern fulfillment when the New Covenant began (Mt. 27:31; Heb. 9:8).

Historically, the literal Jerusalem Temple was fully functioning in 457 B. C. It functioned continuously from Nehemiah's restoration in 515 B.C. until Rome caused it to cease in A. D. 70. The only very noteworthy exception was the 1150 literal days between 167 B. C. and 164 B. C.! Therefore, the *beginning* desolation of the 2300 evening-morning can be historically documented as December 25, 167 B. C.

Ten: SDAs teach that the 2300 "days" were 2300 "years" which reached to 1844. Yet they were neither the first nor the last to apply this period to modern times. In 1452 Krebs of Cusa taught that it started with the rise of Persia (Dan. 8:3) and ended between **1700-1750**. *The Matthew Henry Commentary* mentioned that Cumming placed the end of the 2300 "years" in **1821**. In 1825, the Methodist classic, *Adam Clarke's Commentary,* stated that the little horn of 8:9 was Antiochus IV, but might be pagan Rome. He reasoned that, if the 2300 years began with the emergence of Alexander in 334 B. C., it would end with a Jerusalem sanctuary being built in the A. D. **1966**. Like Adventists, Clarke interpreted the little horn of Daniel 7:25 as the Roman Catholic Church and predicted that its power would last 1260 years from A. D. 755 to **2015**. Views such as Clarke's were well-known to the early Adventists, many of whom came from the Methodist Church. However, Matthew Henry himself, plus Miller's other contemporaries such as *Albert Barnes; Jamieson, Fausset and Brown* and *Keil and Delitzsch* all agreed with the Antiochus Epiphanes explanation of Daniel 8:14.

Historically, the 2300 days were either 2300 literal days between 171-164 B. C., or else 1150 daily sacrifices performed in 1150 literal days between 167-164 B. C. The 2300 *'ereb-boqer* were literal sanctuary burnt offerings in which the "daily sacrifice" (Hebrew *tamid*) had been interrupted by Antiochus IV. This sacrifice was offered twice a day: in the evening, *'ereb*, and in the morning, *boqer*. Therefore the number, 2300, could either refer to 2300 total days, or 6.4 years, or 1150 total sacrifices offered in 3.2 years. Both time periods are historically defensible. The 6.4 years fits the time period when Jewish youth were enticed away from the sanctuary to the Greek gymnasium. The 3.2 years fits the time period between the desecration of the altar with a pig and its rededication after the civil war had ended in 164 B.C. Josephus made three different statements in three different places about this period being 3 years, 3 and one quarter years, and three and one half years. See *Preface to Wars* (3 years 3 months); *Wars* i. 1.1 (3 ½ years); *Antiquities* xii.7.6 (3 years).

Eleven: Unfortunately, in the SDAs' own scenario, nothing really "ended" in 1844, the so-called "end" of the 2300 "years." This seriously contradicts the text [8:14's 'then shall'] and is the opposite end of the preceding discussion.

In practice, SDAs make the answer to the question in 8:13 "After" (not "before" or "not until") 2300 years, then the heavenly sanctuary will "begin to be restored." The verb action is reversed! Instead of something *ending* after the 2300 time period, something *begins*.

Although much of the SDA scenario has ended, none of it ended in 1844. (1) The ripped veil in the Temple at Christ's death both "ended" the significance of the old sanctuary (Heb. 9:8) and "began" the priesthood of believers, thus allowing every believer to boldly enter directly into the Most Holy Place (Heb. 4:16; 7:19-20; 10:19-20). Sadly, though, admitting this truth would force SDAs to correct their doctrine. (2) The A. D. 70 desolation of the Jerusalem

Temple has not ended because it has not been rebuilt. (3) According to Protestants, in the 1500s the Protestant Reformation corrected (or ended by exposing) the false doctrine of the Roman Catholic confessional. (4) The only thing that did not "end" in 1844 is the Investigative Judgment which allegedly only "began" in 1844.

The question in 8:13 was "How long will the vision about the regular sacrifice *apply*, while the transgression causes horror, so as to allow both the holy place and the host to be trampled?" NASU. And the answer in 8:14 is "For 2,300 evenings and mornings; then the holy place will be properly restored" NASU. If the interpretation of the answer does not match the question, then it must be the wrong answer! The question, "how long?," means "how long *until the desolation stops*?" *Wa-ni-tsa-daq* literally means in Hebrew "then shall be restored" (NASU), "restored to its rightful state" (RSV) and "then will be reconsecrated" (NIV). In order for the SDA interpretation to be correct, the verb, *ni-tsa-daq*, would have to mean "shall *begin to be* restored"—and it does not!

Historically, the sanctuary of 8:14 was indeed completely cleansed at the **end** of the 2300 days in 164 B. C. This interpretation follows the logical sequence that the desecrating little horn from 8:9 to 8:13 was part of the Greek he-goat of 8:8 and was not a new empire such as pagan or papal Rome.

Heb. 9:25, 26 "Nor yet that he should offer himself often, as the high priest enters into the [most] holy place every year with blood of others; For then must he often have suffered since the foundation of the world: but *now once* in the end of the world he has appeared to put away sin by the sacrifice of himself."

Twelve: SDAs teach that the anti-typical Day of Atonement has been continuing since 1844.

The worst failure of SDA "pattern-fulfillment" is the *length* of their prophetic "Day" of Atonement itself! While the "day-for-a-year" pattern SDAs use from Numbers 14:34 should only allow for one year (1844-1845), it is evident that they cannot possibly be honest to their own principle of interpretation. They will not accept the fact that Christ fulfilled the pattern when He died on only one day! The most important prophetic "day" in all of Adventism, the "day" which gave birth to their existence as a church movement in 1844 *has already lasted over 160 years*! Evidently, the patterns are not exact patterns after all.

However, fulfillment of the Day of Atonement cannot possibly fit into a period of time lasting more than part of a single day (such as since 1844). Since the Old Covenant cleansing began and ended within minutes of the blood of the sacrificial animal being shed, then the pattern-fulfillment should also require that the cleansing of the heavenly sanctuary both begin and end soon after Christ shed His blood.

In reality, the *"one day"* Day of Atonement in Leviticus 16 was indeed fulfilled in **one day** when Jesus died!

Rev. 14:7 Saying with a loud voice, Fear God, and give glory to him; for the hour [Greek: *hoora*] of his judgment is come...

Rev. 9:15 And the four angels were loosed, which were prepared for *an hour* [SDA: 15 days] [Greek: *hoora*], and a day [SDA: year], and a month [SDA: 30 years], and a year [SDA: 360 years], for to slay the third part of men. [SDA reckoning]

Thirteen: SDAs interpret "hour" in Revelation 9:15 as prophetic time and applied it to Turkey in 1840. Ellen White called it "another remarkable fulfillment of prophecy" which occurred "at the very time specified" (GC334-335). Their "hour" was 15 days, that is, 1/24th of a 360 day year. Yet they do not use the same principle with "hour" in one of their favorite texts, Revelation 14:7. But, following their own time principles, if the Investigative Judgment began on October 22, 1844, then it should have only lasted one hour, or 15 days. "Hour" (*hoora*) occurs 108 times in the N. T. and in Revelation 3:3, 10; 9:15; 11:13; 14:7, 15; 17:12; 18:10, 17, 19.

Fourteen: The SDA doctrine of the 2300 "days" also means that it would have been impossible for Christ to return before 1844. Yet Christians in every century have believed that Jesus could return in their own lifetime. Even the Apostle Paul spoke about Christ's soon return in the first person, "we" (1 Thess. 4:17; 1 Cor. 15:51).

CHAPTER SEVEN

THE CLEANSING OF DANIEL 8:14

Dan. 8:14 "then shall the sanctuary be cleansed" (KJV); "then the holy place will be properly restored" (NASU); "then the sanctuary shall be restored to its rightful state" (RSV); "then the sanctuary will be reconsecrated" (NIV); "*wa-ni-tsa-daq* (then shall be made righteous)" Hebrew.

The Seventh-Day Adventist Bible Dictionary, 1960, "little horn," p 656. "In chapter 8 at the close of the specified period of time <u>the sanctuary is 'cleansed' of the 'transgression of desolation' erected in it by the little horn *(vs 13, 14)*</u>. In chapter 9:26, 27 <u>the same power</u> destroys Jerusalem and the Temple, causing 'the sacrifice and the oblation to cease' and <u>desolating the sanctuary</u>. In chapter 11:30, 31 <u>the same power</u> enters 'the glorious land'—Palestine (vs 16, 41, 45), stands up against 'the prince of the covenant' (vs 22), <u>pollutes the sanctuary</u> and takes away the daily sacrifice, sets up the 'desolating abomination' (vs 30, 31), and conspires to obliterate the worship of the true God (vs 30)—all for a 'time, times and a half' (ch 12:7)." [Author's note: Without adding their explanation, this entire statement, especially the first sentence (8:13, 14), agrees with the SDA **opponents** who teach that the "little horn" (not the sins of the saints) desolated the sanctuary which required cleansing in 8:14.]

One: SDAs teach that the sanctuary cleansed in 8:14 is not the Jerusalem sanctuary mentioned in 8:11; 9:17 or 9:26. However, the nearest, and only, previous time the word, "sanctuary," appears prior to Daniel 8:13 is 8:11. Therefore, 8:11 should be the logical context of the question of 8:13 and the answer of 8:14.

Most Christians teach that the sanctuary of 8:8-14 is the Jerusalem Temple which had been defiled by the little horn, Antiochus Epiphanes in 167 B.C.

As already discussed, SDAs admit that the sanctuary of 9:17 was the Jerusalem Temple which had been destroyed by Babylon in 586 B. C. They then teach that the sanctuary of 8:11 and 9:26 was the Jerusalem Temple that the little horn of pagan Rome destroyed in A. D. 70. However, ignoring the surrounding "sanctuary" texts (8:11and 9:17), SDAs change to teach that the sanctuary of 8:14 is the one in heaven. Even the *S. D. A. Bible Dictionary* (above), "little horn," cannot seem to get this straight because it agrees with everybody else (except its own church) that the little horn defiled the sanctuary in 8:14!

Two: SDAs teach that "cleansed" in 8:14 refers to the Day of Atonement ritual in Leviticus 16 rather than the necessary rededication performed in 164 B. C. However, the problems created by connecting "cleansed" in Daniel 8:14 to the cleansing of the Day of Atonement in Leviticus 16: 19, 30 are multitude. The KJV "cleansed" in 8:14 is an incorrect translation of the Hebrew *tsa-daq*. The NASU reads "properly restored"; RSV "restored to its rightful state"; NIV "reconsecrated." *Tsa-daq* is a very common Old Testament root word meaning "justify," "just," "justified," "justice" or "righteous." Its only other occurrence in Daniel 12:3 is correct as "righteousness." In fact, Daniel 8:14 is the only time (in 41 instances) that *tsa-daq* is translated "cleansed" in the KJV! Desperate for proof-texts, the SDA Biblical Research Committee, in 1989, could only refer to two obscure texts in Job to argue that *tsadaq* might also mean "cleanse" (*Doctrine of the Sanctuary*, p222).

In the Day of Atonement ritual of Leviticus 16, "cleanse" is the Hebrew word, *ta-heer*, not *tsa-daq*. "Cleanse" is *taheer* in all 15 occurrences in Leviticus. This strongly indicates that Daniel 8:8-14 does not refer to the Day of Atonement.

However, while "cleansed" in 8:14 refers to a general restoration, or re-dedication, of the sanctuary, SDAs teach that "cleansed" in Daniel 8:14 refers to the Day of Atonement ritual in Leviticus 16. When Christ did not come to destroy the earth-sanctuary in the autumn of 1844, the small group which later became SDAs redefined their "sanctuary" in 8:14 from earth itself to the heavenly sanctuary. Then they limited the heavenly sanctuary's cleansing to only the Most Holy Place.

Three: SDAs teach that the sins of God's people defiled the sanctuary in Daniel 8:14.

SDAs completely disconnected 8:13-14 from the remainder of the chapter and book context of Daniel. The 2300 days became 2300 years that ended in 1844. The sanctuary changed from the Jerusalem Temple to only one room in the heavenly sanctuary. And, especially, the desolating power changed from the wicked nations and forces of 8:9-12; 9:17, 27; 11:31 and 12:11 to God's own saints!!!!

In the SDAs' own explanation of 8:9-12 (previous chapter), the context of 8:14, they stated that the "little horn" opposed the host of heaven, cast down some of the host and of the stars to the ground, stamped upon them" (8:10), "magnified himself to the prince of the host, took away the daily sacrifice, cast down the place of his sanctuary" (8:11), was against the "daily sacrifice" and "cast down the truth" (8:12). Very clearly, the little horn, and not God's saints, defiled and took away the "daily sacrifice."

However, the SDA explanation of 8:14 ignores 8:9-12 and *reverses the need for the cleansing* of the sanctuary! Although 8:12 says that God allowed the little horn to desolate the sanctuary as punishment for the sins of His people ("by reason of transgression"), it was still the little horn who desolated the sanctuary and not God's saints!

Historically, 8:9-12 is a description of the terrible circumstances in Jerusalem from the time Antiochus IV cast down the Jewish religion to the ground, enticed the Jewish boys to abandon the Temple for the Greek gymnasium, to his desecration of the altar, until its restoration and rededication after the end of the war of independence in 164 B.C.

Four: SDAs teach that defiling the "daily sacrifice" in Daniel 8:14 required a Day of Atonement-type of cleansing.

However, there are at least three different kinds of "cleansings" associated with the sanctuary service and SDAs have chosen the wrong one to explain Daniel 8:14. Using the predominant scriptural terminology, the first "cleansing" would be called the "dedication," the second either "rededication," "dedication" or "cleansing," and the third "atonement."

NEW DEDICATION: The **first** "cleansing," the original "dedication" of the sanctuary was required when the sanctuary, or temple, was initially inaugurated for holy use after its construction. Only Ezekiel calls it a "cleansing." "When you have made an end of **cleansing** it, you shall offer a young bullock without blemish, and a ram out of the flock without blemish" (Ezek. 43:23). The word used here, *chata'* (Strong's 2398), means "removal of sin" and is the most common word used for "purification from sin." Scripture describes this ceremony in great detail, but almost always calls it the "dedication," *cha-nuk-kah* (Strong's 2398). Also compare Exodus 24:3-8's "purification."

This initial dedication-cleansing was performed for the tabernacle in the wilderness, for Solomon's temple and for Ezra's second temple in 515 B. C. Initially priests were consecrated through sin offerings for atonement to "cleanse," "anoint" and "sanctify" the great altar. "And you shall offer every day a bullock for a sin offering for atonement: and you shall cleanse (*chata*) the altar, when you have made an atonement for it, and you shall anoint it, to sanctify it. Seven days you shall make an atonement for the altar, and sanctify it; and it shall be an altar most holy: *whatsoever touches the altar shall be holy*" (Ex. 29:36-37).

After the priests had been cleansed by the sin offering, the whole burnt offering of the "daily sacrifice" was offered. The blood of the daily sacrifice was poured out at the base of the great altar and was not brought into the sanctuary (Ex. 29:38-43).

Finally, *anointing OIL, not blood,* was used to "anoint" (not cleanse) the entire sanctuary! It is important to note that the Most Holy Place was entered on this initial dedication day, not with blood, but with OIL. "And you shall anoint the tabernacle of the congregation therewith, and the ark of the testimony" (Ex. 30:26). Although the blood from the priests' sin offerings (i.e. Christ) was not brought into the sanctuary, it was still sufficient to consecrate the entire new sanctuary. *This is a totally different cleansing, for different reasons, than that on the Day of Atonement* (compare 30:10 with 30:25-26).

In 586 B. C. the Babylonians entered the temple, took war spoil of all its precious articles from all of the sanctuary (including the Most Holy Place), and then they completely destroyed Solomon's Temple. In 515 B. C. a completely different second temple was erected. Ezra 6:14-20 describes the restoration, or dedication (*chanukka'*) of the second temple. The temple was "dedicated" and the priests were "purified." See Exodus 30:23-30, Leviticus 8 and 9, Numbers 7, First Kings 8, Second Chronicles 7, Ezra 6 and Ezekiel 43.

RE-DEDICATION/RESTORATION: A **second** "cleansing" of the sanctuary was required whenever it had been defiled by any unclean person or thing. Whenever the sanctuary had been entered and defiled by an unclean Israelite, or by non-Israelite such as the Greeks in 167 B. C., the entire sanctuary complex was considered "defiled" and required "cleansing." *Again, this is a different "cleansing of the sanctuary," for different reasons, than that performed on the Day of Atonement!* This is very important! And, again, the Most Holy Place was entered for the cleansing.

The 167 B. C. desolation of the second Temple by Antiochus IV, which is described in Daniel 8 and 11 and in the historical books of *First* and *Second Maccabees,* was this second type of cleansing, or re-dedication. Antiochus had offered a pig on the altar of burnt offering and had erected a statute of Zeus inside the temple. A restoration, or rededication, was required in order to start using the temple again. The historian of *First Maccabees* 4:42 wrote, "He [Judas] chose blameless priests devoted to the law, and they *"cleansed the sanctuary"* and removed the defiled stones to an unclean place." This is the cleansing described in Daniel 8:14 (and not that of the heavenly sanctuary). *Both Exodus 30:26 and Ezra 6:16 use "cha-nuk-ka" for "dedication"* rather than *tsadaq* from Daniel 8:14 or even *taheer* from Leviticus 16:19.

ATONEMENT: A **third** "cleansing," actually called "atonement" of the sanctuary, occurred once a year, on the tenth day of the seventh month of the

Hebrew calendar, and is called the "Day of Atonement" or *Yom Kippur.* Leviticus 23:27-32 uses "atonement," or "atone," (*kaphar*, Strong's 3722) three times in verses 27 and 28. Although Leviticus 16 uses "cleanse, clean" (*taheer*, Strong's 2891) twice in verses 19 and 30, it uses "atonement" 13 times, in 16:6, 10, 16, 17, 17, 18, 20, 24, 27, 30, 33, 33 and 34. Again, *taheer* is not the same word used for "cleansed" in Daniel 8:14. (Also see Exodus 30:10.)

The bad news for SDAs is that the Hebrew word translated "cleansed" in Daniel 8:14, *tsa-daq* (Strong's 6663), does not appear in *any* description of the Day of Atonement rituals! Therefore, SDAs incorrectly identify the dedication, or re-dedication, "cleansing" of 8:14 with the Day of Atonement "cleansing."

However, even if it were the Day of Atonement cleansing, in their 1844 pattern-fulfillment scenario, SDAs restrict it to only the Most Holy Place, although it actually applied to the entire sanctuary complex. Leviticus 16:33 "And he shall make an atonement **for the holy sanctuary,** and he shall make an atonement **for the tabernacle of the congregation,** and **for the altar,** and he shall make an atonement **for the priests,** and **for all the people** of the congregation."

Five: By their very inaccurate application SDAs teach that part of the sanctuary could function even though part of it had been defiled—therefore, Christ could minister in the Holy Place while the Most Holy Place remained defiled until 1844 (and beyond until immediately prior to His return to earth). This would have been completely unimaginable in biblical reality.

This SDA error is from deduction of their stated doctrine. Since SDAs at least concede that Christ began ministering inside the Holy Place in the heavenly sanctuary after His ascension, then He must have already first made some kind of dedication of His blood (per Heb. 9:23). However, this SDA solution creates at least two problems. (1) How could Christ present His blood and only dedicate "part" of the heavenly sanctuary? (2) Why did He not dedicate ALL of the heavenly sanctuary on the same day as was done in the "patterned" reality of the earthly sanctuary?

Contrary to SDA doctrine, all three of the "original dedications," "re-dedications," and "atonements" found in God's Word are **total** and not partial! In other words, if *any one part* of the sanctuary were defiled, then **all** of it would be defiled! Therefore, the entire sanctuary, or Temple, was always cleansed at the same time! Again, no part of the sanctuary could function unless all of it had been restored by cleansing.

Exodus 29:38-43 reveals yet another SDA inconsistency. The "daily sacrifice" was offered, or restored, *before* the other dedications, anointings or cleansings could proceed. By taking away the "daily sacrifice," the entire sanctuary service was forced to cease. Likewise, by first restoring the daily sacrifice through ritual cleansing and re-consecration, the entire sanctuary could then be restored. *Even on the Day of Atonement, the "daily sacrifice" never ceased and always preceded (and followed) the other rituals.* This means that the altar of burnt offering was used "first" and "third" for the daily sacrifice even on the Day of Atonement. "First" for the evening (*'ereb*) daily sacrifice, "second" for the Day of Atonement cleansing and "third" for the morning (*boqer*) "daily sacrifice."

Six: SDAs teach that the cleansing of the Most Holy Place in heaven is Christ's final ministry phase which only began there in 1844.

The biblical facts are clear: (1) The entire earthly sanctuary received cleansing on the Day of Atonement, not just the Most Holy Place. (2) On the yearly Day of Atonement, the "daily sacrifice" had never ceased and was still offered to begin the day. (3) Since the sacrificial blood on the Day of Atonement was brought into the Most Holy Place soon after its being shed, then Christ followed this correct pattern.

However, the SDA error of restricting the Day of Atonement "cleansing" to the Most Holy Place is absolutely necessary to fit their Investigative Judgment. Yet their own statements create even more confusion. With no explanation, *The S.D.A. Bible Dictionary,* "Atonement, Day of," reads (following the cleansing of the Most Holy Place) **"In this manner *the holy place was cleansed,* and atonement was made for the sins of the people (Lev. 16:16). In a similar manner *the altar was cleansed* (verses 18, 19)."** Also GC419. Here, SDAs admit that, on the Day of Atonement, not only the Most Holy Place, but also the Holy Place and the altar of burnt offering were "cleansed" with the blood of atonement! Therefore, whatever types of sins were (supposedly) required to be cleansed from the earthly Most Holy Place were also required to be cleansed from both the outer Holy Place and the great altar outside of the sanctuary proper.

Yet this admission contradicts their own doctrine in several ways: (1) As discussed previously, absolutely no ministry could be performed in either the earthly (or heavenly) sanctuary until ALL of it had been restored after defilement. (2) Since the cleansing of the Most Holy Place on the Day of Atonement was immediately followed by the cleansing of the Holy Place and the great altar, the cleansing of these should be explained in SDA theology. (3) Christ could not have begun a ministry in the heavenly sanctuary (in either room) unless the entire sanctuary had first been completely dedicated. Thus it makes no sense to give the impression that Christ only moved from the Holy Place to the Most Holy Place in 1844. If one studies the doctrine carefully, Christ would not have needed to cleanse any part of the sanctuary in 1844 because He had already been ministering there since His ascension. SDAs fail miserably to follow their own pattern-fulfillment.

Seven: SDAs teach that Jesus did NOT enter the Most Holy Place in the heavenly sanctuary and begin ministering there after His ascension. Therefore, by extension SDAs teach that the "right hand of the Father" does not refer to the Most Holy Place.

With the lone exception of Seventh-day Adventism, the Christian world, both Protestant and Roman Catholic, believes that, after Christ's death and resurrection, Jesus ascended into heaven to the throne of God corresponding to *the Most Holy Place* and sat down at the right hand of the Father in the heavenly sanctuary. His sinless life, atoning death, burial, resurrection and ascension to the throne of God fulfilled all of the types of the earthly sanctuary. He fulfilled the types of the many sacrificial animals, the daily ministering priests and the high priest. He also fulfilled the types of the furnishings and furniture within the holy place and most holy place. Having finished his work of atonement, Jesus "sat down" at the right hand of the Father. See the chapter on "Rooms" for a full discussion of this subject.

CHAPTER EIGHT

THE OLD COVENANT DAILY SACRIFICE

Dan. 8:11, 12, 13; 11:31; 12:11 "daily sacrifice" (KJV, NIV); "regular sacrifice" (NAS); "continual burnt offering" (RSV); *tamid* (Hebrew); Strong's 8548
Dan. 8:14 "days" (KJV); "evenings and mornings" (NAS; RSV; NIV); (*'ereb-boqer*) Hebrew

The "daily sacrifice" *(tamid)* in the Hebrew sanctuary was a whole sweet-savor burnt offering which began each evening (*'ereb*) and again began each morning (*boqer*) of the year—including the Day of Atonement. The *tamid* consisted of two lambs of the first year without spot. Since its appeasement-communication with God never ceased, it was also called the "continual," or "perpetual," offering. Because the blood of the *tamid* was neither a sin nor guilt offering, it was always poured out at the base of the great altar and its flesh was never eaten by priests (Numb. 28:1-7).

The *tamid* was the first, or foundational, sacrifice which allowed all of the other sacrifices to follow. Therefore, every part of the sanctuary service depended on the "daily sacrifice." Without the *tamid*, nothing else could be offered. And, conversely, if defilement occurred in any part of the sanctuary, the *tamid* was also considered to be defiled.

The *tamid* made it possible for sin to be atoned and forgiven via the sin offerings which followed it. Again, the *tamid* was not the sin offering itself! Even on the Day of Atonement, like all other days, the *tamid* was offered first and last. Without the *tamid,* there could be no Day of Atonement sacrifice (Numb. 29:11).

In the book of Daniel *tamid* is correctly called the "daily sacrifice" all five times it is used (8:11, 12, 13; 11:31; 12:11). The *tamid* is identical with "evening-morning" (*'ereb boqer*). Its context requires it to be understood as the "evening and morning daily sacrifice" in the Israelite sanctuary service. The "daily ministry" of the priests is *not* the same as the "daily sacrifice." Although their day began and ended with the *tamid*, the "daily ministry" included everything the ordinary priests normally did.

Tamid's first occurrence in Daniel 8:11 is agreed to by all, including SDAs, to be a reference to the "evening-morning" sacrifice (*'ereb-boqer*) of the Jerusalem Temple. The only disagreement about 8:11 is whether the text refers to its defilement by Antiochus IV in 167 B. C. or pagan Rome in A. D. 70. However, 8:12 is very controversial. While most today say it refers to Antiochus, SDAs teach that it now refers to papal Rome which desolated the truth about Christ's ministry in the heavenly sanctuary, especially through priestly confessions.

Therefore, oddly, the SDA interpretation of Daniel 8:11-14 explains the removal of the "daily sacrifice" in three very different ways. (1) In 8:11 it is the Jerusalem Temple which was destroyed by the little horn of pagan Rome in A. D. 70. (2) In 8:12 it is the heavenly sanctuary which was desolated by the little horn of papal Rome when the confessional was made mandatory in A. D. 1215. (3) In 8:14 it is the heavenly sanctuary which was defiled by the confessed and forgiven sins of God's children since Adam's first sin. Again, there is simply no continuity between these three different explanations!

The SDA interpretation of 8:11-14 would require three completely different kinds of cleansings. (1) The *first* would require a non-Day of Atonement dedication when the temple was rebuilt. (2) The *second* defilement (according to SDAs) would be restored by the "truth" taught by the SDA remnant church since 1844 to repudiate the confessional. (However, as Protestants they should teach that this refutation was actually given by the Reformers 300 years earlier.) (3) Only the *third* requires a Day of Atonement type of cleansing similar to Leviticus 16. Again, there is simply too much disconnect (no continuity) between these three concepts. None of these three would correctly require the actual re-dedication of 164 B. C. referred to in 8:14.

As previously discussed, the *tamid* began and ended every day of the year, even on the Day of Atonement. The Bible emphasizes that the little horn of 8:11-12 desolated the "daily" and the entire sanctuary—not merely the Most Holy Place! The daily ministration of priests in the Holy Place was also completely stopped by the little horn.

SDAs greatly contradict themselves here. While they teach that "desolating the daily" in Daniel 8:11-12 caused the entire sanctuary to be defiled, they then teach that defiling the "daily" in 8:13 only required the Most Holy Place to be cleansed in 8:14! This necessary manipulation of the facts allows them to teach that Christ has continued daily ministering inside the Holy Place since His ascension. Yet He could not minister inside the Most Holy Place because it was still defiled!!!

"After 2300 *'ereb-boqer* (daily sacrificial cycles) have passed, then the sanctuary will be restored." The text plainly states that the "daily cycles" will cease *until* the end of 2300 sacrificial cycles.

From a Protestant viewpoint, Seventh-day Adventists are actually more guilty of "casting down the truth" about Christ's High Priestly ministry in the heavenly sanctuary than are Roman Catholics. SDAs deny that Christ has been performing a uniquely high priestly ministry inside the Most Holy Place since His ascension. SDAs have destroyed the "truth" about any activity by Christ *as high priest* before 1844. Yet Roman Catholics teach that the confessional exists because Christ has indeed been ministering in heaven since his ascension and priests are His representatives on earth. Roman Catholics do not teach that the confessional replaced the necessity of Christ's intercessory ministry.

Historically, Antiochus IV "took away the daily sacrifices" (and all others) when he polluted the sanctuary in 167 B. C., as recorded in Daniel 11:31. The reliable (though not without mistake) historical books of *First Maccabees* 1:45-47, *Second Maccabees* 6:1 and Josephus agree. *Even the SDA Bible Dictionary admits *"Jews at the time of Christ applied the prophecy of Daniel to the desolation of the Temple by Antiochus Epiphanes"* and gives references to the writings of Josephus. Then they admit *"Christ applied the expression 'abomination of desolation' to the [pagan] Romans."* See *SDA Bible Dictionary*, 1960, "daily," 243.

The question of Daniel 8:13 asked how long the vision would last before the "daily sacrifice," the *tamid*, would cease "to be trodden under foot." And the answer in 8:14 was that 2300 daily sacrifices, *'ereb-boqer* (not "days," *yom*) would lapse before restoration (*tsadaq*, not *taheer*). **Since the Old Covenant Day of Atonement *did not restore* the "daily sacrifice," but always followed it, then Daniel 8:14 cannot possibly be a reference to the Day of Atonement. A defiled "daily sacrifice" could only be restored by "dedication" (*hanukah*) and not by a Day of Atonement *taheer*.** The "daily" was called the "continual" because it never ceased, not even on the Day of Atonement. The only logical reason for using *tsa-daq* (for re-dedication) in Daniel 8:14 instead of *ta-heer* (from the Leviticus 16 cleansing) is because the defilement of the daily was caused by the little horn and not by the Day of Atonement's general sinfulness of God's people.

Jesus Christ died to fulfill all types of sacrificial offerings. As the "daily" lamb of God, the whole sweet-savor sacrifice, He died wholly for us (Lev. 1:11-13). As the sin and guilt-offering lamb of God, His blood was brought into the sanctuary and sprinkled before the veil (Heb. 12:24). As the Passover lamb of God, His body is symbolically eaten by believers (Mt. 26:26). As the goat of atonement on the Day of Atonement, He died once for all time for all sin (Heb. 9:19-28). As the scapegoat on the Day of Atonement he forever carried away the sins of believers.

CHAPTER NINE

THE CONTROVERSY OVER PATTERN-FULFILLMENT

Seventh-day Adventists use pattern-fulfillment to explain why the Day of Atonement did not occur at Calvary, but, instead, began in 1844. Rater than agreeing with Miller and most early Adventists that nothing happened in 1844, a very small group re-defined the sanctuary of Daniel 8:14 from their first guess of earth itself to the "heavenly" sanctuary. Not knowing Hebrew, they equated the KJV word, "cleansed" (*tsa-daq*), in Daniel 8:14 with the "cleanse" (*ta-heer*) in Leviticus 16:19, 30. Instead of Christ coming to judge the wicked by destroying the earth with fire, they decided that he only moved from the Holy Place to the Most Holy Place of the heavenly sanctuary to begin judging the lives of professed believers in order to determine whom to recreate from annihilation.

Since, until 1844, Christians everywhere (including themselves) had believed that Jesus had entered the Most Holy Place as High Priest at his ascension, then justification was needed for this completely different explanation. The new explanation depended on their use of pattern-fulfillment.

GC417 [Ellen G. White] But the most important question remains to be answered: What is the cleansing of the sanctuary? That there was such a service in connection with the earthly sanctuary is seated in the Old Testament scriptures. In Hebrews 9 the cleansing of both the earthly and heavenly sanctuaries is plainly taught. "Almost all things are by the law purged with blood; and without shedding of blood is no remission. *It was therefore necessary that the patterns of things in the heavens should be purified with these*; but the heavenly things themselves with better sacrifices than these" (Hebrews 9:22, 23), even the precious blood of Christ.

GC418 But how could there be sin connected with the sanctuary, either in heaven or upon earth? This may be learned by reference to the symbolic service; for the priests who offered on earth, served *"unto the example and shadow of heavenly things."* Hebrews 8:5.

GC420 And what was done in type in the ministration of the earthly sanctuary is done in reality in the ministration of the heavenly sanctuary.

Applying SDA Pattern-Fulfillment: Having established the existence of (at least some) pattern-fulfillment, *The Great Controversy* then "proves" that Christ only ascended into the first apartment of the heavenly sanctuary by quoting Revelation 4:5 and 8:3 (GC414-415). Next, a brief statement about Daniel 8:14 says that it "unquestionably refers to a sanctuary in heaven." Moving back to Hebrews 9:23-24, the reality of the "patterns" requires that the heavenly things be purified with the blood of Christ (GC417). The new "light from God" was in their "discovery" that *the cleansing is necessary because of sacrificial blood which defiled the heavenly sanctuary with the forgiven sins of God's people* (GC418-419). This was because the sin had not been canceled by the blood of the sacrifice (GC420). Their pattern-fulfillment then moved from Calvary to 1844 to the second coming because the removal of sin from the heavenly sanctuary must still be accomplished "in reality in the ministration of the heavenly sanctuary" (GC420). Since the sins of the saints still remain on the books of record in heaven, they must be removed before Christ can return. This removal began in 1844 (GC421).

The Truth About Pattern-Fulfillment

One: In context, the book of Hebrews does **not** teach that the Old Covenant sanctuary service provided a must-follow "pattern," "example," "copy" or "shadow" for New Covenant Christians. In fact, in context, it teaches exactly the opposite! Hebrews teaches that the Old Covenant sanctuary *patterns ended at Calvary!* It proves its point by *contrasting* Christ's ministry in the heavenly sanctuary with that of the Old Covenant sanctuary.

The following list contains 48 descriptions of Christ from Hebrews 1:1 to 7:28. With one exception (4:15 to 5:4), all are *contrasts* to the Old Covenant priest—not pattern-fulfillment. There are seven (7) separate references to Christ's High Priesthood after the order of Melchizedek who was not even an Israelite. Contrast, not pattern-fulfillment, is clearly taught. 1:3 Sitting at the right hand of the Majesty; 1:4 So much better than angels; better name; 1:5 Father-Son relationship; 1:6 Worshiped by angels; 1:8 Called "God" by the Father; 1:9 Personally anointed by God; 1:10 Called Creator by the Father; 1:12 Called Eternal by the Father; 2:8 All things are subject to him; 2:9 Dies for all men (greater love); 2:17 As High Priest his person made reconciliation for the sins of the people; 3:1 Both an Apostle and High Priest; 3:3, 5, 6 Greater than Moses; Christ a son; Moses a servant; 3:3, 4 The house-builder; 4:3 Provides rest (Moses and Aaron did not); 4:14 Great High Priest in the heavens; the Son of God; [4:15; 5:1-4 As High Priest sympathizes with our weaknesses]; 4:16 Commands believers to approach the throne of grace with confidence; 5:5 Appointed High Priest by God's oath; 5:6 High Priest after the order of Melchizedek (1st time); 5:9 As High Priest is the author of eternal salvation; 5:10 High Priest after the order of Melchizedek (2nd time); 6:19 Sure, steadfast, anchor of the soul within the veil; 6:20 High Priest after the order of Melchizedek (3rd time); 7:1 Blessed Abraham; 7:2 Received tithes from Abraham; 7:2 Called King of Righteousness; 7:2 Called King of Peace; 7:3 An eternal priest; 7:6 Not related to the Levitical priests; 7:9-10 Received tithes from Levi (thus Aaron); 7:11 High Priest after the order of Melchizedek (4th time); 7:12 His High Priesthood demands the Law be changed; 7:13-14 From Judah, not Levi; 7:15 High Priest after the order of Melchizedek (5th time); 7:16 Priesthood based on eternal principles; 7:17 High Priest after the order of Melchizedek (6th time); 7:18 Necessitated the annulment of laws governing the Levitical priesthood; 7:19 Proved that laws concerning the Levitical priesthood could not perfect anything; 7:19 A better hope providing all direct access to God; 7:20 Became a priest through God's oath; 7:21 High Priest after the order of Melchizedek (7th time); 7:22 Guarantor of a better covenant; 7:23-24 One unchangeable eternal priesthood with no death; 7:25 Eternal intercessor; 7:26 High priest, holy, innocent, undefiled, separated from sinners and exalted above the heavens; 7:27 As High Priest offered one sacrifice; 7:28 Perfected rather than weak. Again, *contrast*, not pattern-fulfillment is the theme.

Two: Seventh-day Adventists are really not that seriously interested in teaching pattern-fulfillment except when it involves their own view of the Day of Atonement. In order for all pattern-fulfillment requirements to be true for New Covenant believers, the heavenly sanctuary would have (1) many Aaronic priests and Levites, (2) daily evening and morning sweet savor offerings, (3) weekly Sabbath-day offerings, (4) monthly new moon offerings, (5) seasonal Passover, Pentecost and the Day of Atonement offerings, (6) replacement of the 12 loaves of bread, (7) refilling of the candlestick oil, (8) burning of incense, (9) a laver for washing and many other comparable pattern-fulfillments. Thus the following statement in GC420 actually causes more problems that it solves—"What was done in type in the ministration of the earthly sanctuary is done in reality in the ministration of the heavenly sanctuary."

Three: When Hebrews 9:9, 23; 8:5; and 9:24 (from GC417-418) are studied *in order and in context,* chapters 8 and 9 also clearly teach that the patterns only lasted as long as the Old Covenant sanctuary and have no continuing relevance to New Covenant believers.

Hebrews 8:1 sums up chapters 1-7 by saying **"Now this is the main point of the things we are saying: We have such a High Priest, who is seated at the right hand of the throne of the Majesty in the heavens."** To use their own terminology, SDAs "desolate" this main point from chapters 1-7 that Jesus has already been ministering, not as an ordinary priest, but as High Priest *since His ascension* to the "right hand of the throne." When they describe his ministry as that of an ordinary priest only inside the holy place until 1844, they completely miss the "main point" of "why" he is "seated at the right hand of the throne." He had already fulfilled His High Priestly Day of Atonement pattern and was/is already in the very Presence of the Father. That is why he is *seated.*

Heb. 8:4 For *if he were* on earth, he should *not* be a priest, seeing that there are priests that offer gifts according to the law. [Note the contrast.]
Heb. 8:5 Who serve *unto the example and shadow of heavenly things*, as Moses was admonished of God when he was about to make the tabernacle: for, See, he said, that you make all things according to the *pattern shown* to you in the mount.
Heb. 8:6 *But now* he has obtained a *more excellent ministry*, by how much also he is the mediator of a *better covenant*, which was established upon *better promises.* [Note the contrast.]
Heb 8:7 For *if that first covenant had been faultless*, then should no place have been sought for the second. [Note the contrast.]
Heb. 8:8 For finding fault with them, he said, Behold, the days come, saith the Lord, when I will make a *new* covenant with the house of Israel and with the house of Judah. [Note the contrast.]

SDAs use 8:5 completely out of context. They quote it to prove that the heavenly New Covenant sanctuary must also follow the same pattern given to Moses for the Old Covenant sanctuary. However, both verse 4 and verse 6 prove the SDA explanation to be wrong.

Hebrews 8:4 repeals patterns. It teaches "pattern-*dissolution*," not "pattern-fulfillment." (1) Christ was "out of Judah; of which tribe Moses spoke nothing [in the law-pattern] concerning priesthood (7:14). (2) Since Christ was after the order of Melchizedek, it was "far more evident" that he was not following the law-pattern (7:15). (3) Christ's priesthood came into existence specifically "not after the law of a carnal commandment, but after the power of an endless life" (7:16)—meaning that it was not patterned "according to the law."

The "example and shadow of heavenly things" (8:5) means "the example and shadow of heavenly things—*for the Old Covenant.*" The priests were still serving even while the words were being written. However, 8:6 begins with "*but now*" which again shows contrast, not pattern. Christ's "*more excellent* ministry," of "a better covenant" "upon *better* promises" was necessary because the former patterns, examples and copies were "*faulty*" (8:7-8). It was a "*new*" covenant, nor a "revision" of the "old" law-pattern (8:8).

Breaking with the old law-pattern, the New Covenant was "*not* according to" the [old] covenant (8:9). In fact, the New Covenant took the moral essence of the Law out of the Old Covenant Most Holy Place and placed it *inside* of the believer (8:10)! And the teaching-hierarchy from priests to Levites to elders to commoners was replaced by the *priesthood of all believers* (8:11).

Heb. 8:12 For I will be merciful to their unrighteousness, and their sins and their iniquities I will remember no more.

Hebrews 8:12 is of particular importance because it refers to the Day of Atonement, "For I will be merciful to their unrighteousness, and their sins and their iniquities will I *remember no more.*" Contrast, not pattern is stressed! The O. T. pattern was repeated because sins and iniquities were still remembered. The fulfillment of this text began at Calvary, not in 1844! When Hebrews 10:3 says "in those sacrifices there is a *remembrance* again made of sins *every year*," it is referring to its context, "For the law having a shadow of good things to come" (10:1). Specifically, the Day of Atonement was the time that Israel "remembered" their sins once a year. The "shadow" of the Day of Atonement met its "reality," not in 1844, but at Calvary! Even Arminians teach that [at the very least] confessed, forgiven and atoned sins of believers have already been forever washed away by the blood of Jesus Christ, never to be remembered again. Yet SDAs apply the final fulfillment of this promise to the end of the Investigative Judgment (GC485).

Heb. 8:13 In that he says, A *new* covenant, he has made the first *old.* Now that which is *decaying* and *waxing old* is ready to *vanish* away.

Chapter 8 ends with the conclusion that the Old Covenant law-pattern was "becoming obsolete, growing old and ready to disappear" (8:13) NASU. Thus, the SDA argument for exact pattern-fulfillment ignores the context of 8:1-13 and only partially quotes 8:5 out of context.

Heb. 9:1 Then verily the first covenant had also ordinances of divine service and a worldly sanctuary [*to hagion*].

Heb. 9:3 And after the second veil, the tabernacle which is called the Holiest of all [*hagia hagioon*].

Heb. 9:7 But into the second went the high priest alone once every year, not without blood, which he offered for himself, and for the errors of the people:
Heb. 9:8 The Holy Spirit this signifying, that the way into the holiest of all [*toon hagioon*] was not yet made manifest, while as the first tabernacle was yet standing:
Heb. 9:9 Which was a figure for the time then present, in which were offered both gifts and sacrifices, that could not make him that did the service perfect, as pertaining to the conscience.

Hebrews, chapter 9, continues **pattern-*dissolution***, as contrasted to pattern-fulfillment. It continues contrasting Christ's New Covenant ministry in heaven with the Old Covenant ministry in the entire earthly sanctuary (*to hagion*, v 1). While verses 2 and 6 describe the daily ministry in the outer holy place, verses 3, 4, 5 and 7 are limited to the inner Most Holy Place.

A Greek word-play exists between verses 1 and 9. "Sanctuary" in verse 1 is *to hagion*, meaning "the holy (place)." "Holiest of all" in verse 3 is *hagia hagioon*, meaning "holy of holies." "Holiest of all" in verse 8 is *toon hagioon*, meaning "the holies." Grammatically and contextually, "holiest of all" in verse 8 is not referring to "holiest of all" in verse 3. Instead, it is a superlative of *to hagion* in verse 1.

Therefore, "signifying" in verse 8 refers to all of verses 1-7 and not merely verse 3. In other words, as long as the *entire* Old Covenant sanctuary ministry from verses 1-7 continued (the O. T. "holy" sanctuary), the Holy Spirit was indicating "that it was not yet time for Christ's's High Priestly ministry in the New Covenant's ("holiest") sanctuary to begin." Most Christians believe that, when the veil of the Temple was ripped open at Christ's death on Calvary, the Old Covenant sanctuary lost its significance. Even some SDA scholars have agreed to this interpretation of verse 8. See *Questions on Doctrine*, 385, footnote.

Heb. 9:9 *Which was a figure for the time then present,* in which were offered both gifts and sacrifices, that could not make him that did the service perfect, as pertaining to the conscience.
Heb. 9:10 Which stood only in food and drink, and various washing, and carnal ordinances, imposed on them *until* the time of reformation.

SDAs part with the majority of Christendom at Hebrews 9:9. The truth is that all of the patterns, examples and shadows given to Moses in the Law were only patterns of Old Covenant pre-Calvary reality! However, according to 9:9, *everything* in the sanctuary mentioned from verse 1 to 8, including the Day of Atonement, was only a *"figure of the time then present"*—the Old Covenant! They were not figures of New Covenant time!

SDAs try to say that the "patterns" were for the Old Covenant, but that the "reality" is for the New Covenant. However, the New Covenant sanctuary where Christ ministers as High Priest does not have "reality counterparts" for many priests, twice-daily burnt offerings, daily animal sacrifices, grain offerings, drink offerings and ritual washings because all of those patterns were only for the Old Covenant which ended "in the time of reformation" (9:10).

Heb. 9:11 But Christ being come an high priest of good things to come, by a greater and more perfect tabernacle, not made with hands, that is to say, not of this building.

The explanation for the Seventh-day Adventist key text of 9:23 begins here at 9:11. Unfortunately (for SDAs) the context is not about Christ entering the heavenly sanctuary to fulfill the Day of Atonement imagery. Instead it is about Christ partially following Moses' example from Exodus 24:3-8 and anointing the heavenly sanctuary **to inaugurate His New Covenant ministry.**

Heb. 9:12 Neither by the blood of goats and calves, but by his own blood he entered in once into the holy place [*ta hagia*], having obtained eternal redemption for us.

Although 9:11-15 might at first appear to be Day of Atonement imagery, 9:19 makes it clear that they are in the context of New Covenant *inauguration* imagery of verses 16-23.

Heb. 9:13 For if the blood of bulls and of goats, and the ashes of an heifer sprinkling the unclean, sanctifies to the purifying of the flesh:
Heb. 9:14 How much more shall the blood of Christ, who through the eternal Spirit offered himself without spot to God, purge your conscience from dead works to serve the living God?

> Ex. 24:3 And Moses came and told the people all the words of the LORD, and all the judgments: and all the people answered with one voice, and said, All the words which the LORD has said we will do.

Ex. 24:4 And Moses wrote all the words of the LORD, and rose up early in the morning, and built an altar under the hill, and twelve pillars, according to the twelve tribes of Israel.

Ex. 24:5 And he sent young men of the children of Israel, which offered burnt offerings, and sacrificed peace offerings of oxen unto the LORD.

Ex. 24:6 And Moses took half of the blood, and put it in basins; and half of the blood he sprinkled on the altar.

Ex. 24:7 And he took the book of the covenant, and read in the audience of the people: and they said, All that the LORD has said will we do, and be obedient.

Ex. 24:8 And Moses took the blood, and sprinkled it on the people, and said, Behold the blood of the covenant, which the LORD has made with you concerning all these words.

Again, in the context of verses 16-23, Hebrews 9:13 is a description of the *inauguration* of the Old Covenant from Exodus 24:3-8. Israel had agreed to enter into the Old Covenant stipulations with God (Ex. 24:3). Since this was before the first sanctuary had been built, Moses erected a temporary altar (24:4) and made burnt offerings and peace offerings (24:5). Those who were ritually clean within the camp were sprinkled with the blood (24:6). Those who had been ritually unclean outside the camp were sprinkled with the ashes of the red heifer (Heb. 9:13).

The Old Covenant inauguration "purified the flesh" through animal sacrifices (9:13). The New Covenant inauguration with the blood of Christ is much more effective. Not only does it purify the flesh, but it also "purges your conscience from dead works" (9:14). In Exodus 24:7-8 half of the blood was sprinkled on the congregation. This is obviously not a law-pattern fulfillment from the Day of Atonement!

Heb. 9:15 And for this cause he is <u>the mediator of the new testament</u>, that by means of death, for the redemption of the transgressions that were under the first testament, they which are called might receive the promise of eternal inheritance. (also Rom. 3:25)

Every sin mediated in the Old Covenant was forgiven because of the future perfect sacrifice of the sinless Lamb of God. *When this sacrifice was made by one whose human lineage was from the tribe of Judah and whose Priesthood was patterned after the Gentile Priest-King Melchizedek, the law-pattern defi-*

nitely ended. Whereas the Old Covenant High Priest could not promise eternal redemption, the New Covenant Priest-King could.

Heb. 9:19 For when Moses had spoken every precept to all the people according to the law, he took the blood of calves and of goats, with water, and scarlet wool, and hyssop, and sprinkled both the book, and all the people,
Heb. 9:20 Saying, This is the blood of the testament which God has commanded you.
Heb. 9:21 Moreover he sprinkled with blood both the tabernacle, and all the vessels of the ministry.
> **Ex. 24:8 And Moses took the blood, and sprinkled it on the people, and said, Behold the blood of the covenant, which the LORD has made with you concerning all these words.**

Again, 9:19-21 is clearly not Day of Atonement imagery! It is that of the Old Covenant inauguration from Exodus 24:3-8! The tabernacle here is the one used by Moses and the elders before God's tabernacle was built from instructions which began in Exodus 30.

Heb. 9:22 And almost all things are by the law purged [NAS, NIV: cleansed] with blood; and without shedding of blood is no remission.

This text brings the discussion from 8:1 to 9:22 to its goal. The Law required almost every ritual to begin with cleansing blood. This is not the Day of Atonement cleansing; it is every-day cleansing. The "almost" refers to rituals such as that of the red heifer and lesser grain offerings for the poor which were not performed on the Day of Atonement.

Heb 9:23 It was therefore necessary that the patterns of things in the heavens should be purified [cleansed] with these; but the heavenly things themselves with better sacrifices than these.

In order to initiate both the Old and New Covenants, blood was required. In 9:19 that blood was used to sprinkle both the book of the covenant and also the people. Therefore, the "patterns" referred o in 9:23 are primarily patterns to be followed in *inaugurating* the New Covenant!!! The "purification" of 9:23 refers to the "purification" of 9:12-14, the "sprinkling" of 9:19, and the "purification" of Exodus 24:3-8. Therefore it refers to the purification which Christ made when He *began* his New Covenant High Priestly ministry (9:12)—and not the Day of Atonement.

Why was it necessary to "purify" the "patterns of things in the heavens"? Not because of the Day of Atonement cleansing, but in order to *inaugurate* the New Covenant with the reality of the patterns necessary to *replace* the Old Covenant!

Heb. 9:24 For <u>Christ is *not*</u> entered into the holy places [*hagia*] made with hands, [which are] the figures of the true, but into *heaven itself* [*auton ton ouranon*], now to appear in the presence of God for us.
Heb. 9:25 <u>Nor yet</u> that he should offer himself often, as the high priest entering into the holy place every year with blood of others.

"Christ is not!"—the patterns have ended; the contrast now begins. The Old Covenant sanctuary had been replaced by "heaven itself." The Aaronic priesthood has been replaced with the Melchizedek priesthood (Heb. 7). The every day shadow rituals of the literal altar of burnt offering, the water laver, the loaves, the candlestick, and the altar of incense—all have ended in the reality of Christ.

"Nor yet"—even the yearly Day of Atonement has been replaced by the contrasting "once for all" perfect "entering into" heaven itself. Christ became a contrasting High Priest-King after the order of Melchizedek of which the Law and the Old Covenant pattern said absolutely *nothing* (7:12-19)! The "main point" is still that Christ is *now* seated at the right hand of God in heaven itself because He had finished His atonement (8:1). What did it take to place him there? *It took completely replacing the law-patterned priesthood with a Melchizedek priesthood patterned after eternal principles (7:16, 19-22).* It was "**necessary to change**" the law-pattern and to bring in a newer better covenant (7:12; 8:7).

> 1 Kings 8:27 But will God indeed dwell on the earth? Behold, the heaven and heaven of heavens cannot contain You; how much less this house that I have built?

> Isaiah 40:22 "It is He that sits upon the circle of the earth, and the inhabitants thereof are as grasshoppers; [it is he] that stretches out the heavens as a curtain, and spreads them out as a tent to dwell in."

SDAs want to place God into a literal room in heaven in order to justify their pattern-fulfillment scheme. However, the old sanctuary pattern of God's dwelling place was always merely symbolic. The Most Holy Place of the tabernacle was fifteen foot square (15' x 15') and the Most Holy Place of Solomon's

Temple was thirty foot square (30' x 30') (1 Kg. 6:16). Are we to believe that the God of the Universe lives in a house smaller than our own?

The writer of Hebrews is telling the reader to "stop thinking about the New Covenant using Old Covenant terminology." Christ is not in a tiny building in heaven that has compartments like that of the Old Covenant. "Christ is not." Again, he "is not." He is "in heaven itself." He is already in the "presence of God for us."

Heb. 9:26a For then he must have often suffered since the foundation of the world...

"For then he must"—if Christ did not *end* the patterns, *then he must repeat them*! Is not that what the text says? If Christ did not end the daily sacrifices, then he must still die daily? If Christ did not end the yearly sacrifices (Day of Atonement), then he must still die yearly.

Heb. 9:26b...but now once in the end [consummation] of the world [ages] he has appeared to put away sin by the sacrifice of himself.

On the one hand the Old Covenant inauguration law-pattern needed to be fulfilled in order to bring in a New Covenant. On the other hand Christ did exactly that and now ministers using "new" covenant principles. The one important pattern-fulfillment carried over from the Old to the New Covenant is that remission is only obtained through the shedding of blood (9:16-22).

"But now—once—in the end of the ages"—contrast, not pattern fulfill-ment. In a one-time event which occurred about 2000 years ago, all sacrificial ends (*sun-teleo*) of all the ages were brought together and fulfilled by Jesus Christ. This includes the daily, monthly, seasonal and yearly Day of Atonement sacrifices! As far as believers are concerned, the patterns of blood-sacrificial time from Adam's first sin until the last daily morning sacrifice before Calvary have all ended in the "now." Christ's sacrifice of Himself at Calvary reached from the "foundation of the world [*kosmos*]" to the "end of the world."

"The LORD said to my Lord, Sit at my right hand, until I make your ene-mies your footstool" (Ps. 110:1). "The LORD has sworn, and will not repent, You are a priest for ever after the order of Melchizedek" (Ps. 110:4). These are Calvary events which forever ended the Old Covenant patterns.

Hebrews 9:25-26 clearly tells everybody (except SDAs) "how" Christ "cleansed" all of the heavenly things (not in 1844), but at His death, ascension and enthronement. When 9:25 says "as the high priest entered into the holy place every year," there can be absolutely no doubt that it is referring to the

Most Holy Place on the Day of Atonement. *Ta hagia*, translated "holy place" in the KJV can also be translated "the holies" and is translated "Most Holy Place" in both the New KJV and the NIV.

While SDAs proclaim 1844 as the Day of Atonement and as a "last day event" warning about the nearness of the "end of the age," they ignore 9:26b which clearly places the event at the "now" of Calvary. This same "end of the age," "fulness of time" and "these last days" application of Calvary is also found in Acts 2:17; First Corinthians 10:11; Galatians 4:4; Ephesians 1:10; Hebrews 1:2 and First Peter 1:20—and none of these refer to 1844.

Heb. 9:27 And as it is appointed unto men once to die, but after this the judgment [*krisis*].
Heb. 9:28 So Christ was once offered to bear the sins of many; and unto them that look for him shall he appear the second time without sin [not to deal with sin: RSV] unto salvation.

On the one hand, when believers are not involved, the normal sequence is for all men to die and face God in an after-death judgment similar to that of Revelation 20:11-13. Without Christ, all men will eventually be judged by the works they did while they were living (9:27).

On the other hand, for believers, Jesus Christ the Melchizedek High Priest-King broke the law-pattern and died "once." This is still all-inclusive terminology which began in verse 25. *The "end of the age" "judgment" appointment for believers in verse 27 is missing in verse 28 because the believers' sins were judged in Christ at Calvary.* The "judgment" for believers was brought forward from the end of literal time to the "end" of salvation-time at Calvary. Since only the sins of believers were involved in the sanctuary ministry, then Christ's death at Calvary fulfilled the Day of Atonement for believers. Unbelievers still face the "great white throne" judgment of Revelation 20.

This is also the meaning of John 3:16. The judgment decree of "eternal life" brings the decree from the end of literal time forward to the moment one "believes." John 5:24 says "He that hears my word, and believes on him that sent me, [already] has everlasting life, and shall not come into condemnation [*krisis*: judging process] but has passed [already] from death unto life." Romans 8:1 says "There is therefore now no condemnation [*kata-krima*: contrary judgment sentence] to them which are in Christ Jesus." SDAs attempt to change the meaning of *krisis* in John 5:24 from "judgment" into "condemnation.." However, *kata-krisis* and *kata-krima* are the terms for "condemnation" or "judgment *against*." See *Questions on Doctrine*, 418-419.

Believers were looking for Christ to return even in the first century, not because of an Investigative Judgment which did not begin until 1844, but because he had already completely dealt with their sins at Calvary, had applied His atonement at the moment they accepted Him as Lord and Savior and, under the New Covenant terms, had claimed the promise that "their sins and iniquities will I remember no more"—forgotten even in the first century.

CHAPTER TEN

THE ERROR OF SIN TRANSFER INTO THE SANCTUARY

GC418: [Ellen G. White] The ministration of the earthly sanctuary consisted of two divisions; the priests ministered daily in the holy place, while once a year the high priest performed a special work of atonement in the most holy, for the cleansing of the sanctuary. Day by day the repentant sinner brought his offerings to the door of the tabernacle, placing his hand upon the victim's head, confessed his sin, thus in figure transferring them from himself to the innocent sacrifice. The animal was then slain. "Without shedding of blood," says the apostle, there is no remission of sin. "The life of the flesh is in the blood." Leviticus 17:11. The broken law of God demanded the life of the transgressor. The blood, representing the forfeited life of the sinner, whose guilt the victim bore, was carried by the priest into the holy place, and sprinkled before the veil, behind which was the ark containing the law that the sinner had transgressed. _By this ceremony the sin was, through the blood, transferred in figure to the sanctuary._ In some cases the blood was not taken into the holy place, but the flesh was to be eaten by the priest, as Moses directed the sons of Aaron saying "God has given it unto you to _bear the iniquity_ of the congregation." Leviticus 10:17. Both ceremonies alike symbolized the _transfer of the sin from the penitent to the sanctuary_."

GC419 Such was the work that went on day by day throughout the year. _The sins of Israel were thus transferred to the sanctuary, and a special work became necessary for their removal._ God commanded that an atonement be made for _each_ of the sacred apartments. 'He made an atonement for _the holy place [Most Holy Place]_ because of the _uncleanness_ of the children of Israel and because of their transgressions _in all their sins_: and so shall he do for _the tabernacle of the congregation [Holy Place]_ that remaineth among them in the midst of their _uncleanness.'_ An atonement was also to be made for _the altar_ to 'cleanse it and hallow it from the _uncleanness_ of the children of Israel.' Leviticus 16:16, 19.

GC420"Important truths concerning the atonement are taught by the typical service. A substitute was accepted in the sinner's behalf, *but the sin was not canceled by the blood of the victim*. A means was thus provided by which *it was transferred to the sanctuary*. By the offering of blood the sinner acknowledged the authority of the law, confessed his guilt in transgression, and expressed his desire for pardon through faith in a Redeemer to come; *but he was not yet entirely released from the condemnation of the law*. On the Day of Atonement the high priest, having taken an offering from the congregation, went into the most holy place with the blood of this offering, and sprinkled it upon the mercy seat, directly over the law *to make satisfaction for its claims*. Then, in his character of mediator, *he took the sins upon himself and bore them from the sanctuary*. Placing his hands upon the head of the scapegoat, he confessed over him *all these sins, thus in figure transferring them from himself to the goat*. The goat then bore them away, and they were regarded as forever separated from the people.

The underlined portions above are the heart of the Seventh-day Adventist cultic doctrine. To condense GC417-420, SDAs, unlike any other Christian denomination, teach that sacrificial blood which was carried into the sanctuary literally defiled it with sin and literally caused the "transfer of the sin from the penitent to the sanctuary." "The sin was not canceled by the blood of the victim," but "it was transferred to the sanctuary." "He [the sinner] was not yet entirely released from the condemnation of the law." On the Day of Atonement the high priest entered the Most Holy Place "to make satisfaction for its [the Law's] claims." Then, "he took the sins upon himself and bore them from the sanctuary.""He confessed over him [Satan, the scapegoat] all these sins, thus in figure transferring them from himself to the goat."

Only SDAs teach that both the earthly Old Covenant and the heavenly Old and New Covenant sanctuaries were literally defiled by the confessed, forgiven and atoned sins of God's children and required "cleansing" from these sins. They then use the Old Covenant sanctuary's yearly cleansing pattern on the Day of Atonement in Leviticus 16 to interpret Daniel 8:14 as a reference to the heavenly sanctuary. Beginning on October 22, 1844 (they teach) Jesus began His final ministry to remove those sins from His Most Holy Place.

CHAPTER ELEVEN

THE TRUTH ABOUT THE BIBLICAL SANCTUARY

ONE: Only General and Accidental Sins Were Daily Confessed in the Sanctuary

Sin Offering: Atonement for specific unintentional sin; included confession, forgiveness and cleansing from defilement; Lev. 4:1-5:13; 6:24-30; 8:14-17; 16:3-22; per *The NIV Study Bible*

Lev. 4:2 If *a person* shall *sin through ignorance* against any of the commandments of the LORD…
Lev 4:3 If *the priest that is anointed* do sin according to the sin of the people….
Lev 4:12 When *a ruler* has sinned, and done somewhat *through ignorance* against any of the commandments of the LORD….
Lev. 4:13 And if *the whole congregation* of Israel sin through ignorance, and the thing be hid from the eyes of the assembly, and they have done somewhat against any of the commandments of the LORD concerning things which should not be done, and are guilty;
Lev. 4:14 When the sin, which they have sinned against it, is known, then the congregation shall offer a young bullock for the sin, and bring him before the tabernacle of the congregation.
Lev. 5:1 Now if a person sins after he hears a public *adjuration to testify* when he is a witness, whether he has seen or otherwise known, if he does not tell it, then he will bear his guilt. NASU
Lev. 5:2 Or if a soul *touch any unclean thing*, whether it be a carcase of an unclean beast, or a carcase of unclean cattle, or the carcase of unclean creeping things, and if it be *hidden* from him; he also shall be unclean, and guilty.

Lev. 5:3 Or if he touch the uncleanness of man, whatsoever uncleanness it be that a man shall be defiled withal, and it be *hid* from him; when he knows of it, then he shall be guilty.

Lev. 5:4 Or if a soul swear, pronouncing with his lips to do evil, or to do good, whatsoever it be that a man shall pronounce with an oath, and it be *hid* from him; when he knows of it, then he shall be guilty in one of these.

Lev. 5:5 And it shall be, *when he shall be guilty in one of these things, that he shall confess that he as sinned in that thing.*

Lev. 5:15-16; 22:14-16 [unintentionally eats a gift which had been promised to God]

Guilt Offering: Atonement for Unintentional Sin Requiring Restitution; Lev. 5:14-16:7:1-6; per *The NIV Study Bible. The Wycliffe Bible Commentary* adds "The sin offering (chap. 4) stressed the sins of which one became conscious. The trespass or guilt offering emphasized that situation in which one felt guilt but was unable to specify it exactly."

Lev. 6:2 [deception regarding a deposit]
Lev. 6:3 [lie about finding something which was lost]
Lev. 6:4, 5 [restitution plus one fifth]

With very limited exceptions, only specific accidental sins (sins of ignorance) and non-high-handed sins were atoned by individual sin and trespass offerings in the normal sanctuary routine. Another exception was a goat for a general sin offering which was offered every Sabbath and on seasonal sabbaths (Numb. 28:15).

These biblical facts destroy the entire SDA doctrine of sin transfer because (at least in the Old Testament) deliberate. high-handed and wilful sins were never confessed over sacrificial animals and, therefore, were never brought into the sanctuary (as SDAs claim) to "defile" it. Our practice of confessing and receiving forgiveness of all sins (high-handed, deliberate, wilful, general and accidental) does not follow the Old Covenant sanctuary pattern at all. Yet the book of Leviticus makes it clear that (normally) only unintentional non-high-handed sins committed accidentally or in ignorance could be atoned through individual confession and sacrifice. Where another's property was involved, confession required restitution plus an offering (Lev. 5:16; 6:4-5).

Therefore, when Seventh-day Adventists include confessed and forgiven *deliberate* sins among those which (they say) defile the most holy place during the daily ministration of the sanctuary service (Old and New Covenant) they blatantly misunderstand the nature of the sins involved.

TWO: Pre-meditated, High-handed, Intentional, Deliberate, Wilful Sins Could Not be Atoned by Daily Personal Sacrifices.

Numb. 15:30 But the person that does anything presumptuously [defiantly], whether he be born in the land, or a stranger, the same reproaches the LORD; and that person shall be cut off from among his people. [Note that no sacrifice was prescribed.]

Numb. 15:31 Because he has despised the word of the LORD, and has broken his commandment, that person shall utterly be cut off; his iniquity shall be upon him.

Numbers 15:30-31 makes it clear that there was no sacrifice permitted for deliberate pre-meditated wilful sin under the Old Covenant pattern. This even applied to people, like lepers, who continued to be unclean beyond their own control.

When a person committed most pre-meditated sins, there was no pre-scribed sacrifice to bring. No appeasement could be made to God. That person must suffer the disciplinary consequences and responsibility of his/her sin. He/she was totally at the mercy of God, the judges, their accusers and those whom they had sinned against.

Ex. 21:23 And if any mischief follow, then you shalt give life for life,
Ex. 21:24 Eye for eye, tooth for tooth, hand for hand, foot for foot,
Ex. 21:25 Burning for burning, wound for wound, stripe for stripe.

When a serious high-handed deliberate sin had been committed, death, or cutting off, was often the penalty, or consequence. The judges declared a "life for life, eye for an eye, tooth for a tooth." **No sacrifice was acceptable! Death—not a sacrifice—was the punishment for** idolatry (Ex. 22:20), blaspheme of God's name (Lev. 24:16); adultery (Lev. 20:10), incest (Lev. 20:11), homosexuality (Lev. 20:13), working on the Sabbath Day (Ex. 31:14); cursing parents (Lev. 20:9), child sacrifice (Lev. 20:2), sex with animals (Lev. 20:15) and witchcraft (Ex. 22:18). This also explains why God did not command a sacrifice when Moses struck the rock (Numb. 20), when Achan became a thief (Josh. 7), when David was declared guilty of murder (2 Sam. 12), when Herod accepted praise as a god (Acts 12), and when Ananias and Sapphira lied to God (Acts 5). God did not provide a sacrifice; instead, he judged and punished the sin. The guilty persons "bore their own iniquity." See Numb. 5:31; 30:15 ; Eze. 18:20.

THREE: Pre-meditated Sins of Believers Bring God's Discipline

1 Cor. 11:27 Wherefore whosoever shall eat this bread, and drink this cup of the Lord, unworthily, shall be guilty of the body and blood of the Lord.
1 Cor. 11:28 But let a man examine himself, and so let him eat of that bread, and drink of that cup.
1 Cor. 11:29 For he that eats and drinks unworthily, eats and drinks damnation to himself, not discerning the Lord's body.
1 Cor. 11:30 For this cause many are weak and sickly among you, and many sleep.

Heb. 2:2 For if the word spoken by angels was steadfast, and every transgression and disobedience received a just recompense of reward;
Heb. 2:3 How shall we escape, if we neglect so great salvation; which at the first began to be spoken by the Lord, and was confirmed unto us by them that heard him.

Heb. 10:26 For if we sin wilfully after that we have received the knowledge of the truth, there remains no more [NKJ, NAS, RSV: no longer remains] sacrifice for sins,
Heb. 10:27 But a certain fearful looking for of judgment and fiery indignation, which shall devour the adversaries.

The Hebrew sacrificial system was not designed to convert non-Israelites into Israelites. Those who brought sacrifices were already Israelites through birth, circumcision, genealogy and/or the Passover event. In other words, they were *already* in a special covenant **relationship** with Yahweh. God gave them His law, holiness code and sacrificial system in order to keep them in **fellowship** with Him and to restore fellowship with Him. As His children, if they committed accidental sins, there was a means to receive forgiveness and escape discipline. However, when they committed wilful and deliberate sins against his known will, then they could expect often severe discipline as his children.

The correct explanation of the controversial verse, Hebrews 10:26, may possibly be found in the discussion of wilful sin and the sanctuary. The point is that, even if the SDA doctrine that confessed sins defiled the sanctuary was correct (and it is not), a great many sins committed by Old Covenant Hebrews and New Covenant Christians do not qualify as "accidental sins" and the entire doctrine again becomes unnecessary and irrelevant.

Heb. 10:30 For we know him that has said, Vengeance belongs to me, I will recompense, says the Lord. And again, The Lord shall judge his people.
Heb. 10:31 It is a fearful thing to fall into the hands of the living God.

Heb. 12:8 But if you are without chastisement, whereof all are partakers, then you are bastards, and not sons.

Jesus can only die once for the sins of believers. Comparable to Old Testament Israelites, once one becomes a Christian, he/she is a member of God's family and has a **relationship** with Him. Punishment for sins committed after becoming a member of God's household fall under the category of discipline to restore **fellowship** (Prov. 23:14; Heb. 10:30, 31; 12:8). Such discipline might even include death (1 Cor. 11:30). The child of God cannot re-sacrifice Christ to cover willful sin. He/she can confess sins, ask for mercy and pray for reconciliation into God's fellowship without subsequent discipline, or he/she can expect judgment and strict discipline. Discipline is God's prerogative!

FOUR: Un-Atoned Sins Defile the Sanctuary

Lev. 15:31 Thus shall you separate the children of Israel from their uncleanness that they do not die in their uncleanness when *they defile my tabernacle that is among them.* (See 15:25-31; women's issue of blood.)

Lev. 18:28 That the land does not spit you out also when *you defile it,* as it spat out the nations that were before you. (See 18:1-28.)

Numb. 5:2 Command the children of Israel that they put out of the camp every leper, and every one that has an issue [of blood] and whosoever is defiled by the dead.
Numb. 5:3 Put out both male and female. Put them outside the camp that they *do not defile their camps in the MIDST whereof I dwell.*

Numb. 19:13 Whosoever touches the dead body of any man that is dead and does not purify himself *defiles the tabernacle* of the LORD and that person shall be cut off from Israel...(See also 19:20.)

Numb. 35:34 Do not defile the land which you shall inhabit wherein I dwell. For I the LORD dwell among the children of Israel.

Ezra 2:62 (also Neh.7:64): These sought their register among those that were reckoned by genealogy but they were not found. Therefore were they, *as polluted*, put from the priesthood.

While SDAs emphatically stress that the sanctuary was defiled *by the confessed, forgiven and atoned sins* of God's people, exactly the opposite is true! The sanctuary was defiled by *un*-atoned sins. In fact the atoned sins were the only ones that did *not* defile the sanctuary!

First, Leviticus 15:25-31 teaches that Israelite women *who do not ritually purify themselves* from their "issue of blood" "*defile the sanctuary*"—thus the sanctuary was defiled by *not* being cleansed through its use. **Second,** in its context, Leviticus 18:28 and Numbers 35:34 teach that the land itself was *defiled* by deliberate wilful sin (which could not be brought into the sanctuary as unintentional sins). **Third,** like unclean women, Numbers 5:2-3 also teaches that lepers *defile* the camp. Yet, as long as they remained leprous, there was no sacrificial offering for them in the sanctuary. **Fourth,** in Numbers 19:13, 20 a person who touched dead animals or persons "*and does not purify himself defiles the tabernacle*." **Fifth,** Ezra 2:62 teaches that "polluted" priests could not minister in the sanctuary—which proves that they could not carry sin into it.

Therefore, contrary to what SDAs teach, there is no Bible text which says that *atoned* sins defile the sanctuary!!! The land, the camp and the tabernacle were all defiled by either deliberate sin or other sins which could not be atoned by sacrifice! Thus exactly the opposite of what SDAs teach is true.

The atoned sins were washed away by the sinless blood of the sacrificial animal, a type of Christ. This death occurred at the "doorway" of the inner court which was reserved for the Levites and priests (Lev. 1:3; 3:2; 4:4; etc). Neither the penitent nor the live animal entered into the sanctuary proper.

FIVE: The Day of Atonement Ritual Only Removed General Sinfulness Which Remained

Lev. 16:16 And he shall make an atonement for the holy place [MHP], *because of the uncleanness [NAS: impurities] of the children of Israel, and because of their transgressions in ALL their sins*: and so shall he do for the tabernacle of the congregation [NAS: tent of meeting; HP], that remains [NAS: abides] among them in the MIDST of their uncleanness.
Lev 16:17 And there shall be no man in the tabernacle of the congregation [HP] when he goes in to make an atonement in the holy place [MHP], until he comes out, and has made an atonement *for himself, and for his household, and for all the congregation of Israel.*

Lev 16:18 And he shall go out unto the ALTAR that is before the LORD, and make an atonement for it; and shall take of the blood of the bullock, and of the blood of the goat, and put it upon the horns of the ALTAR round about. [Note: This is the altar of burnt offerings inside the entrance of the open courtyard.]
Lev. 16:19 And he shall sprinkle of the blood upon it [altar of burnt offerings] with his finger seven times, and cleanse it, and hallow it *from the uncleanness of the children of Israel.*
Lev. 16:20 And when he has made an end of reconciling the *holy place*, AND the *tabernacle of the congregation*, AND the *altar*, he shall bring the live goat.
Lev. 16:30 For on that day shall the priest make an atonement for you, to cleanse you, that you may be clean *from all your sins* before the LORD.

In their 1844 pattern-fulfillment scheme, SDAs teach that only the Most Holy Place required cleansing from the defilement of sacrificial blood which had carried confessed and atoned sins into it.

However, the preceding verses (16-20, 30) from the Day of Atonement's most important chapter, Leviticus 16, prove that exactly the opposite is true. **First**, this was a general, all-inclusive, cleansing of ALL of the remaining un-atoned sins of Israel. It was a new beginning for the new year immediately prior to entrance into God's rest (symbolized by the fall harvest and the entrance into Canaan).

"And he shall make an atonement for the holy place, because of *the uncleanness* of the children of Israel, and *because of their transgressions in all their sins*: and so shall he do for the tabernacle of the congregation, *that remains [abides] in the midst of their uncleanness* (16:16). "And he shall sprinkle of the blood upon it with his finger seven times, and cleanse it, and hallow it *from the uncleanness* of the children of Israel" (16:19). "*All the iniquities* of the children of Israel, and *all their transgressions in all their sins*" (16:21). "For on that day shall the priest make an atonement for you, to cleanse you, *that you may be clean from all your sins before the LORD*" (16:30). Since only non-high-handed sins were allowed to be atoned through individual blood sacrifices, then these texts must not be referring to those specific sins which had already been forgiven and atoned. Besides, God does not require two different atonements for the same sins.

Second (and this is very important), unlike the heavenly sanctuary, the earthly sanctuary required this cleansing because it was located in the "*midst of*," in the middle of, a wicked and perverse nation. Comparable to being located in the middle of a sandstorm of sinfulness, the earthly sanctuary was surrounded by several million Israelites who habitually sinned in every conceivable way, both deliberately and accidentally. Although it was the most un-defiled place in the nation, the earthly sanctuary still became defiled merely because of its very *location* in the middle of sinners.

"Uncleanness" is Hebrew *tumot,* also meaning "filthiness." "Transgressions" is *peeshah,* also meaning "rebellion." "Sins" is *khataah,* also meaning "offense." However, the key phrase for this point is "*that remains [abides] in the midst of their uncleanness*" (16:16; also 15:3; Numb. 5:3). The pre-meditated un-confessed sins included in these four texts had not been daily confessed and had not been specifically atoned. This cleansing went far beyond merely cleansing accidental sins. Therefore, the sanctuary required a yearly cleaning, not because of confessed non-high-handed sins and not because (as SDAs teach) the priests had been transferring sin into the most holy place, but simply because of its location on earth in the middle of a sinful people.

Unger's Bible Dictionary says "The day appointed for a yearly, general, and perfect expiation for all the sins and uncleanness that might remain, despite the regular sacrifices. The Levitical ritual was a constant reminder that "the Law...can never by the same sacrifices year by year, which they offer continually, make perfect those who draw near" (Heb. 10:1). Even with the most scrupulous observance of the prescribed ordinances *many sins and defilements would still remain unacknowledged and therefore without expiation. This want was met by the appointment of a yearly, general, and perfect expiation of all the sins and uncleanness that had remained un-atoned for and uncleaned in the course of the year (Lev. 16:33)."* Nelson's Bible Dictionary* adds "The only fasting period required by the Law (Lev. 16:29; 23:31), the Day of Atonement was a recognition of man's *inability* to make any atonement for his sins." The *International Standard Bible Encyclopedia* adds "The atonement takes place for the sanctuary which has been defiled by the contamination of the Israelites."

Heb. 10:1 "For the law having a shadow of good things to come, and not the very image of the things, can never with those sacrifices which they offered year by year continually make the comers thereunto perfect.
Heb. 10:2 For then would they not have ceased to be offered because that the worshipers once purged should have had no more conscience of sins.
Heb. 10: But in those sacrifices there is a *remembrance* again made of sins every year."

These verses best explain the reason for the failure of the earthly Day of Atonement." Sins were still "*remembered,*" not because they were still on the books, but because the entire sequence of rituals must be repeated year by year until a perfect sacrifice was made.

SIX: The Entire Sanctuary Was Cleansed on the Day of Atonement

In their application of pattern-fulfillment beginning on October 22, 1844, SDAs teach that only the Most Holy Place required cleansing on the Day of Atonement.

However, Leviticus 16:16-20 (see above) clearly point out how much cleansing was required on the single Day of Atonement.

16:16, 17, 20, 33 the **Most Holy Place** (SDAs agree); called the "holy place" in KJV

16:16, 17, 20, 33 the **Holy Place,** called the tabernacle (tent) of the congregation (meeting)

16:18, 19, 20, 33 the **Altar** of burnt offerings (inside the entrance)

SDAs pattern-fulfillment theology must ignore the Bible fact that the Holy Place (the first tent) and the altar of burnt offering also required the cleansing ritual. They must ignore this in their explanation because Christ had already been ministering inside the Holy Place since his ascension. See discussion on pattern-fulfillment.

SEVEN: Sin/sinners Cannot Survive in the Presence of God

Ex. 33:22 And it shall come to pass, while my glory passes by, that I will put you in a cleft of the rock and will cover you with my hand while I pass by.
Ex. 33:23 And I will take away my hand and you shalt see my back parts, but my face shall not be seen.

Lev. 16:13 And he shall put the incense upon the fire before the LORD that the cloud of the incense may cover the mercy seat that is upon the testimony— that he die not.

Isa. 6:3 Holy, holy, holy, is the LORD of hosts. The whole earth is full of his glory.
Isa. 6:4 And the posts of the door moved at the voice of him that cried and the house was filled with smoke.
Isa. 6:5 Then I said, Woe is me! for I am undone because I am a man of unclean lips, and I dwell in the midst of a people of unclean lips—for mine eyes have seen the King, the LORD of hosts.

2 Chron. 26:19 Then Uzziah was angry, and had a censer in his hand to burn incense: and while he was angry with the priests, the *leprosy* even rose up in his forehead before the priests in the house of the LORD, from beside the incense altar.

The Hebrew sanctuary and Temple were designed to reveal the holiness and purity of their God who cannot tolerate sin in His presence. The sinner and sin stopped at the doorway, or entrance, to the holy ground. And only after the innocent sacrificial animal had died could its (now most holy) blood and flesh be brought beyond the doorway. The SDA doctrine that the sin itself was deliberately brought inside the dwelling place of God by either the sacrificial blood or sacrificial flesh eaten by the priests violates everything we know about the holiness of God.

When Moses asked to see God's glory (Ex. 33:18), he was only allowed to see the distant recession as God passed (33:22-23). In Leviticus 16:13 the High Priest could not enter the Most Holy Place on the Day of Atonement unless the room was first filled with dense smoke of incense. In Isaiah 63:3-5 the prophet became aware of his horrible sinfulness when confronted with the throne of God. In Second Chronicles 26:19, when King Uzziah dared to enter the Holy Place and offer incense, God struck him with leprosy. In Ezekiel 1:1-23 and Revelation 1:12-18 the prophets are equally struck with the holiness of God and His throne. Yet SDAs make God's throne room into the storage room for all confessed and atoned sins since Adam.

2 Thess. 2:8 And then shall that Wicked be revealed, whom the Lord shall consume with the spirit of his mouth and shall destroy with the brightness of his coming.

Rev. 22:3 And there shall be no more curse [of sin]: but the throne of God and of the Lamb shall be in it. And his servants shall serve him.

During the Passover ritual, no leaven (or sin) was allowed inside the houses of believers. "Put away leaven out of your houses" (Ex. 12:15) because "A little leaven leavens the whole lump (Gal. 5:9). In Second Thessalonians 2:8 it is the very presence of God's glory and holiness that will destroy the wicked when Jesus returns. *Although the earthly sanctuary was located in the middle of a wicked and sinful people, that cannot be said of the sanctuary in heaven.* It is inconceivable to think that God would allow the Most Holy Place of the entire universe to be corrupted by sin for any length of time—much less since Adam! Yet this is exactly what SDAs teach.

EIGHT: Clean-to-Unclean Defilement Laws

Lev. 5:2 Or *if a soul touch any unclean thing,* whether it be a carcase of an unclean beast, or a carcase of unclean cattle, or the carcase of unclean creeping things, and if it be hidden from him; *he also shall be unclean and guilty.*

Under the normal day-to-day circumstances of Old Testament life, the "unclean" defiled anything "clean" which it touched (Lev. 5:2). Most of us realize that this is the normal way in which infection spreads. When something dirty touches something which is not antiseptically clean, then usually both items/persons become dirty. *Sin and sin-laden blood normally defile!*

NINE: Unclean-to-Clean Sacrificial Laws

Ex. 29:37 "[The great altar] it shall be an altar most holy. Whatsoever touches the altar shall be holy [RSV: 'become holy'; already qualified to touch it]."

Lev. 6:17 It [the grain offering] shall not be baked with leaven. I have given it unto them for their portion of my offerings made by fire; *it is most holy, as is the sin offering, and as the trespass offering*
Lev. 6:18 All the males [priests] among the children of Aaron shall eat of it. It shall be a statute for ever in your generations *concerning the offerings of the LORD made by fire: every one that touches them shall be holy.*

Lev. 6:25 This is the law of the sin offering. In the place where the burnt offering is killed shall the sin offering be killed before the LORD. *It is most holy.*
Lev. 6:26 The priest that offers it for sin shall eat it: in the holy place shall it be eaten, in the court of the tabernacle of the congregation.
Lev. 6:27 Whatsoever shall *touch the flesh thereof shall be holy* [NAS: become consecrated; NIV become holy]: and when there is sprinkled of the blood thereof upon any garment, you shall wash that whereon it was sprinkled in the holy place.

Numb. 18:9 This shall be yours of *the most holy things,* reserved from the fire: every oblation of theirs, every grain offering of theirs, and every sin offering of theirs, and every trespass offering of theirs, which they shall render to me, *shall be most holy* for you and for your sons.

NORMAL   SACRIFICIAL
clean plus defiled = defiled   defiled plus sacrifice = most holy
touch dead animal = defiled   touch dead sacrificial animal = holy

It is extremely important to realize that the "clean to unclean" law (Lev. 5:2) was reversed when offerings were involved at the sanctuary or Temple. And this reversal destroys the SDA logic about the priests carrying and transferring sin into the sanctuary!

Depending on the translation, according to Exodus 29:37, any person (priest) who even touched the (most holy) altar of burnt offerings must either first "be" holy [KJV, NKJ, NAS, NIV] or will "then become holy" [RSV] or even more holy merely by touching it.

According to Leviticus 6:17, 25, all offerings which touched the sacrificial fire, including the grain offerings, were "most holy." Leviticus 6:18, 27 both say that *"every one that touches them shall be holy."* Especially after the sacrificial animal had died, everything about it was "holy"—the altar, the priest, the blood and the garment on which blood was spilled. If the blood were indeed sin-laden (which it was not),then the garment could have been washed anywhere.

Numbers 18:9 is even more clear! "Every offering" given to the priests became *most holy*, and, only as *most holy,* could it then be brought into the sanctuary! This includes both sin and trespass offerings. Therefore, far from transferring sin, sacrificial blood was *most holy*. The sin-offering itself became "most holy." The "sin" and "trespass" offerings became such, not because their blood could carry sin into the sanctuary, but because they were innocent and holy and could bear the guilt of sin by destroying it through their death. Compare also Lev. 16:19 and Ezekiel 43:20.

Ezra 2:62 These sought their register among those that were reckoned by genealogy, but they were not found: therefore were they, as *polluted* [NAS, RSV, NIV: *unclean*; NKJ: *defiled*) unclean, put from the priesthood.

Why would God command priests (as SDAs teach) to actually carry SIN into the sanctuary and defile it when He would not even allow defiled, unclean or polluted priests to minister inside it?

TEN: Sacrificial Blood Washed Away Sin When Shed at the Doorway

Lev. 4:20...and the priest shall make an atonement for them and it shall be forgiven them.

Lev. 5:6 "…and the priest shall make an atonement for him concerning his sin.
Lev. 6:7 And the priest shall make an *atonement* for him before the LORD: and it shall be *forgiven* him for any thing of all that he has done in *trespassing therein.*
See also Lev 4:26, 31, 35; 5: 10, 13, 16, 18.

When the sacrifice died as a sin offering at the entrance of the sanctuary, the payment for the confessed sin was complete. The ministering priest collected its blood which had become *most holy* (Lev. 4:20; 5:6; 6:7, 25-27; Numb. 18:9). The fat portions of the animal were placed on the altar of burnt offering, thus again confirming its holiness (Ex. 29:37). Depending on the circumstances, either the blood or portions of its flesh (eaten by the priest) were also brought into the sanctuary—again making them most holy (Numb. 18:9).

The blood was brought inside the sanctuary, not to defile it, but as a proof (receipt of payment rendered) that the redemption price had already been fully paid. The priest announced to the penitent that "an atonement for him before the LORD" had been made and that he was "forgiven" of his "trespass" (Lev. 4:20; 5:6 and 6:7).

The blood was not brought into the sanctuary, as Ellen White wrote, "*to make satisfaction for its claims*" (GC420).The "satisfaction" had *already* been made and announced when the sacrificial animal's blood was shed! Even at Calvary the atonement was made when Jesus shed his blood, pronounced forgiveness, announced "it is finished" and died.

SDAs seriously err here in two ways. First, they teach that "sin-transfer" blood literally carries the actual confessed sins into the sanctuary to defile it. Second, they teach that this *same* blood then makes atonement, or satisfaction. However, the life-blood was accepted, not because it was carrying sin, but (like Christ) because it had already washed away sin and was "most holy."

Lev. 14:19 And the priest shall offer the sin offering, and make an atonement for him [the leper] that is *to be cleansed from his uncleanness*; and afterward he shall kill the burnt offering.

Heb. 9:13 For if *the blood* of bulls and of goats, and the ashes of an heifer sprinkling the unclean, *sanctifies to the purifying of the flesh*:
Heb. 9:14 How much more shall the *blood* of Christ, who through the eternal Spirit offered himself without spot to God, *purge your conscience* from dead works to serve the living God?"

Sacrificial blood "purifies"; it does not defile! As discussed in the previous section on pattern-fulfillment, in the context of verses 16-23, Hebrews 9:13 is a description of the *inauguration* of the Old Covenant from Exodus 24:3-8. In Exodus 24 Moses began the Old Covenant with a purification ritual. Next, turning to the New Covenant inauguration, the blood of Christ's new covenant ministry purges, or purifies, the conscience of the believer (9:14).

Contrary to SDA theology, sacrificial blood always "cleansed" or "washed away" sin. Sacrificial blood did not transfer sin to another place (to be dealt with later) only to defile that other place—the Most Holy Place in heaven!

Sacrificial blood is the redemption price for sin (Eph. 1:7; Heb. 9:12). The sinner does not "give" his/her sins to God—the sinner asks God to wash them away and forget them. Why would God want or need sins? Redemption blood brings the sinner "near" to God by reconciliation—not by defiling His dwelling place (Eph. 2:13). God would not declare "peace through the blood" if that same blood had defiled His throne (Col. 1:20).

Why would believers want to boldly "enter into the holiest by the blood of Jesus" if that "holiest" contained the accumulated sins of every believer since Adam—thus making it the most unholy and most sinful place in the entire universe (Heb. 10:19 cf GC418-421)?

ELEVEN: O. T. Priests Did Not Carry Sins into the Sanctuary

NORMAL	SACRIFICIAL; PRIESTLY
"bear sins" = suffer consequences	"bear sins" = bear away via atonement

Ex. 28:38 And it [the mitre] shall be upon Aaron's forehead, that Aaron may *bear [NAS: bear away] the iniquity* of the holy things which the children of Israel shall hallow in all their holy gifts; and it shall be always upon his forehead that they may be accepted before the LORD.
[RSV: take upon himself any guilt incurred in the holy offering]
Ex 28:43 And they [consecrated priests' garments] shall be upon Aaron, and upon his sons, when they come in unto the tabernacle of the congregation, or when they come near unto the altar to minister in the holy place that they *bear not iniquity*, and die. It shall be a statute for ever to him and his seed after him.

Lev. 17:11 For the life of the flesh is in the blood: and I have given it to you upon the altar to make an atonement for your souls: for it is the blood that makes an atonement for the soul.

Numb. 18:1 And the LORD said to Aaron, You and your sons and your father's house with you shall bear the iniquity [guilt; responsibility] of the sanctuary: and you and your sons with you shall bear the iniquity of your priesthood.

Numb. 18:7 I have given your priest's office to you as a service of gift: and the stranger that comes near shall be put to death.

Numb 18:22 Neither must the children of Israel henceforth come near the tabernacle of the congregation, *lest they bear sin [inside the sanctuary],* and die.

Isa. 53:6 All we like sheep have gone astray; we have turned every one to his own way; and the LORD has *laid on him the iniquity* of us all.

Isa. 53:12 "...he bare the sin of many [until death], and made intercession for the transgressors."

As soon as the O. T. priest received the sin offering, that sin offering became *most holy* (Numb. 18:9). And merely touching the dead flesh of the sin offering also transferred more holiness to the priest (Lev. 6:27). *Therefore, instead of transferring sin into the sanctuary via the priests (as SDAs teach), the most holy sacrifice actually transferred more HOLINESS to the priests and into the sanctuary!* The holy priest was only allowed to touch, handle and work with holy things and most holy things! Exodus 28:38 explains that the priest's ministry bore away the sin from the offering, thus making the sacrifice most holy. In fact, the death penalty awaited any priest who dared to bring anything defiled into the sanctuary (Exod. 28:43).

For the priest, "bearing sin" as part of his service meant *"bearing sin away."* Since no thing (nor person) unclean or defiled was allowed to enter the sanctuary, then the sanctuary was not defiled through the normal daily ministry itself. Both the penitent and the animal being offered were first ritually purified through washing before even approaching the entrance of the inner court to present the sacrificial animal to the priest at the gate. Again, neither the live animal nor the penitent Israelite were allowed past the gate to enter inside the holy inner court and its nearby most holy altar. The priest met the penitent at the entrance where confession was made over the animal, where the slaying of the innocent victim occurred, and where atonement was proclaimed.

The vicarious death of the innocent sacrificial animal allowed the priest to grant forgiveness (Rom. 3:25; Heb. 9:15). *The sin had disappeared! The sin itself had been washed away! The sin itself never entered beyond the entrance of the inner court into that sanctuary itself.* This is a very important detail to remember.

The priest then "bore," or carried his portion of the flesh and the fatty parts of the carcase and its blood into the inner sanctuary itself to the altar of burnt offering. There the *now-"most holy" sacrifice* was either burned or partially eaten and the *now-"most holy" blood* was either poured out at the base of the altar or else brought into the Holy Place to be sprinkled before the veil of the Most Holy Place <u>as a testimony that the redemption price had been paid</u>.

Contrary to what SDAs teach, the priest did not "bear SIN" nor did he "transfer sin" into the sanctuary. Like Christ, he typically bore the GUILT (or punishment) of sin for the sinner. The blood was "proof of payment" which was presented to God. Just as Adam was punished by thorns and sweat for his sin, even so the priest's ministry of the sacrifices, his necessary job, his service, was also a type of punishment! The Aaronic priest was performing a ritual which had formerly been a required punishment by every male head-of-household. The priest was performing a sanctified and necessary act of reconciliation—not defilement.

Since any stranger, or non-priest Levite, or impure priest who entered the sanctuary was to be put to death, it is extremely illogical to teach (as SDAs do) that the pure priests routinely transferred sin into it through (of all things) the most holy sacrificial blood. Compare Numbers 18:3, 4, 7 and 22.

TWELVE: Jesus Did Not Carry Sin into the Heavenly Sanctuary

Isa. 53:6 All we like sheep have gone astray; we have turned every one to his own way; and the LORD hash laid on him the iniquity of us all.

Matt. 8:16-17 When the evening was come, they brought to him many that were possessed with devils. And he cast out the spirits with his word and healed all that were sick that it might be fulfilled which was spoken by Esaias the prophet, saying, Himself took our infirmities, and *bare our sicknesses.*

John 1:29 Behold the Lamb of God, which *takes away the sin* of the world.

Heb. 9:26…but now once in the end of the world he has appeared *to put away sin* by the sacrifice of himself.
Heb. 9:28 So Christ was once offered *to bear the sins* of many; and unto them that look for him shall he appear the second time *without sin* unto salvation.

1 Peter 2:24 Who his own self *bare our sins* in his own body on the tree.

[compare with]

GC421: [Ellen G. White]"As anciently the SINS of the people were placed by faith upon the sin offering and through its blood *transferred*, in figure, to the earthly sanctuary, so in the new covenant the SINS of the repentant are by faith placed upon Christ and *transferred, IN FACT, to the heavenly sanctuary.*

As a priest—as our High Priest—as the sinless God-man Jesus died on the cross of Calvary to pay the redemption price of sin (Heb. 9:28). Jesus carried (or bore) our sins to Calvary (and not beyond). There he died. Next he arose from the dead! Why? Because he had already "put away sin" (9:26). Because sin could not hold him in the grave! Why? Because he was still "holy, harmless, undefiled and separate from sinners" (Heb. 7:26). Jesus did not carry sins beyond the cross (1 Pet. 2:24).

All sacrificial animals were types of Jesus Christ. *SDAs are wrong when they teach that the daily, weekly, monthly and seasonal blood sacrifices defiled the temple while the yearly Day of Atonement blood cleaned it.* Shockingly, SDA theology teaches that Jesus Himself was, and still is, the greatest polluter of the heavenly sanctuary because he bore, and is still transferring sins into it (GC421).

Again, all sacrificial animals represented our perfect, pure, sinless, substitute—Jesus Christ, the Lamb of God. John the Baptist understood this when he saw Jesus and proclaimed in John 1:29, "Behold the Lamb of God, which *takes away* the sin of the world." Therefore, whatever sins had been "taken away" by the "lamb" (and other animals) prior to the Day of Atonement remained "taken away" and did not require "taking away" a second time on the Day of Atonement! *Sacrificial blood of the sin and trespass offerings was most holy and washed away sin—it did not transfer sin into the sanctuary.*

Concluding Remarks

The great Bible promises associated with forgiveness apply to the moment the blood is shed and not to a so-called Investigative Judgment which would not begin until 1844. "When I see the blood, I will pass over you" (Ex. 12:13). "Wash me, and I shall be whiter than snow" (Ps.51:7). "As far as the east is from the west, so far has he removed our transgressions from us" (Ps. 103:12). God did not store up our sins in His personal closet to bring them out again in 1844.

The Gospel of Jesus Christ is the real judgment message. Those who believe in Christ already have received the verdict of the final judgment which is "eternal life" (Jn. 3:16). The Greek word for "condemned" relates to judgment. When John 5:24 says "He that hears my word, and believes on him that sent me, has everlasting life, and *shall not come into condemnation*; but is passed from death unto life"—it means in the Greek "already has everlasting life," "*shall not come into judgment* (krisin)" and "has already passed from death to life." When Romans 8:1 says "There is therefore now *no condemnation* to them which are in Christ Jesus," it means in the Greek "*no contrary judgment sentence*" (*kata-krima*). Hebrews 9:27-28 relates to the judgment, "And as it is appointed unto men *once* to die, but after this the *judgment*: So Christ was *once* offered to bear the sins of many; and unto them that look for him shall he appear the second time without sin unto salvation." The believer's appointment to meet God at a judgment to determine guilt of innocence has already been met by Jesus Christ at Calvary. That verdict of "righteous in Christ" is placed on the believer, not after 1844, but at the moment of conversion. These great New Covenant texts applied over 1800 years before 1844. Yet SDAs teach that all believers must wait until the end of an Investigative Judgment which began in 1844 before they can be assured of their salvation.

Seventh-day Adventists do not explain *why* God waited so long to begin cleansing the heavenly sanctuary. They spend most of their efforts trying to explain *when*. This is not a trivial matter! If your favorite room were found to be incredibly defiled, how long would you wait before cleaning it? Common sense would dictate that any defilement of God's personal dwelling place would result in an immediate cleansing. Therefore, in any situation in which the sanctuary would be defiled, the priests would make every effort to clean it as soon as possible. For example, after Babylon had defiled the temple in 586 B. C. it was the very highest (to the point of being fanatical) priority of Ezra to rebuild and rededicate the Temple. And also the time of the Maccabees—even while the war was still raging around them, the Temple was restored to its rightful state in 164 B. C.

Why did not God take the very first opportunity He had to cleanse the heavenly sanctuary? And our Omniscient God must still be cleaning it today because (SDAs teach) sin is still entering! This questions brings us to the books.

CHAPTER TWELVE

THE BOOKS OF HEAVEN
Three Different SDA Explanations

SDAs really confuse the matter of books in heaven. How many different books exist? Are all of the books in the Most Holy Place in heaven, or are some kept someplace less holy, but nearby God's throne? Is there one set of books for professed believers and another set of books for unbelievers? Is the "book of life" in the O. T. the same as the "book of life" in the N. T.? Do the books contain actual "sins" or merely the "records" of sins? If they only contain the "records" of sins, then do the "records" defile God's very Presence? Since Ellen White and SDAs argue among themselves when trying to answer the above questions, it is impossible to understand precisely what they teach.

GC421: [Ellen G. White] "For eighteen centuries this work of ministration continued [only] in the <u>first apartment</u> of the sanctuary [the holy place]. The blood of Christ, pleaded in behalf of penitent believers, secured their pardon and acceptance with the Father, *yet their SINS still remained upon the books of record.* As in the typical service there was a work of atonement at the close of the year, so before Christ's work for the redemption of men is completed there is a work of atonement *for the removal of SIN from the sanctuary. This is the service which began when the 2300 days ended.* At that time, as foretold by Daniel the prophet [GC479; Dan. 7:9, 10], <u>our High Priest entered the most holy,</u> to perform the last division of His solemn work—to cleanse the sanctuary." [This paragraph follows quotations of Heb. 6:19, 20 and 9:12.] [no gaps] GC421-422: "As anciently the SINS of the people were placed by faith upon the sin offering and through its blood *transferred,* in figure, to the earthly sanctuary, so in the New Covenant the SINS of the repentant are by faith placed upon Christ and *transferred, in fact, to the heavenly sanctuary.* And as the typical cleansing of the earthly was accomplished by the removal of the SINS by which it had been polluted, so the actual cleansing of the heavenly is to be accomplished by the removal, or blotting out, of the SINS which are there recorded. But before this can be accomplished, there must be *an exami-*

nation of the books of record to determine who, through repentance and faith in Christ, are entitled to the benefits of his atonement. The cleansing of the sanctuary therefore involves a work of investigation—a work of judgment. This work must be performed prior to the coming of Christ to redeem His people; for when He comes, His reward is with Him to give to every man according to his works. Revelation 22:12."

One: When you carefully read *The Great Controversy,* Chapter 23, *What is the Sanctuary?*, pages 409-422, you will conclude SDAs teach that, in the Old Covenant, the only sins while defiled the sanctuary were those which had been (1) confessed over sacrificial blood, (2) forgiven, (3) atoned and (4) brought into the sanctuary by the priests. Therefore, the Old Covenant books should only contain the *forgiven* sins of professed believers.

GC480: "So in the great day of final atonement and investigative judgment the only cases considered are those of the professed people of God. The judgment of the wicked is a distinct and separate work and takes place at a later period. ' [For the time is come that] **Judgment must begin at the house of God: and if it first begin at us, what shall the end be of them that obey not the gospel of God?'** 1 Peter 4:17. [no gaps] [Notice the omission from 1 Peter 4:17.]

GC480: "The books of record in heaven, in which the names and <u>the deeds of men</u> are registered, are to determine the decisions of the judgment. Says the prophet Daniel: *'The judgment was set and the books were opened'* [Dan. 7:10]. The Revelator, *describing the same scene,* adds: 'Another book was opened, which is the book of life; and the dead were judged out of those things, which were written in the books, according to their works.' Revelation 20:12."

Two: When you next carefully read Chapter 28, *Facing Life's Record,* 479-491, the books being examined inside the Most Holy Place contain *all* sins, or "deeds," of professed believers, not merely the sins which had been confessed, forgiven and received atonement (GC480-482). Yet we are not told how the un-confessed and un-forgiven sins have now violated the SDA's own pattern-fulfillment (from Chapter 23) and are now inside the Most Holy Place in heaven!

Actually in the O. T. the real "investigation" by Israelites began BEFORE the Day of Atonement. It began on the first day of the tenth month (Trumpets) in connection with a call to fasting and contrition of heart. The "investigation" had been completed before the congregation presented their two goats to the

High Priest (Lev. 23:24-29). In other words, the "investigation" began "before" the Day of Atonement and "ended" on the Day of Atonement. SDAs have the investigation "beginning" on the Day of Atonement and still continuing.

SDAs have invented an "investigation" of unconfessed sin *after death* in order to determine who will remain saved. Chapters 23 and 28 contain some of the most absurd teachings ever presented to mankind in the name of Christianity.

Three: In Chapter 42, *The Controversy Ended,* 662-678 (esp. 666), the same books of record (supposedly in the Most Holy Place in heaven) are now being used to judge the *unbelievers* at the Great White Throne Judgment.

Again notice the confusion found in these statements:

GC480: "The books of record in heaven, in which the names and the deeds of men are registered, are to determine the decisions of the judgment. Says the prophet Daniel: '*The judgment was set and the books were opened*' [Dan. 7:10]. The Revelator, *describing the same scene,* adds: 'Another book was opened, which is the book of life; and the dead were judged out of those things, which were written in the books, according to their works.' Revelation 20:12."

Therefore, the contents of the books inside the Most Holy Place have changed from (1) only confessed sins of saints in Chapter 23, (2) to include all sins of saints in Chapter 28, and (3) to include all sins, including unbelievers in Chapter 42. Therefore, SDAs are inconsistent with their own teachings.

The Truth About the Books

One: THE BOOK OF LIFE. There is a difference between the Old and New Covenants' use of the term, "book of life." With the questionable exception of Daniel 12:1, in the Old Covenant, it is the "book of the living" and has little or no direct reference to afterlife. Entrance into the Old Covenant community was gained by the Passover event, genealogy and circumcision. The Law was added, not to create a *relationship*, but to maintain *fellowship*. "And it shall come to pass, that he that is left in Zion, and he that remains in Jerusalem, shall be called holy, even every one that is *written among the living* in Jerusalem" (Isa. 4:3).

Also, in the Old Covenant, "blotting out" usually meant "put to death," or "cut off from the living" with no relevance to the soul or afterlife. For example, in Exodus 32:32-33, when Moses told God "if you will not forgive Israel's sin then "blot me out of your *book*," he was neither asking to be eternally separated from God, nor was he asking to be sent to lower *Sheol*. Instead, Moses was asking God to accept himself as an innocent substitute for the sins of the guilty. God's answer, "Whosoever has sinned against me, him will I *blot out of my book*," meant that He would not accept Moses' substitute for deliberate high-handed sin. The penalty of defiant sin was being "cut off from the living" (Ex. 31:14; Lev. 17:9).

Two: THE REGISTER OF GENEALOGY. The O. T. "books" which determined access to God were the books of genealogy. The genealogies contained the names of all qualified Israelites, especially those of the priestly house of Aaron. "The LORD shall count, when he *writes* up the people, that this man was born there" (Ps. 87:6). "These are now the chief of their fathers, and this is the *genealogy* of them that went up with me from Babylon, in the reign of Artaxerxes the king" (Ezra 8:1). "And my God put into my heart to gather together the nobles, and the rulers, and the people, that they might be *reckoned by genealogy*. And I found *a register of the genealogy* of them which came up at the first, and found written therein" (Neh. 7:5). "So all Israel were reckoned by *genealogies*; and, behold, they were written in the book of the kings of Israel and Judah, who were carried away to Babylon for their transgression" (1 Chron. 9:1). "*The book of the generation* of Jesus Christ, the son of David, the son of Abraham" (Mt. 1:1).

Three: The Old Testament does not reveal a required examination of lists of sins in order to determine which had been forgiven. Again, the books which were examined at the entrance of the assemblies were the books of genealogies. Those who could not prove that they were true Israelites (community members in good standing) were not allowed full-fledged worship in the assemblies, nor full access to the sanctuary or temple. Again, this was especially true of priests. "They could not show their father's house, and their seed, whether they were of Israel" (Ezra 2:59). Those who could not prove that they were true descendants of Aaron could not enter the priesthood. Ezra 2:62 and Nehemiah 7:64 describe the removal from the "register" of those who failed to qualify for the priesthood: "These sought their *register* among those that were reckoned by *genealogy*, but they were not found; therefore were they, *as polluted,* put from the priesthood." Even the prophets were not exempt. Ezekiel 13:9, "And my hand shall be upon the prophets that see vanity, and that divine lies: they shall not be in the assembly of my people, *neither shall they be written in the writing* of the house of Israel, neither shall they enter into the land of Israel; and you shall know that I am the Lord GOD."

Four: In the New Testament, the "book of life" already contains the names of those who are true believers. The names have been written there while the believers are still living. "Rejoice because your names are written in heaven" (Lk. 10:20). "Whose names are in the book of life" (Phil. 4:3). Comparable to the Old Covenant genealogy, "To the general assembly and church of the first-born, which are written in heaven" (Heb. 12:23). In Revelation 13:8 those suffering during great tribulation already have their names "written in the book of life."

GC421: [Ellen G. White] "…before Christ's work for the redemption of men is completed there is a work of atonement *for the removal of SIN from the sanctuary. This is the service which began when the 2300 days ended.*" [in 1844]
GC421: "…so in the New Covenant the SINS of the repentant are by faith placed upon Christ and *transferred, in fact, to the heavenly sanctuary.*"

Five: "Sins" has been capitalized by this author in the Ellen White quotes for a reason. Some SDA theologians try to lessen the impact of her statements by saying she only meant "the *record* of sins" when she wrote "*their SINS still remained upon the books of record.*" Yet this cannot possibly be the meaning of all of her statements about "sins." Such claim destroys her point that "sins" were transferred into the Most Holy Place of the entire universe and that "sins" defiled it. Mere judicial "records" of pardons of sin would not defile! EGW plainly teaches that "sins" "in fact" entered the Most Holy Place in heaven.

GC479, 661
Dan. 7:10 A fiery stream issued and came forth from before him: thousand thousands ministered unto him, and ten thousand times ten thousand stood before him: the judgment was set, and the books were opened.

Dan. 7:22 until the Ancient of Days came and judgment was passed in favor of the saints of the Highest One, and the time arrived when the saints took possession of the kingdom. NASU

Six: SDAs point to Daniel 7 in an attempt to find texts which support their claim that the lives of the righteous (to determine salvation) will be investigated after their death. However, the sins of God's people are not on trial in Daniel 7. Instead, *God's people are the ones being persecuted and rescued.* The context makes it so evident that this is a judgment of, and against, the little horn and the kingdoms which have persecuted Israel that it is marginally worth discussing.

After describing the kingdoms which have persecuted God's people in verses 1-8, a judgment scene is described in verses 9-10 in which those kingdoms were punished in verses 11-12. A second look at the heavenly judgment is in verses 13-14 which has the same result of the Son of man replacing the persecuting nations with His own eternal kingdom. In verses 15-20 Daniel is not concerned about the saints being judged. Instead he is worried about the little horn. The little horn is "waging war with the saints and overpowering them" in verse 21 "until the Ancient of Days came and judgment was passed in favor of the saints" in verse 22. This obviously means "in favor of the saints" because it was "against the little horn." Yet, incredibly, the SDA Biblical Research Committee wrote in 1989, "Nowhere in Daniel 7 does the 'Son of man' judge either the little horn or the beast," *Doctrine of the Sanctuary*, 223.

According to their own *initial* explanation (GC409-422), the SDA Investigative Judgment doctrine on the Day of Atonement is an investigation of the previously recorded *forgiven* sins of professed believers which have been recorded inside the Most Holy Place through blood sacrifice and have consequently defiled it. The sins of the persecuting powers and the little horn from Daniel 7 have absolutely no relevance to this version of the SDAs' investigation.

GC480
Rev. 20:12 And I saw the dead, small and great, stand before God; and the books were opened: and another book was opened, which is the book of life: and the dead were judged out of those things which were written in the books, according to their works.
Rev. 20:15 And whosoever was not found written in the book of life was cast into the lake of fire.

Seven: Seventh-day Adventists also have no legitimate reason for quoting Revelation 20:12 in order to prove their Investigative Judgment doctrine because it occurs 1000 years after their Investigative Judgment has ended with Christ's second coming. Yet EGW calls it *"the same scene"* as Daniel 7:10, 13 in order to justify using it to explain their Investigative Judgment scenario. See especially GC480. Compare also GC548-549, 660 and 661.

Therefore, Daniel 7:10 and Revelation 20:12, the two most important texts used by SDAs to validate the presence of books at the pre-advent investigative judgment are both invalid. Daniel 7:10 is clearly a judgment against the little horn which rescues the saints and Revelation 20:12 is a post-advent judgment of unbelievers. However, if their doctrine were true, one would expect solid biblical verification.

"If God alone were concerned, there would certainly be no need of records. But that the inhabitants of the whole universe, the good and evil angels, and all who have ever lived on this earth might understand His love and His justice, the life history of every individual who has ever lived on the earth has been recorded, and in the judgment these records will be disclosed—for every man will be judged according to what is revealed in 'the books' of record (Dan. 7:10; Rev. 20:12)." *Seventh-day Adventists Answer Questions on Doctrine, 420-421*, entire paragraph quoted.

Eight: SDAs explain the delay in Christ's return by changing the "examiner" of the books from Jesus to the "**inhabitants of the whole universe, the good and evil angels, and all who have ever lived.**" Will evil angels be inside the Most Holy Place examining the life history of everybody who has ever lived? *The Great Controversy* often portrays human life in terms of a controversy, or dialog, between God and Satan. Satan challenged God with unfairness in saving some and not others. Satan has placed a doubt in the minds of all of God's creation about God's fairness. Therefore, the Investigate Judgment vindicates the righteousness of God by opening the books of record for all to view and convince themselves that God is just and fair.

However this explanation creates another huge problem. As God the Son, Christ is Omniscient and does not require researching books—He knows everything! God can very quickly personally review every record. However, the *myriads* of "other intelligent creatures" who need to research the records in order to satisfy themselves that God is just *are not omniscient!* Even the evil angels take their turns. This means that casting them into Gehenna will be delayed.

How much faith do the un-fallen angels have that God is just? On the one hand, if they (any many others) have a lot of faith in God, then they do not need to research books! On the other hand, if they (and many others) do not trust God, do they dare to leave any of the books un-researched? Therefore, how long will it take the myriads of these non-omniscient created beings to read every page of every book of every person who has ever lived? Yet this investigation must be complete before Christ can return.

Another reason for the delay of Christ's return since 1844 is the SDA doctrine of perfection among last day Seventh-day Adventists. EGW's many references to "standing before God without a mediator" refer to the 144, 000 SDAs who have achieved character perfection. They cannot recall a single sin or thought that has been unforsaken. Sadly, SDAs have forgotten that Christ comes as a Melchizedek-type **priest**-king and not only as a king. They teach that, when he removes his priestly garments and puts on his kingly garments he can no longer function as a priest and, therefore, those redeemed when he returns must be able to stand without a mediator. When the 144, 000 SDAs can prove to the world that the Ten Commandments can be perfectly observed without a mediator, then Christ will come. See GC425, 613-634.

**GC482: "Every man's work passes in review before God and is registered for faithfulness or unfaithfulness. Opposite each man's name in the books of heaven is entered with terrible exactness every wrong word, every selfish act, every unfulfilled duty, and every secret sin, with every artful dissembling. Heaven-sent warnings or reproofs neglected, *wasted moments, unimproved opportunities,* the influence exerted for good or for evil, with its far-reaching results, all are chronicles by the recording angel."

**GC483: "Names are accepted [since 1844], names rejected [since 1844]. When any have *SINS* remaining upon the books of record, *un-repented of* and *un-forgiven,* their names will be blotted out of the book of life [*salvation lost after death*], and the record of their good deeds will be erased from the book of God's remembrance" [quotes Exod. 32:33 and Ezek. 18:24]."

GC485: "The work of the investigative judgment and the blotting out of SINS is to be accomplished before the second advent of the Lord. Since the dead are to be judged out of the things written in the books, *it is impossible that the SINS of men should be blotted out until after the judgment* at which their cases are to be investigated." [quotes Acts 3:19-20] (Compare GC417-426 with 479-493.)

Nine: Again, EGW's chapter 28 (pages 479-491) contradicts her previous chapter 23 (pages 409-422). While in chapter 22, only forgiven sins are brought by blood into the sanctuary to defile it—in chapter 28 "every man's work," including unconfessed and unforgiven sins are defiling the books of heaven. And there are unforgiven sins there which now cause the forgiven sins to be erased!

How can anybody be saved? From GC483 it is clear that Seventh-day Adventists teach that God will *un-forgive* previously forgiven sin. The "record of their good deeds" must include previous sincere confessions of sin. If any un-forgiven and un-forsaken sins go to the grave, then God will "erase" those sins which have been previously forgiven. Ellen White here used the word, "erase," instead of "blotted out." Since the book of remembrance contains all good actions, then it definitely must also contain the sincere confessions of sin (GC481).

This is the reason why SDAs teach that forgiven sins must still remain on the books of heaven until immediately before Christ returns (GC420-421).

While those who have completely confessed and forsaken every sin will have their "sins" blotted out, those believers who failed to confess and forsake every sin will have the record of pardon against their confessed sins erased and their names will be blotted out of the book of life (GC483, 486).

GC483

Ezek. 18:24 But when the righteous turns away from his righteousness, and commits iniquity, and does according to all the abominations that the wicked man does, shall he live? *All his righteousness that he has done shall not be mentioned*: in his trespass that he has trespassed, and in his sin that he has sinned, in them shall he die.

Ten: Ezekiel 18:24 is quoted by Ellen White in GC483 to prove that previously forgiven sins can be reversed and unforgiven. However, Ezekiel 18 is a discussion of discipline of God's people which can (and often does) result in physical death. EGW is confusing the O. T. concept of "blotting out of the book of life" (meaning physical death) with eternal spiritual separation from God.

As discussed earlier, when Moses wanted God to "blot me out of your book" (Ex. 32:32), he was asking to be physically slain (with no relevance to his soul or to an eternal presence with God). Yet Ellen White only quoted God's reply to Moses (Ex. 32:33) when she quoted Eze. 18:24.

Ezekiel 18:24 is actually stating that previous forgiveness does not negate discipline for current and future sin! In other words, sins committed before conversion do not affect God's discipline or treatment of the person in the present. How one acts in the present determines how God disciplines in the present. This is not a discussion about unforgiving previously forgiven sins.

GC483, 484

Rev 3:1 And to the angel of the church in Sardis write; These things says he that has the seven Spirits of God, and the seven stars; I know your works, that you have a name that you live, and are dead.
Rev. 3:4 You have a few names even in Sardis which have not defiled their garments; and they shall walk with me in white: for they are worthy.
Rev. 3:5 He that overcomes, the same shall be clothed in white raiment; and I will not blot out his name out of *the book of life*, but I will confess his name before my Father, and before his angels.

Eleven: Revelation 3:1-5 are battleground texts between Calvinists and Arminians and are interpreted two different ways. On the one hand, Calvinists (Presbyterians, Reformed, and many Baptists) say that, once your name has been written in the "book of life," it cannot be removed and (they teach) these texts do not affirm that it can be removed. While the "dead" name from verse one is only on the church register on earth, the names in verse four are worthy over-comers whose names are not in jeopardy of being removed from God's book.

On the other hand, Arminians teach that the names of those who do not continue to live a Christian life can be blotted out of the book of life. However, this does not mean that God "un-forgives" forgiven sins of the past. Even though a defiant lifestyle pursued after conversion can cause one to fall from grace (they teach), Arminians do not teach that God will ever "re-investigate" previously forgiven sins before finally blotting names out of the book of life. This is an SDA oddity from GC, chapter 23.

Historically, the church at Sardis did disappear very early. Although its name as a church was blotted out, the names of the faithful within it were not blotted out.

GC418: "Remission, or the putting away of sin, is the work to be accomplished." [since 1844]

GC421, 422: "Their SINS still remained upon the books of record." "In the New Covenant the SINS of the repentant are by faith placed upon Christ and transferred, in fact, to the heavenly sanctuary." "There must be an examination of the books of record to determine who, through repentance and faith in Christ, are entitled to the benefits of his atonement."

GC484: "Jesus does not excuse their sins, but shows their penitence and faith...."

GC485: "Thus will be realized the complete fulfillment of the New Covenant promise, 'I will forgive their iniquity and I will remember their sins no more.'" [Heb. 8:12]

GC485: "It is impossible that the sins of men should be blotted out until after the judgment at which their cases are to be investigated."

GC486: Sins that have not been repented of and forsaken will not be pardoned and blotted out of the books of record, but will stand to witness against the sinner in the day of God.

Twelve: Seventh-day Adventists go far beyond the Arminian position (that sins committed after salvation can cause one to fall from grace). The above incredible statements from *The Great Controversy* are repeated for emphasis. The SDA doctrine is a denial of the New Covenant promise in Hebrews 8:12 that God chooses not to remember (at the least) sins of the past. In GC485 Ellen White places the fulfillment of this promise to long after death. Also the perfection requirements of the final section (GC482-486) make it impossible for anybody to be saved because nobody can remember all of his/her sins and control the influences of personal sins after death.

GC484: "*...when* the names entered in the book of life come up in review [after 1844] before the Judge [the Father] of all the earth. The divine Intercessor [then] presents the plea that all who have overcome though faith in his blood [then] be forgiven their transgressions...He asks for his people not only pardon and justification, full and complete [not yet granted], but a share in his glory and a seat upon his throne [not yet granted]."

Thirteen: What has Christ been doing since his ascension? To any person who really knows the gospel message, the above statement is simply ridiculous.

Rom. 3:25 Whom God has set forth to be a propitiation through faith in his blood, to declare his righteousness for the remission of sins that are past, through the forbearance of God.

Heb. 9:15 And for this cause he is the mediator of the new testament, that by means of death, for the redemption of the transgressions that were under the first testament, they which are called might receive the promise of eternal inheritance.

Fourteen: Based on Christ's eventual sacrifice, each sacrificial animal redeemed the penitent from the penalty and curse of sin (Rom. 3:25; Heb. 9:15). The redemption was effective because it granted full and complete forgiveness of sin. "Remission" means that the consequences of the sin have already been released, or canceled. However, SDAs place the "remission" of sins at the end of the Investigative Judgment, *"Remission, or the putting away of sin, is the work to be accomplished [after 1844]" (GC418).* Yet forgiveness brings remission. The pronouncement by the Old Covenant priest after the redemption for sin had been offered was *"it shall be forgiven"* (Lev. 4:20; 5:10; 6:7). SDAs cannot grasp this simple formula which occurs ten times in the Leviticus ritual alone. Contrary to EGW's statement in GC483, previously forgiven and atoned sins are never in jeopardy of being either erased or blotted out by subsequent sin.

1 John 1:3 That which we have seen and heard declare we to you, that you also may have *fellowship* with us: and truly our *fellowship* is with the Father, and with his Son Jesus Christ.

1 John 1:6 If we say that we have *fellowship* with him, and walk in darkness, we lie, and do not the truth:
1 John 1:7 But if we walk in the light, as he is in the light, we have *fellowship* one with another, and the blood of Jesus Christ his Son cleanseth us from all sin.
1 John 1:9 If we confess our sins, he is faithful and just to forgive us our sins, and to cleanse us from all unrighteousness.

GC486-487: "Our acts, our words, even our most secret motives, all have their weight for deciding our destiny for weal or woe. Though they may be forgotten by us, they will bear their testimony to justify or condemn."

Fifteen: In GC482-487 EGW says that our forgotten sins and even those which we cause by our influences after death will testify against us in the Investigative Judgment. But, un-confessed and un-forgiven *forgotten and influenced sins* would place every person under nothing but damnation.

However, the New Covenant, activated at Calvary, states "For I will be merciful to their unrighteousness, and their sins and their iniquities I will remember no more" (Heb. 8:12). Paul promised in his lifetime, "Therefore being justified by faith, we have peace with God through our Lord Jesus Christ" (Rom. 5:1). "There is therefore now no condemnation [contrary judgment] to them which are in Christ Jesus" (Rom. 8:1). "For you are dead, and your life is hid with Christ in God" (Col.3:3). These texts are not describing those who have achieved sinless perfection, but those who have achieved the *imputed* sinless perfection of Jesus Christ through faith.

First John 1:9 is a description of how believers stay in *fellowship* (not relationship) with God. Yet SDAs teach that forgotten sins, unconfessed sins and even influences of sins that continue after one dies can cause names of believers to be blotted out (GC486-487). This is garbage theology! Actually, if we confess our **known** sins (*hamartia*), then God will not only forgive those known confessed sins, but He will also "cleanse us from **all unrighteousness** (*a-dikia*).

When one (sooner or later) sins after accepting Christ, then fellowship (not relationship) is immediately broken. "Fellowship" occurs four (4) times in First John 1:3, 6 and 7. This simple teaching is why God could (and did) grant an all-inclusive forgiveness both at Passover and at the Day of Atonement.

CHAPTER THIRTEEN

ROOMS IN THE HEAVENLY SANCTUARY

GC414-415: [Ellen G. White] "The holy places of the sanctuary in heaven are represented by the *two apartments* of the sanctuary on earth. As in vision, the apostle John was granted a view of the temple of God in heaven, he behold there '*seven lamps of fire burning before the throne.*' Revelation 4:5. He saw an angel 'having a golden censer, and there was given unto him much incense, that he should offer it with the prayers of all saints upon *the golden altar which was before the throne.*' Revelation 8:3. Here the prophet was permitted to behold the *first apartment* of the sanctuary in heaven; and he saw there the 'seven lamps of fire' and 'the golden altar' represented by the golden candlestick and the altar of incense in the sanctuary on earth,"

GC421: "For eighteen centuries this work of ministration continued [only] in the *first apartment* of the sanctuary [the holy place]....so before Christ's work for the redemption of men is completed there is a work of atonement *for the removal of SIN from the sanctuary. This is the service which began when the 2300 days ended* [in 1844]. At that time, as foretold by Daniel the prophet [GC479; Dan. 7:9, 10], our High Priest *entered the most holy*, to perform the last division of His solemn work—to cleanse the sanctuary."

SDAs are forced by their Investigative Judgment doctrine to offer an extremely unusual interpretation of where Jesus went at his ascension and what he has been doing since his ascension. **First,** they teach that the heavenly sanctuary must be an exact representation of the Old Covenant sanctuary and Temple. **Second,** that means it must have rooms, or compartments, which correspond to the Holy Place and Most Holy Place of the earthly. **Third,** when Jesus ascended into heaven, sat down at the right hand of the Father and began his priestly ministry, he was only inside the corresponding Holy Place and was not in the Most Holy Place of the heavenly sanctuary. **Fourth,** Jesus did not enter into the corresponding Most Holy Place until October 22, 1844 when he began investigating the books there to determine who is qualified to be re-created when he returns. Therefore, the rooms become an important part of SDA theology.

Heb. 9:3 And after the second veil, the tabernacle which is called the Holiest of all; Heb. 9:4 Which had the golden censer, and the ark of the covenant…"

Rev. 4:2 I was in the spirit: and, behold, a throne was set in heaven, and one sat on the throne.

Rev. 5:6 And I beheld, and, lo, in *the midst of the throne* and of the four beasts, and in the midst of the elders, stood a Lamb as it had been slain, having seven horns and seven eyes, which are the seven Spirits of God sent forth into all the earth. Rev. 5:7 And he came and took the book out of the right hand of him that sat upon the throne….

AT GOD'S RIGHT HAND: For all except SDAs, the fifteen (15) "right hand" texts make it absolutely clear that Jesus was in His Father's presence *inside the Most Holy Place* in the heavenly sanctuary since His ascension. The texts are self-explanatory and unambiguous in their destruction of SDA theology. **Acts 2:33,** "Therefore being by the right hand of God exalted." **Acts 2:34,** "The LORD said unto my Lord, Sit on my right hand." **Acts 5:31,** "Him has God exalted with his right hand to be a Prince and a Savior." **Acts 7:55,** "But [Stephen], being full of the Holy Spirit, looked up steadfastly into heaven, and saw the glory of God, and Jesus standing on the right hand of God." **Acts 7:56,** "Behold, I see the heavens opened, and the Son of man standing on the right hand of God." **Romans 8:34,** "[Christ] is even at the right hand of God, who also makes intercession for us." **Ephesians 1:20,** "[God] set him at his own right hand in the heavenly places." **Colossians 3:1,** "Christ sits on the right hand of God." **Hebrews 1:3,** "[Christ] sat down on the right hand of the Majesty on high." **Hebrews 1:13,** "But to which of the angels said he at any time, Sit on my right hand." **Hebrews 8:1,** "We have such an high priest, who is set on the right hand of the throne of the Majesty in the heavens." **Hebrews 10:12,** "But this man, after he had offered one sacrifice for sins for ever, sat down on the right hand of God." **Hebrews 12:2,** "[Christ] is set down at the right hand of the throne of God." **First Peter 3:22,** "Who is gone into heaven, and is on the right hand of God." **Revelation 5:7,** "And [Christ] came and took the book out of the right hand of him that sat upon the throne."

Wherever God is—there His throne is also—and there the Most Holy Place is also! It is God's Presence, His glory, that makes the Most Holy Place into the Most Holy Place! What a simple concept! When Revelation 5:7 says, "And

[Christ] came and took the book out of the right hand of him that sat upon the throne," it is clearly telling the reader that Jesus Christ was *already* at the right hand of the Father inside the throne room after His ascension.

BETWEEN THE CHERUBIM: Likewise, the eleven (11) "between the cherubim" texts are also self-explanatory in their destruction of SDA theology. Exodus 25:22, "I will commune with you from above the mercy seat, from between the two cherubim which are upon the ark of the testimony." Numbers 7:89, "[Moses] heard the voice of one speaking unto him from off the mercy seat that was upon the ark of testimony, from between the two cherubim: and he spoke unto him." "The LORD of hosts, which *dwells between the cherubim*," First Samuel 4:4; Second Samuel 6:2; Second Kings 19:15; First Chronicles 13:6; Psalm 80:1; Isaiah 37:16. "[God] sits between the cherubim," Psalm 99:1. [God's throne is] "between the cherubim," Ezekiel 10:1-7.

Seventh-day Adventists, especially Ellen G. White, have taught that Christ did not enter into the Most Holy Place of the heavenly sanctuary at His ascension, but entered there for the first time in 1844. However, it is obvious from reading changes in their various statements of faith, baptismal certificates, apologetics and current theological statements that the discussion of "rooms" in heaven is embarrassing and should be replaced with "phases" of Christ's ministry.

Doctrine of the Sanctuary [SDA], Editor Frank Holbrook, 1989, 218. "There is *basic agreement* that Christ at His ascension entered into the very presence of God, as symbolized by the earthly high priest's entrance on the Day of Atonement. There is also *general acceptance* that neither Daniel nor a two-phased ministry are referred to in the Epistle to the Hebrews. But we do deny that His entrance into the presence of God precludes (1) a first-apartment phase of ministry or (2) marks the beginning of the second phase of his ministry." [Author's note: Parts of this SDA leadership statement will be considered as heresy among many Adventists.]

However, the statements from pages 414-421 in *The Great Controversy* are unambiguous about their teaching of "apartments" in the heavenly sanctuary. Ellen White's statements clearly contradict those of the Biblical Research Committee in the 1989 statement.

When Ellen White wrote that the "*seven lamps of fire burning before the throne*" are only in the "*first apartment*" of the heavenly sanctuary, she ignored the context of Revelation 4 and 5. In 4:2 John was caught up in the spirit to the very throne of God the Father, "And immediately I was in the spirit: and, behold, a *throne* was set in heaven, and one sat on the *throne*." From 4:1 to 5:5 there is absolutely no doubt that the throne of heaven is being described. And from 5:6 to 5:14 Jesus Christ is very clearly at the throne in the presence of the Father.

"The golden altar which was before the throne" has also been located at the throne and is not merely in an outer apartment (compare Heb. 9:3-4). The previous discussion of Hebrews 8 and 9 revealed that God's place in heaven is not a building, or room, as we know it. Since Christ began opening the seals at the throne in chapter five of Revelation, then He must still be at the throne as the seventh seal is opened in chapter eight. ("At the throne" is more appropriate than "inside the throne room.")

In the first century the Apostle John witnessed this vision of Christ un-sealing the scroll of final judgment. The historical school of interpretation allegedly followed by Seventh-day Adventists places the fulfillment of many of the seals and trumpet judgments of Revelation prior to 1844 as proof of the soon second coming. SDAs even place the end of their 1260 prophetic years at 1798. However, by doing this, they are admitting that much of the final judgment of the wicked has already taken place prior to 1844. If Christ's presence inside the Most Holy Place in Revelation 4 and 5 are indicative of the fulfillment of the anti-typical Day of Atonement, then these sequences of judgments would make sense. However, since SDAs deny this, then they are not following their own historical school of prophetic interpretation.

Some very orthodox-sounding SDA statements mean something very different when read in the light of their 1844 Investigative Judgment doctrine. For example, GC415, "In the temple in heaven, the dwelling place of God, his throne is established in righteousness and judgment. In the Most Holy Place is His Law, the great rule of light by which all mankind are tested. The ark that enshrines the tables of the Law is covered with the mercy seat, *before which Christ pleads His blood in the sinner's behalf.*"

First, this statement is subtle deception. For SDAs it really means *"before which Christ NOW, ONLY SINCE 1844, pleads His blood in the sinner's behalf."* If God's throne and dwelling place are inside the Most Holy Place, then how could Christ have been ministering before the Law from Calvary until 1844 when he was supposedly only inside the Holy Place? **Second**, some SDA theologians want to say that God's throne is moveable and was only inside the Holy Place until 1844. However, this argument destroys the entire SDA argument distinguishing between the Holy Place and the Most Holy Place before 1844. If Christ has been ministering before the Law and mercy seat since His ascension, then he has also been ministering *as high priest* (the Day of Atonement being fulfilled) since His ascension. No matter how loudly SDAs deny it, wherever God is, His throne is, and the Most Holy Place is. The SDA distinction between the Holy Place and the Most Holy Place apartments of the heavenly sanctuary are wrong.

CHAPTER FOURTEEN

INSIDE THE VEIL IN HEAVEN

GC420-421: [Ellen G. White] "The ministration of the priests throughout the year in the first apartment of the sanctuary, _'within the veil,' which formed the door and separated the holy place from the outer court_, represents the work of ministration upon which Christ entered at his ascension. It was the work of the priest in the daily ministration to present before God the blood of the sin offering, also the incense which ascended with the prayers of Israel. So did Christ plead his blood before the Father in behalf of sinners, and present before Him also, with the precious fragrance of His own righteousness, the prayers of penitent believers. Such was the work of ministration _in the first apartment_ of the sanctuary in heaven."

GC421: "Thither [only the first apartment] the faith of Christ's disciples followed Him as He ascended from their sight. Here [only the first apartment] their hopes centered, 'which hope we have,' said Paul, 'as an anchor to the soul, both sure and steadfast, and which enters into that _within the veil_; whither the forerunner is for us entered, even Jesus, made a high priest forever.' 'Neither by the blood of goats and calves, but by his own blood he entered in _once into the holy place_, having obtained eternal redemption for us.' Hebrews 6:19, 20; 9:12."

Inseparable from the discussion of rooms in the sanctuary is the discussion about the veil. SDAs teach that, at his ascension, Jesus only entered inside the first, or outer veil, that separated the Holy Place room from the courtyard containing the water laver and altar of burnt offering. This means that, at his ascension, Jesus did not enter the inner veil which separated the Holy Place from the Most Holy Place. Thus he did not enter into the room which contained the Ten Commandments, the cherubs and the glory and presence of God. This is because (SDAs teach), in fulfilling the Day of Atonement prophecy of Daniel 8:14, he did not enter the inner veil until October 22, 1844.

Heb. 6:19 Which hope we have as an anchor of the soul, both sure and steadfast, and which enters into that _within the veil_;

Heb. 6:20 Whither the forerunner is for us entered, even Jesus, made an *high priest* for ever after the order of Melchisedec.

Heb. 10:19 Having therefore, brethren, *boldness* to enter into the *holiest* by the blood of Jesus,
Heb. 10:20 By a new and living way, which he has consecrated for us, *through the veil*, that is to say, *his flesh*.

The purpose of the book of Hebrews is to convince Jewish Christians to stop worshiping at the Jerusalem Temple and accept the high priesthood of Jesus. The highlight of Hebrews is that, because Jesus had abolished the old pattern, He is now a high priest in heaven serving after the order of Melchizedek, an Old Testament "Gentile" priest-king from Genesis 14.

When Hebrews 6:19-20 says that Christ is (after his ascension to the right hand of the Father) "within the veil," it means "within the inner veil as high priest" like that of Melchizedek. And when Hebrews 10:19 says that we also (in the first century) already have "boldness (or confidence) to enter into the holiest by the blood of Jesus," it is also referring to believers having the same authority as the Old Covenant high priest to enter the Most Holy Place on the Day of Atonement. With the exception of SDAs, these are universally accepted interpretations of Hebrews 6:19-20 and 10:19.

This should not be difficult to understand. **First,** since Christ's "flesh" was the "veil" of the Old Covenant sanctuary, then that divider-flesh was in *both* compartments at the same time. **Second,** since only one "veil" is mentioned, it is certainly the most important "veil" which separated the two compartments. **Third,** since that "veil" (Christ) is now seared at the right hand of the Father, then there is no longer a separating "veil." **Fourth,** without a separating veil the old idea of "two" compartments (since Calvary) is now only "one" compartment (if we must speak of God's dwelling place as compartments). **Fifth,** "Within the veil" clearly refers to the Day of Atonement in Leviticus 16:2, 12 and 15. The quotations by Ellen White twist the obvious truth into the lie that Jesus only ministered as an ordinary priest in the heavenly sanctuary's outer compartment and separated from the Father until 1844.

With one exception (Heb. 9:3), five of six references to "veil" in the New Testament refer to the veil between the Holy Place and the Most Holy Place—not to the curtain separating the Holy Place from the courtyard. Matthew 27:51, Mark 15:38 and Luke 23:45 all clearly refer to the veil to the Most Holy Place that was ripped in two when Christ died. The ripped veil exposed the Most Holy Place to all onlookers. Not only the high priest, but ordinary priests, ordinary Levites, ordinary Jewish men, and ordinary Jewish women inside the

Temple could "boldly" look inside the Most Holy Place because the new priesthood of believers was being inaugurated. There was no longer any necessity for a two-roomed ministry either on earth or in heaven.

"Veil" (KJV: vail) in the Old Testament is the Hebrew *paa-ro-ket* (Strong's 6532) and refers to the veil between the Holy Place and the Most Holy Place. *Paaroket* is translated "veil" 25 of 25 times in the KJV. See Exodus 26:31-35; 27:21; 30:6; 35:12; 36:35; 38:27; 39:34; 40:30; 40:21, 22, 26; Lev. 4:6, 17; 16:2, 12, 15; 21:23; 24:3; Numb. 4:5; 18:7; 2 Chron. 31:14;

The phrase, "within the veil (inside the vail)" occurs six (6) in the Old Testament and *always* refers to the Most Holy Place, particularly on the Day of Atonement in Leviticus 16. See Ex. 26:33; Lev. 16:2, 12, 15; Numb. 18:7. The phrase, "without the veil (outside the vail)" occurs four (4) times in the Old Testament and always refers to the Most Holy Place. See Ex. 26:35; 27:21; 40:22; Lev. 24:3.

This is important!—even though they are made of the same material, both the "veil" between the Holy Place and outer court and the "veil" at the entrance of the outer court are a different Hebrew word, **maa-saak** (Strong's 4539). This word is *never* translated as "veil" in the King James Version used by early Adventists or in any other version! Instead, these two veils are called the "hangings" or "coverings" (KJV), "screens" (NKJ, NAS, RSV) and "curtains" (NIV). *Maasaak* is called "hanging" or "covering" 25 of 25 times in the KJV. See Exodus 26:36, 37; 27:16; 35: 15, 17, 36, 18; 39:38, 40; 40:5, 8, 28, 33; Numb. 3:25,31; 4:25, 26. It is the "*hanging* for the door of the tent" in Exodus 26:36; 35:15; 36:37; 39:38; 40:5; 40:28 and Numbers 3:25; 4:25. It is the "*hanging* for the gate of the court" in Exodus 27:16; 35:17; 38:18; 39:40; 40:8; 40:33 and Numbers 3:26; 4:26. It is the "veil of the *covering*" for the mercy seat in Exodus 35:12; 39:34; 40:21 and Numbers 3:31; 4:5. Again, whenever *maasaak* is associated with the Most Holy Place, the wording is "veil of the covering"—"*paaroket* of the *maacaak*." See Ex. 39:34;

This tedious listing would be totally unnecessary for any Bible study group other than the Seventh-day Adventists. Yet, in the light of overwhelming evidence, SDAs cannot change what Ellen G. White has written that "within the veil" in Hebrews 6:19 refers to the hanging at the entrance of the tabernacle. **"The ministration of the priests throughout the year in the first apartment of the sanctuary, 'within the veil,' which formed the door and separated the holy place from the outer court, represents the work of ministration upon which Christ entered at his ascension"** (GC420).

CHAPTER FIFTEEN

LEVITICUS 16: THE DAY OF ATONEMENT
and
THE SCAPEGOAT: JESUS or SATAN?

Lev. 16:1 And the LORD spoke to Moses after the death of the two sons of Aaron, when they offered before the LORD and died.

In chapter 10 God killed Aaron's sons, Nadab and Abihu, because they had failed to observe holiness rules. They had defiled the sanctuary by bringing something (strange fire) into it which had been forbidden. Again, the facts of this event challenge the SDA claims that priests routinely brought SIN itself into the sanctuary as part of God's will without receiving punishment.

Lev. 16:2 And the LORD said to Moses, Speak to Aaron your brother, that he does not come at all times into the holy place [MHP] *within the veil* before the mercy seat, which is upon the ark; that he does not die: for I will appear in the cloud upon the mercy seat.

While SDAs do not deny that "the holy place" here refers to "the most holy place," they do deny that "within the veil" in Hebrews 6:20 refers to Leviticus 16:2, 12 and 15. (See previous chapter.)

Lev. 16:3-4 Thus shall Aaron come into the holy place [MHP]: with a young bullock for a sin offering, and a ram for a burnt offering. He shall put on the holy linen coat, and he shall have the linen sash upon his flesh, and shall be girded with a linen girdle, and with the linen mitre shall he be attired: these are *holy garments*; therefore shall he *wash* his flesh in water, and so put them on.

Lev. 16:11-14 And Aaron shall bring the bullock of the sin offering, which is for himself, and shall *make an atonement for himself,* and for his house, and shall kill the bullock of the sin offering which is for himself: And he shall *take a censer full of burning coals of fire from off the altar before the LORD,* and his hands full of *sweet incense* beaten small, and bring it *within the veil:* And he shall put the incense upon the fire before the LORD, that the *cloud of the incense* may cover the mercy seat that is upon the testimony, THAT HE DIE NOT: And he shall take of the *blood* of the bullock, and sprinkle it with his finger upon the mercy seat eastward; and before the mercy seat shall he sprinkle of the blood with his finger seven times.

Contrary to SDA theology, the Most Holy Place was so undefiled that:
A. Only the holy high priest could enter.
B. The high priest could only enter one day a year—the holiest day!
C. The high priest must first bathe in holy water.
D. The high priest must be wearing holy garments.
E. The high priest must first fill the room with dense smoke of holy incense.
F. The fire of the incense and the incense must meet very holy standards.
G. The high priest must enter with the blood of his own most holy sin offering.

If, according to SDAs, the MHP contained the combined atoned sins of all Israel, then it would be the most defiled place in the nation. Therefore, the above holiness ritual would make no sense. Since God killed Nadab and Abihu for using unholy fire, then he certainly would also kill any priest who dared to carry sin into the sanctuary.

Lev. 16:5-6 And he shall take *of the congregation of the children of Israel two kids of the goats for a sin offering,* **and one ram for a burnt offering. And Aaron shall offer his bullock of the sin offering, which is for himself, and make an atonement for himself, and for his house.**

After the high priest had offered his personal household sin offering, he received two goats for ONE sin offering from the congregation. Both goats had been chosen by the holy congregation during the previous 9 days of prayer, fasting and deep contrition. Since the congregation did not know which goat the LORD would choose, then both goats must have been equally qualified to die as the most holy sin offering of atonement for Israel. This alone should disqualify one of the goats as being Satan himself (as SDAs teach). Remember that both goats made one sin offering and that the sin offering was most holy (Numb. 18:9).

Lev. 16:7-9 And he shall take the two goats, and present them before the LORD at the door of the tabernacle of the congregation. And Aaron shall cast lots upon the two goats; one lot for the LORD, and the other lot for the scape-

goat [RSV: for *Azazel*]. And Aaron shall bring the goat upon which the LORD's lot fell, and offer him for a sin offering.

In 16:7 both goats were "*presented before the LORD at the door of the taber-nacle of the congregation.*" Therefore, as sin offerings, both goats became "most holy." "This shall be yours of *the most holy things...*every sin offering of theirs, and every trespass offering of theirs, which they shall render unto me, *shall be most holy* for you and for your sons" (Numb. 18:9).

Since both goats were presented *"before the LORD,"* before Yahweh, then it is inconceivable to think that Yahweh would have allowed the congregation of Israel to present an adversary before Him as a possible blood sacrifice!

Lev. 16:10 But the goat, on which the lot fell to be the scapegoat [RSV: for Azazel], shall be presented alive before the LORD, *to make an atonement* with him, and to let him go for a scapegoat [RSV: to *Azazel*] into the wilderness.

In 16:8 one of the goats was chosen for immediate death and the other was chosen as the [KJV] "*scapegoat.*" Yet both were chosen as ONE sin offering in verse 5. Rather than translate the Hebrew word, the RSV says that he was cho-sen "*for Aza'zel*" and was subsequently to be led out into the desert "*to Aza'zel*" in verse 10. This interpretation does not demand that the scapegoat actually be *Aza'zel*, or Satan. Jesus Christ, like Yahweh's goat, was condemned to die inside the holy city of Jerusalem, but, like *Aza'zel's* goat, actually died outside of it to prevent defiling it. This is why Hebrews 13:12 says **"Wherefore Jesus also, that he might sanctify the people with his own blood, suffered outside the gate."** The difference is that *Aza'zel* could not hold Jesus in death.

For the second time, in 16:10, the text says that the scapegoat is *"presented alive before the LORD."* Again, this could never be said of Satan or of sin sur-viving in the Presence of God. However, this contrasts with the SDA idea that sin itself can exist in the "heavenly" sanctuary in the very Presence of God until cleansed by the Investigative Judgment.

"*To make an atonement*" means exactly what it says! Animals used to "make atonement" must be "most holy," pure, clean and set-apart types of Christ. The high priest accepted the goat "for *Aza'zel*" because he had been selected by the entire congregation, and accepted by Yahweh, as a "most holy sin offering." Unclean and defiled animals (and Satan) certainly did not qualify "to make atonement" of any kind! Finally, "*into the wilderness*" has two comparisons to Christ. First, after being presented before Yahweh at His baptism, Jesus went "into the wilderness," into Satan's territory. Second, "into the wilderness" could also refer to Christ's descent into Hades immediately after His death (Eph. 4:8-10).

Lev. 16:15 Then he shall kill the goat of the sin offering that is for the people and bring his blood *within the veil,* and do with that blood as he did with the blood of the bullock, and sprinkle it upon the mercy seat and before the mercy seat.
Lev. 16:17 And no man shall be in the tabernacle of the congregation [the holy place] when he goes in to make an atonement in the holy place [MHP], until he comes out, and has made an atonement for himself and for his household and for all the congregation of Israel.

The holiness requirements previously described for the high priest's personal sin offering are repeated for the congregation's sin offering. Absolutely no opportunity for defilement was allowed during this most solemn holy ritual.

SDAs fail to realize that the order of events on this Day of Atonement essentially follows the same sequence as every other day! (1) The sacrificial animals (high priest's bullock and congregation's goats) were presented before the LORD at the doorway of the sanctuary. (2) By being accepted by the LORD, they became 'most holy' (Numb. 18:9). (3) When the blood was shed, when the life was given, then the atonement was accepted and the guilt of the offence had been released. And (4) the blood was then brought before the LORD (Yahweh) as proof that the penalty required for the cleansing of sin had already been met. (5) The major difference was that the blood was brought inside the Most Holy Place.

For a full description of the nature of the sins removed on the Day of Atonement, see chapter 11 of this book. SDAs greatly err when they teach that the blood of the sin offerings throughout the year *defiled* the sanctuary by bringing sin into it—but the blood of the sin offering on the Day of Atonement *cleansed* it!!! However, all sin offerings represented the sinless blood of Jesus Christ which only cleanses from sin.

Lev. 16:18 And he shall go out unto the ALTAR that is before the LORD, and make an atonement for it; and shall take of the blood of the bullock, and of the blood of the goat, and put it upon the horns of the altar round about.
Lev. 16:19 And he shall sprinkle of the blood upon it with his finger seven times, and cleanse [*taher*] it, and hallow it from the uncleanness of the children of Israel.

Lev. 16:20 And when he has made an end of reconciling the HOLY PLACE, and the TABERNACLE of the congregation, and the ALTAR, he shall bring the live goat.

As pointed out several times already, SDA theology fails to include the altar and the tabernacle of the congregation (the holy place) in its 1844 scenario. This is because they admit that Christ had (at the very least) already been ministering in the holy place since his ascension and (they teach) that only the Most Holy Place required (over a century of) cleansing beginning in 1844.

Lev. 16:21 And Aaron shall lay both his hands upon the head of the live goat, and confess over him ALL the iniquities of the children of Israel, and ALL their transgressions in ALL their sins, putting them upon the head of the goat, and shall send him away by the hand of a fit man into the wilderness.

"ALL" refers to "all remaining un-atoned sins." God does not require double payment for the same sins. Most Christian denominations teach that the scapegoat in Leviticus 16 represents Jesus Christ who forever bears our sins away. However, Seventh-day Adventists teach that the scapegoat used on the Day of Atonement ritual represented **Satan**, the originator of sin. Since Satan (SDAs teach) is ultimately responsible for all sin, then Satan must be the final sin-bearer who will bear sins out of the presence of God's people. However, it is very obvious that the high priest did not become defiled by placing both of his hands on it.

GC420: [Ellen G. White] "Then, in his character of mediator, *he [the high priest] took the SINS upon himself and bore THEM from the sanctuary.* Placing his hands upon the head of the scapegoat, he confessed over him *ALL THESE SINS,* thus in figure transferring them from himself to the goat. The goat then bore THEM away, and they were regarded as forever separated from the people."
GC422: "It was seen, also, that while the sin offering pointed to Christ as a sacrifice, and the high priest represented Christ as a mediator, the *scapegoat* typified Satan, the author of sin, *upon whom <u>the SINS of the finally penitent</u> will finally be placed.* When the high priest, by virtue of the blood of the sin offering, *removed the SINS from the sanctuary,* he *placed THEM upon the scapegoat.* When Christ, by virtue of His own blood, <u>*removes the SINS of his people from the heavenly sanctuary*</u> at the close of His ministration, *He will place THEM upon Satan* who, in the execution of the judgment, will bear the final penalty. The scapegoat was sent away into a land not inhabited, never to come again into the congregation of Israel. So will Satan be forever banished from

the presence of God and His people, and he will be blotted from existence in the final destruction of SIN and sinners."

GC485: "As the priests, in removing the SINS from the sanctuary, confessed THEM upon the head of the scapegoat, so Christ will place all these SINS upon Satan, the originator and instigator of sin."

Emphasis again is made upon the words, "SINS of the finally penitent" and "THEM." This is because some SDA theologians try to lessen the impact of these words by saying that Christ was our sin-bearer, and Satan only bore "*his part*" of the sins which he caused others to commit. However—and this is a strong "however"—that is NOT what Ellen G. White (incorrectly) wrote, nor is it what God's Word really says.

In 16:20 the high priest "shall *bring* the live goat" (KJV), "offer" (NAS), "present" (RSV), "bring forward" (NIV) (Strong's 7126 *qarab*). This is an extremely important Hebrew word which also means "approach," "come near" and "offer"—*for sacrifice*! It is used in the texts which forbid anything unqualified or unholy from "coming near" anything holy inside the sanctuary complex (with violators being put to death for defiling it). See Numbers 18:3, 4, 7, 15 and 22. The goat "for *Aza'zel*" is clearly a "sin offering" presented as a "living sacrifice" but surely destined to die as an atonement for sin in *Aza'zel's* territory.

As previously discussed in great detail, the earthly sanctuary was defiled by general un-atoned sins of Israel because it was located in the middle of a sinful multitude. These are not previously-atoned sins! Neither is this true of God's dwelling place in heaven. Again, God does not require double atonement for the same sins.

Lev. 16:22 And the goat shall bear upon him ALL their iniquities unto a land not inhabited: and he shall let go the goat in the wilderness.

Heb. 13:11 For the bodies of those beasts, whose blood is brought into the sanctuary by the high priest for sin, are burned outside the camp.

Heb. 13:12 Wherefore Jesus also, that he might sanctify the people with his own blood, suffered outside the gate.

Heb. 13:13 Let us go forth therefore to him outside the camp, bearing his reproach.

In 16:21-22 the high priest used the second half of the one most holy "sin offering" (from 16:5) to carry the sins forever away from God's redeemed. The entire sanctuary complex had already been cleaned (16:20, 30) and now the residue was being removed.

The difference between normal worship and the Day of Atonement is important here. Whereas, normally non-high-handed accidental sins and sins of ignorance were confessed over **daily** sin offerings, on the **Day of Atonement** only general sinfulness was confessed over both the high priest's bullock, and the congregation's goat for the LORD. This was a *general* confession of all remaining unconfessed sins. This compared to the single goat general sin offering made every Sabbath and every holy day (Numb. 28:15, 22, 30; 30:5). Again, see chapter 11 of this book.

The goat "for *Aza'zel*" is another exception. While sins were confessed over it, it was not immediately put to death. The live goat's participation in atonement was probably a visual demonstration that God will both forgive *and forget* atoned sin. God's people could personally visibly watch their sins forever disappearing into the distance as the goat was led away to its eventual death. Again, this Old Covenant ritual was a general cleansing. While only confessed non-high-handed sins were ordinarily daily cleansed, this event atoned for "all iniquities," "all transgressions" and "all sins" which remained within the congregation.

The New Covenant sanctuary in heaven is not located in the midst of a sinful multitude. All of this was symbolic ritual designed by God to last only until the New Covenant reality of Christ's heavenly ministry would begin, *"The Holy Spirit this signifying [through Old Covenant patterns], that the way into the holiest of all [the heavenly sanctuary] was not yet made manifest, while as the first tabernacle was yet standing" Hebrews 9:8.* What purpose then does the law serve? "It was added because of transgressions, *until* the Seed should come to whom the promise was made" Galatians 3:19. NKJV.

Lev. 16:23 And Aaron shall come into the tabernacle of the congregation [HP], and shall put off the linen garments, which he put on when he went into the holy place [MHP], and shall leave them there.
Lev. 16:24 And he shall wash his flesh with water in {that} holy place, and put on his garments, and come forth, and offer his burnt offering, and the burnt offering of the people, and make an atonement for himself, and for the people.

Note that this occurs AFTER the high priest literally touched the goat 'for Aza-zel.' Yet he was not defiled, neither was he required to offer another sin offering. Thus the second goat could not have represented Satan. Neither did he literally handle sins!

Lev. 16:26 And he that let go the goat for the scapegoat shall wash his clothes, and bathe his flesh in water, and afterward come into the camp.

Again note that the person who led away the goat 'for Aza-zel' was not considered defiled by sin. He was not required to offer a sin offering. He did not even have to wait until sunset to come back into the camp. Thus he also could hot have handled Satan and could not have been considered defiled by sin. The comparison between verses 24, 26 and 28 should confirm that both goats had the same value and both goats equally affected their three different handlers—none were required to make sin offerings afterwards.

Lev. 14:52 And he shall *cleanse* the house *with the blood of the bird*, and with the running water *and with the living bird,* and with the cedar wood, and with the hyssop, and with the scarlet.
Lev. 14:53 But he shall *let go the living bird* out of the city into the open fields, and *make an atonement* for the house: and it shall be clean.

Lest SDAs still object, a similar ritual is found in the cleansing of a leper with two birds in Leviticus 14:1-53, especially verses 52-53. Both birds made one atonement.

CHAPTER SIXTEEN

ANTIOCHUS IV (EPIPHANES) AND 164 B. C.

The great majority of Bible commentaries, past and present, have interpreted the "little horn" of Daniel 8 as Antiochus IV (Epiphanes) of the Greek Seleucids who ruled from Syria. Since Daniel 11:3-4 uses the same terminology as Daniel 8:8-9, 22, it is certain that both texts refer to the same kingdom. It is noteworthy that even William Miller (in a strange way) connected Daniel 9:23 with First Maccabees 8 and 9. See #6 of Miller's *Time Proved in Fifteen Different Ways* found in *Cultic Doctrine* by Dale Ratzlaff.

One of the four kingdoms which emerged from the Grecian goat after Alexander's death was the Greek Seleucid Kingdom, described in Daniel 11:4-20. Antiochus IV reigned from 175 to 164 B. C. Most commentators agree that his hatred of the Jews and desecration of their Temple is recorded in great detail in Daniel 11:21-35.

Although insignificant in history as a whole, in Daniel's history of nations which persecute Israel, Antiochus IV is a key figure. As such, he is also a type of the last-day Antichrist (Matt. 24:15; Mark 13:14).

The Jews living during Antiochus' reign understood and interpreted Daniel 8:8-14 to their time. The two historical books of Maccabees detail the desolations that Antiochus inflicted on Israel from 171 to 164 B. C. Although neither inspired nor canonical, *First* and *Second Maccabees* are accepted by historians as mostly reliable accounts of the events of that time period. Serious Bible students are encouraged to read these books and compare them with Daniel 8 and 11.

From Daniel and other sources, the contextual and historical meaning of the "abomination of desolation" is the desecration of the Temple when Antiochus erected a statue of Zeus inside the temple and sacrificed a pig on the altar on December 25, 167 B. C. in honor of the birth of the Sun god. This single act of desolation so incited the Jews that it began a revolt which ended in Jewish independence for the first time since 586 B. C. This end of foreign rule has been celebrated as the important Jewish festival of *Hanukkah*, meaning "dedication" (of the sanctuary) from 164 B. C. until today.

In Daniel 8:13 the "host" is national Israel who is "trodden under foot" by Antiochus IV, the little horn of Daniel 8. The "host" would cease to be "trodden under foot" when the Maccabean rebellion overthrew Antiochus in 164 B. C.

First Maccabees 1:10-15 "From them came forth a sinful root, Antiochus Epiphanes, son of Antiochus the king; he had been a hostage in Rome. He began to reign in the one hundred and thirty-seventh year of the kingdom of the Greeks. In those days lawless men came forth from Israel, and misled many, saying 'Let us go and make a covenant with the Gentiles round about us, for since we separated from them many evils have come upon us.' This proposal pleased them, and some of the people eagerly went to the king. He authorized them to observe the ordinances of the Gentiles. So they built a gymnasium in Jerusalem according to the Gentile custom, and removed the marks of circumcision, and abandoned the holy covenant. They joined with the Gentiles and sold themselves to do evil."

Matthew Henry's Commentary of 1825 applied Daniel 8:9-14 to Antiochus IV. "But it is less forced to understand them of so many natural days; 2300 days make six years and three months, and about eighteen days; and **just so long they reckon from the defection of the people, procured by Menelaus the high priest** in the 142nd year of the kingdom of the Seleucids, the sixth month of that year, and the 6th day of the month (so Josephus dates it), **to the cleansing of the sanctuary,** and the reestablishment of religion among them, which was in the 148th year, the 9th month, and the 25th day of the month, 1 Mac. 4:52. God reckons the time of his people's afflictions he is afflicted."

The Jamieson, Fausset, and Brown Commentary says "Six years and 110 days. This includes not only the three and a half years during which the daily sacrifice was forbidden by Antiochus (Josephus, 'Bellum Judaicum,'i.1, sec.1), but the whole series of events whereby it was practically interrupted: beginning with the 'little horn waxing great toward the pleasant land,' and 'casting some of the host' (Dan. 8:9-10); namely, when in **171 B. C.,** or the month Sivan in the year 142 of the era of the Seleucids, the sacrifices began to be neglected, owing to the high priest Jason introducing at Jerusalem Grecian customs and amusements—the palaestra and gymnasium; ending with the death of Antiochus, **165 B. C.,** or the month Shebath in the year 148 of the Seleucid era. Compare 1 Macc. 1:11-15; 2 Macc. 4:7-14. After the death of Seleucus, when Antiochus called Epiphanes took the kingdom, Jason, the brother of Onias, labored underhand to be high priest, promising unto the king, by intercession, three hundred and threescore talents of silver, etc., if he might have license to set him up a place for exercise, and, for the training up of youth in the fashions of the pagan, and to write them of Jerusalem by the name of Antiochians: which, when the king had granted, and he had gotten into his hand the rule, he forthwith brought his own nation to the Greekish fashion—he brought up new customs against the law—and made them wear a hat."

This explanation says that the entire defilement lasted 2300 days, or six years plus.

1 Mac 1:10   175 B. C.; 137th Seleucid year; Antiochus begins reign
1 Mac 1:10-15   *171 B. C. desolating covenant to worship Greek gods
2 Mac 4:7-18   neglected sacrifices
1 Mac 1:16-19   Antiochus plunders Egypt
1 Mac 1:20-28   169 B. C.; plunders temple
1 Mac 1:29-64   167 B. C. plundered Jerusalem
1 Mac 1:39   completely stopped sanctuary services
1 Mac 1:43-53   sacrificed pig; death decree
1 Mac 1:54-64   sets up a desolating sacrilege inside the temple
2 Mac 6:1, 2   "compel the Jews to forsake the laws of their fathers and cease to live by the laws of God, and also to **pollute the temple** in Jerusalem and call it the temple of Olympian Zeus."
1 Mac 4:42-58   **164 BC; sanctuary cleansed; Antiochus died
2 Mac 10:1-8   sanctuary purified

The following sources are a very small representation which agree with *Matthew Henry* and *Jamieson, Fausset, and Brown*. The *Scofield Reference Bible*, (Congregational), 1909; *The New Bible Commentary*, (Presbyterian influence), Inter-Varsity, 1953 Fellowship; *The Wycliffe Bible Commentary*, Moody Press, 1962; *The Ryrie Study Bible*, Moody Press, 1986.

CHAPTER SEVENTEEN

THE SINLESS CREATION SABBATH REST

1:5…evening and the morning…first day.
1:8…evening and the morning…second day.
1:13…evening and the morning…third day.
1:19…evening and the morning…fourth day.
1:23…evening and the morning…fifth day.
1:31…evening and the morning…sixth day.
2:1 Thus the heavens and the earth were finished, and all the host of them.
2:2 And on the seventh day God ended his work which he had made; and he rested on the seventh day from all his work which he had made.
2:3 And God blessed the seventh day, and sanctified it: *because that in it he had rested from all his work which God created and made.*
2:4 These are the generations of the heavens and of the earth when they were created, *in the day* that the LORD God made the earth and the heavens.

Seventh-day Adventists teach that the creation Sabbath was twenty-four hours long and has never been lost in history. Since God rested with Adam and Eve on the first creation Sabbath day, then it must have been set apart for all of the descendants of Adam and Eve. The Seventh-day Sabbath, first observed by God with Adam before sin entered must also be at the heart of a moral expectation from God. Since it had been instituted before either the nation of Israel, or the Mosaic Law, then it could not have been confined to Israel or its Old Covenant set of laws.

ANOTHER VIEW OF THE CREATION SABBATH

First, SDAs make an unfounded claim on Genesis 2:3 and Exodus 20:11 and call the Sabbath a "memorial _of creation._" Although this may seem like 'splitting hairs' over something very insignificant, the texts do not say that the Sabbath was/is a "memorial of creation." Instead, it is a memorial "<u>of the *rest* of creation</u>." Genesis 2:3 reads "**And God blessed the seventh day, and sanctified it**—*because that in it he had rested from all his work which God created and* *made.*" God began resting from His creative activity on the first Sabbath day and God commanded Adam to join in His rest—until Adam sinned. The emphasis is on "rest, not "creation." Also, while "creation" is again mentioned in the Sabbath commandment found in Exodus 20:11, it is noticeably absent from the final version found in Deuteronomy 5:15.

Second, the Bible does not state that the sinless rest which began on the original creation Sabbath day *ended* after only twenty-four hours. While Genesis, chapter one, states that each of the first six days of creation were bounded by an "evening and a morning," it does not state the very same thing about the Sabbath! Why? Obviously, God was trying to indicate that the first Sabbath was somehow different from the other six days of creation and continued beyond one day.

Third, there is some internal textual evidence suggesting that the original Sabbath rest could have lasted for many years until man sinned. God watered the earth (2:6), planted the garden (2:8), prepared the soil for the garden to grow (2:9) and placed Adam in the garden "to dress and keep it" (2:15). "Dressing" and "keeping" the garden did not constitute a violation of the original sinless Sabbath rest because God and Adam continued face-to-face fellowship on a daily (full rest) basis until sin entered (3:8). Only after Adam had sinned and separated himself from God did his sharing of God's original Sabbath sinless rest change to a life of work and sweat (3:17-19). While the original Sabbath day may have ended with sunset, the original Sabbath REST continued. Not until the original Sabbath rest ended did separation and death resulting from sin enter (3:21-24). The Bible does not state how long the original rest which began on the first Sabbath lasted.

Fourth: "But of the tree of the knowledge of good and evil, you shall not eat of it: for *in the day that you eat thereof you shall surely die* (Gen. 2:17). The countdown of the days until Adam's death did not begin when he was created without sin. Genesis 5:3 says that "Adam lived a hundred and thirty (130) years" before Seth was born. Genesis 5:4 says that he lived another eight hundred (800) years producing children after Seth was born. Genesis 5:5 says "And all the days that Adam lived were nine hundred and thirty (930) years: and he died." "All the days" probably does not include the indeterminate sinless time of rest spent in the garden before the fall. *Adam did not start aging until he sinned (Gen. 2:17; Rom. 3:23)!* Therefore Adam's nine hundred and thirty years (930) probably began their calculation *when* he sinned!

Fifth, a memorial can point both ways. After falling away from sharing God's perfect sinless rest and fellowship because of sin, perfect rest in the garden ended. The original Sabbath rest was an every-day rest. *The Sabbaths are primarily types of the original every-day rest before Adam sinned and not of a one* *day a week rest.* Therefore, the one-day Sabbath rest given to national Israel in Exodus 20:8-11 is best explained as a reminder of Adam's indeterminate every-day rest period in the garden *before* he sinned. Likewise, the seventh-day Sabbath rest of Deuteronomy 5:13-15 reminded Israel of its *current every-day* rest from Egyptian bondage. The two sabbath days of the Feast of Booths' rest of Leviticus 23:39-43 also reminded Israel of its *current every-day* rest from Egyptian bondage. The New Covenant believer is also restored, not to a one-day-a-week rest, but to the same kind of *current every-day rest* which Adam had enjoyed in the garden *before he sinned.* Again, the believer's rest is in the presence of God *every day* of the week (Heb. 4:3; Rom. 5:1; 8:1; Heb. 4:16). It is also an imputed every-day *sinless* rest granted on the sinlessness of Jesus Christ.

Sixth, no rest day or Sabbath is mentioned in God's Word from Genesis 2 until Exodus 16 (at least 2500 years). Sinless Sabbath-day rest and subsequent every-day sinless rest ended when sin entered. Mankind sinned and toiled without rest, either physical or spiritual. No rest and much sin led to the flood, "And GOD saw that the wickedness of man was great in the earth, and that every imagination of the thoughts of his heart was only evil continually" (Gen. 6:5). God's anger again fell in Genesis 11 at the tower of Babel. From Genesis 12 until Exodus 16 (Abraham to Moses) the Bible tells us of toil, and more toil, but no rest at all.

Seventh, there is no evidence that the seven-day weekly cycle was either given to, or observed by, nations around the globe before Exodus 16. The SDA claim that the Sabbath was given to all mankind before the Mosaic Law is false.

If God had wanted all mankind to observe a Sabbath day at the end of each week, then He would have made such a day inherent in the conscience of man. This has not happened. Although the ancient Sumerians and Babylonians had a seven-day (7) week, this was most likely from the divisions of the phases of the moon. Their days were assigned to the names of their seven "heavenly bodies" circling Earth, such as the Sun, Moon, Venus, Mars, Jupiter, Uranus and Saturn. Their numbering system used six (6) rather than (10) as the base of its calculations. Six, sixty and multiples of six evidently influenced Hebrew thought (compare Gen. 7:6; Numb. 7:88; 1 Kg. 10:14; Dan. 3:1.)

The frequency of market days, not an innate call to worship on the seventh-day Sabbath, determined the amount of days in a "week" for ancient civilizations. Some tribes in West Africa adopted four-day (4) intervals between market days. The Assyrians adopted five-day (5) intervals. Ancient Rome adopted eight-day (8) intervals. And the ancient Egyptians adopted ten-day (10) intervals. It was not until the first century B.C. that Rome adopted the seven-day weekly cycle. This information is found in most large encyclopedias under "calendar."

The point is that, while some moral attributes of God appear to be known to all mankind, the seventh-day Sabbath ending a seven-day week was not. Therefore, the seventh-day Sabbath is not an eternal innate moral law for all mankind.

CHAPTER EIGHTEEN

THE WEEKLY SABBATH DAY

Ex. 16:23 And he said to them, This is that which the LORD has said, Tomorrow is the rest of the holy Sabbath to the LORD: bake that which you will bake today, and boil that which you will boil; and that which remains over lay up for you to be kept until the morning.

Ex. 16:24 And they laid it up till the morning, as Moses said: and it did not stink, neither was there any worm in it.

Ex. 16:25 And Moses said, Eat that today; for today is a Sabbath to the LORD: today you shall not find it in the field.

Ex. 16:26 Six days you shall gather it; but on the seventh day, which is the Sabbath, in it there shall be none.

Ex. 16:27 And it came to pass, that there went out some of the people on the seventh day to gather, and they found none.

Ex. 16:28 And the LORD said unto Moses, How long do you refuse to keep my commandments and my laws?

Ex. 16:29 See, for that the LORD has given you the Sabbath, therefore he gives you on the sixth day the bread of two days; *abide every man in his place, let no man go out of his place on the seventh day.*

Ex. 16:30 So the people rested on the seventh day.

Exodus 16:23-30 is the first mention of the word, Sabbath, in the Bible. It is also the first time since sin entered that any people of any nation are said to "rest" on a particular day of the week. This is at the very least 2500 years since Genesis 4 and is clearly a new revelation from God. Only the Israelites were given this special revelation. "**Tomorrow is the rest of the holy Sabbath to the LORD** (Yahweh)" was not given to, and does not include, any other race of people. Pharaoh had previously said in Exodus 5:2 "Who is the LORD, that I should obey his voice to let Israel go? I know not the LORD, neither will I let Israel go." Not only was the Sabbath rest not known universally, but God as LORD, Yahweh, was not known universally. The Sabbath *"unto the LORD"* was now made known only to Jacob's descendants by divine revelation!

The Israelites did not know how to act properly on this very first divinely revealed Sabbath day and some immediately ignored it. "The LORD has given you [Israel] the Sabbath" means *only Israel*. When Israel had transgressed God's commandments about gathering, baking and boiling the manna, God asked "How long do you refuse to keep my commandments and my laws?" Thus the Sabbath-rest commandment became not only the very first commandment of the Law officially given, but it also became the very first one transgressed! Transgression of it did not yet carry the death penalty because the Old Covenant had not been ratified.

Notice that the exact wording of the Sabbath commandments does not even command corporate worship! "Abide every man in his place, let no man go out of his place on the seventh day. So the people rested on the seventh day." It was a day of total rest inside one's own residence! Since the Jewish and SDA concept of corporate worship at the Temple, in the synagogues or in their churches are greatly evolved concepts from Exodus 16, it should be self-evident that the current concept of Sabbath worship cannot possibly reflect an eternal moral principle of the character of God.

Ex. 19:3 And Moses went up to God, and the Lord called to him from the mountain, saying, Thus you shall say to the house of Jacob and tell the *sons of Israel*;
Ex. 19:4 You yourselves have seen what I did to the Egyptians, and how I carried you on eagles wings, and brought you to Myself.
Ex. 19:5 Now then, IF *you* [Israel] will indeed obey My voice and keep My covenant, THEN *you* [Israel] shall be My own possession *among all the peoples*, for all the earth is Mine.
Ex. 19:6 and *you* [Israel] shall be to Me a kingdom of priests and a holy nation. *These are the words that you shall speak to the sons of Israel.*

From the creation account in Genesis to Exodus 16 the Sabbath day played absolutely no part in the Abrahamic Covenant and its confirmations in Genesis chapters 12, 13, 15, 17 and 22. The Sabbath was not mentioned in God's dealings with Israel's forefathers, Abraham, Isaac and Jacob. Even though violations of the other nine commandments are evident and punished, Sabbath-breaking was never included in the lists of transgressions and punishments.

Immediately before giving His Law in Exodus 20 onward, God made it clear in Exodus 19 that the Old Covenant, or Mosaic Covenant, in scripture is addressed *only* to the nation Israel! **No other nation was ever commanded to obey the terms of the Old Covenant (19:3-6).** The identifying reference point is specifically "deliverance as a nation from Egypt." This theme is repeated often in Scripture. Only the nation Israel meets this physical description (19:4). The phrase "to the sons of Israel" is repeated for emphasis many times, at almost every address concerning the Mosaic Law, or Old Covenant.

Unlike the *unconditional* Abrahamic Covenant, **this Mosaic Covenant was** *conditional* upon national Israel's obedience (19:5). Every commandment, every statute, every ordinance, and every Sabbath in this covenant was to end (as a covenant) if its conditions were not met by literal Israel (and they were not met). **This passage, Exodus 19:4-6, is extremely important!** Either Israel was to be saved under this covenant (and it was not), or by the New Covenant (which terms were met by Christ and is unconditional to true believers in national Israel).

TWO DIFFERENT SABBATH COMMANDMENTS

Ex. 20:1 And God spoke all these words, saying,
Ex. 20:2 I am the LORD your God who has brought you out of the land of Egypt, out of the house of bondage.

Deut. 5:1 And Moses called all Israel and said to them, Hear, O Israel, the statutes and judgments which I speak in your ears this day, that you may learn them and keep and do them.
Deut. 5:2 The LORD our God made a covenant with us in Horeb.
Deut. 5:3 The LORD did not make this covenant with our fathers, but with us, even us, who are all of us here alive this day.
Deut. 5:4 The LORD talked with you face to face in the mountain out of the midst of the fire.
Deut. 5:5 (I stood between the LORD and you at that time, to show you the work of the LORD: for you were afraid by reason of the fire, and went not up into the mount.)
Deut. 5:6 I am the LORD your God, which brought you out of the land of Egypt, from the house of bondage.

There are two different versions of the Ten Commandments in God's Word. While most Christians make the Exodus 20 version their standard, few place more importance on the second and final version found in Deuteronomy 5.

When the introductions in Exodus 20:1-2 and Deuteronomy 5:1-6 are compared, it is clear that the LORD (Yahweh) was giving His entire Law only to the nation Israel (Deut. 5:1) whom He had just delivered from Egyptian slavery (Ex. 20:2; Deut. 5:6). The Law is the same as the Mosaic, or Old, Covenant (Deut. 5:3).

When Deuteronomy 5:3 says **"The LORD did not make this covenant with our fathers,"** Moses is referring to Abraham, Isaac, Jacob and their descendants up until deliverance from Egypt. Again, there is no reason to conclude that the seventh-day Sabbath, a key part of the Mosaic Covenant, had previously been given to, or observed by, previous generations prior to Exodus 16. In Deuteronomy Moses made it clear that the Ten Commandments which he was about to re-read were part of the whole Law, the entire Covenant, including statutes and judgments. These laws were only for national Israel and had not been given to Abraham, Isaac and Jacob, their forefathers, "as a set of laws."

ONE: Ex. 20:3/Deut. 5:7 You shall have no other gods before me…..
TWO: Ex. 20:4/Deut. 5:8 You shall not make any graven image…..
THREE: Ex. 20:7/Deut. 5:11 You shall not take the name of the LORD your God in vain…..
………………………
FOUR: Ex. 20:8 *Remember* the Sabbath day, to keep it holy…..
FOUR: Deut. 5:12 *Keep* [NAS, RSV: observe] the Sabbath day to sanctify it…..
………………………
FIVE: Ex. 20:12/Deut. 5:16 Honor your father and your mother……
SIX: Ex. 20:13/Deut. 5:17 You shall not kill.
SEVEN: Ex. 20:14/Deut. 5:18 You shall not commit adultery.
EIGHT: Ex. 20:15/Deut. 5:19 You shall not steal.
NINE: Ex. 20:16/Deut. 5:20 You shall not bear false witness against your neighbor.
TEN: Ex. 20:17/Deut. 5:21 You shall not covet your neighbor's…..

The Ten Commandments shown above are the shortened version which appears on most "official" displays. Except for numbers 7-9 which add one consonant to change "not" into "neither," they are almost identical in Hebrew. However, the fourth (Sabbath) commandment changes "remember" (*zaakor*) into "observe" (*shaamor*).

The short version above is most likely closer to the original version given by God to Moses. Careful reading, comparison and internal evidence indicates that the extra words which are usually omitted are probably "explanatory" commentary by Moses.

Ex. 20:10 But the seventh day is the Sabbath of the LORD your God—in it you shall not do any work, you, nor your son, nor your daughter, your *manservant,* nor your *maidservant,* nor your cattle, nor your stranger that is within your gates.

Deut. 5:14 But the seventh day is the Sabbath of the LORD your God—in it you shall not do any work, you, nor your son, nor your daughter, nor your *manservant,* nor your *maidservant, nor your ox, nor your ass,* nor any of your cattle, nor your stranger that is within your gates; *that your manservant and your maidservant may rest as well as yourself.*

Notice the italicized words. Either they are Moses' commentary on God's Words, or else Moses had taken unimaginable liberty in changing God's exact wording. The commandment also indirectly approves of **bond-slavery** which was accepted as part of the Old Covenant. This alone should define the Sabbath as a temporary cultic "ordinance."

Ex. 20:11 For in six days the LORD made heaven and earth, the sea, and all that in them is, and rested the seventh day: wherefore the LORD blessed the Sabbath day, and hallowed it.

Deut. 5:15 And remember that you were a servant in the land of Egypt, and that the LORD your God brought you out from there through a mighty hand and by a stretched out arm: therefore the LORD your God commanded you to keep the Sabbath day.

IMPORTANT! The two sets of explanations for the Sabbath are completely different in the two sets of Ten Commandments! Why? If the creation were such an important part of the Sabbath commandment, as SDAs claim, then why was it not included in the final version, the most important version, of the Ten Commandments found in Deuteronomy? Unless Moses knew that God's intention of "remember" was "observe," then we have no explanation for the change in the basic commandment. However, the every-day rest from Egyptian slavery in Deuteronomy 5:15 must be seen as an improvement on the reason for national Israel to observe the Sabbath. Thus, the "rest" from creation in Exodus 20:11 may not have been an actual part of God's handwriting on the stones—otherwise Moses was guilty of an extremely serious change in God's Ten Commandment Law!

Almost 40 years had passed between Exodus 20 and Deuteronomy 5. Except for Moses, Joshua and Caleb, all older adults who had been present in Exodus 20 had died. The new generation was about to enter and conquer Canaan with almost the same numerical strength in which the previous generation had refused.

Deuteronomy has much more importance than Exodus in Judaism. In fact, it is the most important book in all of the Bible! Therefore, its list of Ten

Commandments should be more important than the list in Exodus. And, for this reason, the difference between the Sabbath commandment of Exodus 20 and Deuteronomy 5 is important. The Ten Commandments immediately followed the covenant conditions of Exodus, chapter 19. They began the entire Old Covenant presentation and re-presentation of both Exodus and Deuteronomy. **They should not be separated from their Old Covenant context.** That covenant was an indivisible whole, and the Ten Commandments are wholly in the context of that Old Mosaic Law Covenant. As such, the Ten Commandments are only addressed to the nation of Israel which was brought out of Egypt. This is a difficult truth to accept, but no Old Testament or New Testament writer would imagine separating the Ten Commandments from the remainder of the Mosaic Law.

Again, the *one day* Sabbath of Exodus 20 is a reminder of God's *every-day* sinless creation rest until sin occurred. However, the Sabbath of Deuteronomy 5 ignores the creation altogether, and is a reminder of *every-day* freedom from Egyptian slavery. Crucial to a proper perspective and understanding of the covenants is the point that **this is not the same covenant that God made with Abraham, Isaac, and Jacob (Deuteronomy 5:3). The Abrahamic Covenant was unconditional** concerning the existence of the nation in the land, concerning Abraham's descendants and the Seed, which was to be Christ (Galatians 3:16). **The Mosaic (Old) Covenant was conditional** and temporary until "faith" arrived, which is Christ. Disobedience delayed God's unconditional promises, but did not annul them (Gal. 3:19-25).

Ex. 23:9 Also you shall not oppress a stranger: for you know the heart of a stranger, seeing you were strangers in the land of Egypt.
Ex 23:10 And *six years* you shall sow your land and shall gather in the fruits thereof:
Ex. 23:11 But the *seventh year* you shall let it rest and lie still; that the poor of your people may eat: and what they leave the beasts of the field shall eat. In like manner you shall deal with your vineyard, and with your olive yard.
Ex. 23:12 *Six days* you shall do your work, and on the *seventh day* you shall rest: that your ox and your ass may rest, and the son of your handmaid, and the stranger, may be refreshed.

In Exodus 23:10-11 and 23:12 the reason for both the seventh-YEAR *every-day* Sabbath rest of the land and the seventh-DAY Sabbath rest is in the major context of providing rest to the poor and the "stranger"—not because of creation rest, because "**you know the heart of a *stranger*, seeing you were *strangers* in the land of Egypt** (23:9). Therefore, it was just as much a transgression to ignore the seventh-YEAR *every-day* rest of the land (23:10-11) as it was to ignore the seventh-day rest of man and beast. Thus the reason for resting in Deuteronomy 5 is also found in Exodus 23. Sabbath-teachers who stress one reason and ignore the other are being incomplete with their interpretation. Also, does this authorize having children by slave ownership?

Ex. 23:32 You shall *make no covenant with them* [other nations] or with their gods. Ex. 23:33 They shall not live in your land in case they would make you sin against Me; for if you serve their gods, it will surely be a snare to you.

Deut. 7:2 And when the LORD your God shall deliver them before you; you shall strike them, and utterly destroy them; you shall *not make any covenant with them, nor show mercy unto them:*
Deut. 7:3 Furthermore you shall not inter-marry with them....
Deut. 7:6 For you are a holy people to the LORD your God; the LORD your God has chosen you to be a people for His own possession out of all the peoples who are on the face of the earth.

Three chapters after giving the Ten Commandments in Exodus 20, and only two chapters after giving them in Deuteronomy 5, **national Israel was specifically told not to share its special covenant with any other nation and not to make any kind of covenant with any other nation.** God commanded Israel not to live with, inter-marry with, share with, or worship with other nations. Neither was it to make military alliances with them. As Israel ignored these restrictions, the other nations became snares. The Mosaic Law itself became a "hedge" or "partition" between Israel and other nations. This was especially true of the Sabbath commandment (Mark 12:1; Eph. 2:14).

"Do not make a covenant with them" must include the Sabbath because it was meaningless to non-Israelites outside of their covenant relationship. One cannot observe the Sabbath and ignore the remainder of the covenant—or the other way around! Therefore, none of the Mosaic Law of the Old Covenant (its commandments, judgments, statutes/ordinances) such as the Sabbath was to be compulsory for others, unless such were inside Israel's towns (political control) and inside Israel's homes! Strange as it may seem, Israel did not go out and deliberately evangelize and convert others to its covenant and lifestyle (see Matthew 10:5-6). Therefore, it can hardly be said that the "Sabbath" day, as understood in the Ten Commandments, was to be for all nations.

Notice "observe" from Deuteronomy 5:12 rather than "remember" from Exodus 20:8.

Ex. 31:13 But as for you, speak *to the sons of Israel*, saying, You shall surely observe My sabbaths: for *this is a sign between me* and you throughout your generations, that you may know that I am the LORD who sanctifies you.

Ex. 31:14 Therefore you are to observe the sabbath, for it is holy *to you*. Every one who profanes it shall *surely be put to death*; for whoever does any work on it, that person shall be cut off from among his people.

Ex. 31:15 For six days work may be done, but on the seventh day there is a sabbath of [NAS: complete; RSV: solemn] rest, holy to the LORD; whoever does any work on the sabbath shall *surely be put to death*.

Ex. 31:16 So *the sons of Israel* shall observe the sabbath, to celebrate the sabbath throughout their generations as a perpetual covenant.

Ex. 31:17 *It is a sign between Me and the sons of Israel* forever; for in six days the LORD made heaven and earth, but on the seventh day He ceased from labor, and was refreshed.

Ex. 31:18 And when He had finished speaking with him upon Mount Sinai, He gave Moses the two tablets of the testimony, tablets of stone, written by the finger of God.

Exodus 31:13-18, a favorite with SDAs, is addressed specifically to the "sons of Israel" and only to national Israel! Verses 13 and 17 point out that the seventh-day Sabbath was only a sign of the Old Covenant between Yahweh and the sons of Israel! If the Sabbath were for all nations, then it could not (at the same time) be a unique sign of God's covenant with Israel. Neither was the Sabbath ever given to the church as a sign of the New Covenant. Thus, at the very least, God did not intend for other nations to keep the Sabbath during the time of the Old Covenant.

Unlike the other nine commandments which were repeated to the church in terms of grace after Calvary, there is no holy day mentioned under the terms of the New Covenant. The "day" has been replaced by the "Person" of Jesus Christ who again provides *every-day* sinless rest to the believer (Heb. 4:3)—a restoration to Adam's state before he sinned.

Concerning 31:15, present-day so-called "Sabbath-keepers" almost always sin against the original description of the Sabbath by not having "complete and solemn" rest (31:15). Among zealous Seventh-day Adventists the seventh-day is often the least restful and the busiest day of the week! Their many Sabbath activities cause both themselves and others to work (such as electric, fire, natural gas, police, telephone and water suppliers—evan maintenance at SDA radio and television stations).

"Whoever does any work on the sabbath shall *surely be put to death*" (31:15). Sabbath-breaking was punishable by death. Why do not strict

Saturday-Sabbath and Sunday-Sabbath observers urge that violators be put to death? The death penalty was also specifically attached to violations of most of the Ten Commandments. Is the "commandment" New Covenant and the "penalty" for violating it only Old Covenant? Where is this principle found? Do any have the right to call themselves "commandment-keepers" if they do not attempt to prosecute violators as the commandment stipulations also require? Logic demands that, either Sabbath-day laws were abolished when the Old Covenant was dissolved, or else the death penalty should still be enforced.

Concerning 3:18, the "**tablets of stone**" should be compared to Second Corinthians 3:7 and 10. "**But if the ministry of death, in letters engraved on stones, came with glory, so that the sons of Israel could not look intently at the face of Moses…For indeed what had glory in this case has** *no glory* **on account of the glory that surpasses it.**" The covenant symbolized by the Ten Commandments has "no glory" in comparison to the surpassing glory of the New Covenant of the Holy Spirit. (Also compare Romans 8:1-3.)

Ex. 34:21 Six days you shall work, but on the seventh day you shall rest: in plowing time and in harvest you shalt rest.

Like Exodus 23:9-12, the Sabbath commandment here is surrounded by various judgments and statutes/ordinances such as the firstborn and yearly festivals. They all had the same value as part of the indivisible Law!

Ex. 35:2 Six days shall work be done, but on the seventh day there shall be to you an holy day, a Sabbath of rest to the LORD: *whosoever does work therein shall be put to death.*
Ex. 35:3 You shall kindle no fire throughout your habitations upon the Sabbath day.

The context of this Sabbath text is the building of the tabernacle. Even this important project for God would stop on the Sabbath day. Not even rubbing sticks together or striking flint to kindle a fire was allowed for warmth. Transgression was to be punished by death! The Sabbath also applied to strangers within the Israelites' control and household. Again, in modern applications, this would apply to causing strangers at the electric and gas companies to work in order to provide heat on the Sabbath.

It is not enough to argue that modern SDAs do not have to work in order to warm their residence on the Sabbath day. SDAs teach that all people of all nations of all time should observe the Sabbath rest. Thus, even before their existence began after 1844, they trace the history of pre-existing Sabbath-keepers all over the world. Yet this would have been impossible in cold climates where it has always been essential to work to build fires for survival.

Lev. 23:2 Speak to the children of Israel, and say to them, Concerning the feasts of the LORD, which you shall proclaim to be holy convocations, even these are my feasts.
Lev. 23:3 Six days shall work be done: but the seventh day is the Sabbath of rest, an holy convocation; you shall do no work therein: it is the Sabbath of the LORD in all your dwellings.
Lev. 23:4 These are the feasts of the LORD, even holy convocations, which you shall proclaim in their seasons.

In Leviticus 23 the seventh-day Sabbath is only the first of many equally important feasts and holy convocations which the LORD (Yahweh) had given only to Israel. Beginning with the weekly Sabbath day, the chapter progresses to the seasonally required feasts and their Sabbath days. However, since the Sabbath days of the festivals were determined by the beginning of the month (the new moon) and not by the weekly cycle, then none necessarily fell on the same day as the seventh-day weekly sabbath.

Deut. 6:20 When your son asks you in time to come, saying, What do the testimonies and the statutes and the judgments mean which the LORD our God commanded you?
Deut. 6:21 then you shall say to your son, We were slaves to Pharaoh in Egypt and the LORD brought us from Egypt with a mighty hand.

What is the basic "meaning" of the entire Mosaic Law—the testimonies, or Ten Commandments, the statutes and the judgments? When the Hebrew child asked this question, the answer was the same as the most important reason for the Sabbath given in Deuteronomy 5: "Then you shall say to your son, we were slaves to Pharaoh in Egypt and the LORD brought us from Egypt with a mighty hand." Since that covenant and its laws were only given to national Israel, the correct answer could only be given by Israelites. Redemption is the foundation behind ALL of the Mosaic Law, including the Ten Commandments (testimonies)—especially *every-day* redemption from Egyptian slavery (6:21) which provided *every-day* rest from that bondage.

Numb. 15:32 And while the children of Israel were in the wilderness, they found a man that gathered sticks upon the Sabbath day.

Numb. 15:33 And they that found him gathering sticks brought him to Moses and Aaron, and to all the congregation.

Numb. 15:34 And they put him under guard, because it was not declared what should be done to him.

Numb. 15:35 And the LORD said to Moses, The man shall be surely put to death: all the congregation shall stone him with stones outside the camp.

Numb. 15:36 And all the congregation brought him outside the camp and stoned him with stones and he died; as the LORD commanded Moses.

Seventh-day Adventists would rather not discuss these texts. They prefer to talk about how wonderful the Sabbath is and how God wants everybody to observe it. Yet Israelites did not expect those outside their covenant to be put to death for Sabbath-breaking. In reality, the seventh-day Sabbath was at the heart of a very strict old covenant relationship between Yahweh and national Israel. The death penalty was equally prescribed for transgression against most of the Ten Commandments. Israel was a very disobedient nation under a theocracy, the direct rule of God. As God's chosen nation, Israel had awesome revelations, awesome possibilities, awesome responsibilities and *awesome penalties*. This was the nature of the old covenant which they agreed to in the Pentateuch. On the other hand, the New Covenant Christian was never offered such a choice as that of the old covenant relationship, including the Sabbath. Although the "wages of sin" are still "death," physical death has only been prolonged outside of the theocracy.

Ezek. 20:3 Son of man, speak to the elders of Israel, and say to them....

Ezek. 20:5…On the day when I chose Israel and swore to the descendants of the house of Jacob and made Myself known to them in the land of Egypt...

Ezek. 20:10 So I took them out of the land of Egypt and brought them into the wilderness.

Ezek. 20:11 And I gave them My statutes and informed them of My ordinances, by which if a man observes them he will live.

Ezek. 20:12 And *also I gave them My sabbaths to be a SIGN between me and them, that they might know that I am the LORD who sanctifies them.*

Ezek. 20:13 But the house of Israel rebelled against Me in the wilderness. They did not walk in My statutes and they rejected My ordinances, by which if a man observes them, he will live; and *My Sabbaths* they greatly profaned...

Ezek. 20:10-24 [much repetition for emphasis]

The Old Covenant relationship with the house of Jacob did not officially begin until the Egyptian redemption. God next gave national Israel a written code of laws. He then gave them his statutes (ceremonial worship ordinances) and *His Sabbaths. All of them, not just the seventh-day Sabbath, were "signs" of the unique covenant made only with Israel.*

Whereas all of the Sabbath days and Sabbath years in Leviticus 23 and 25 were "signs" of God's Old Covenant promises to national Israel, the Holy Spirit is the "sign," or "seal" of God's sure promises to the church. Old Covenant Israel did not have the indwelling Spirit. To the church, God promised "In Him [Christ], you also, after listening to the message of truth, the gospel of your salvation—having also believed, you are **sealed** in Him with the Holy Spirit of promise" (Eph. 1:13). While Israel received its weekly, seasonal and yearly "sabbaths" to remind them of their every-day redemption rest from Egypt, the church received the Holy Spirit seal to remind it of past, continuing, and future every-day redemption rest, "And do not grieve the Holy Spirit of God, by whom you **sealed** for the day of redemption" (Eph 4:30).

Neh. 9:2 And the seed of Israel separated themselves from all strangers, and stood and confessed their sins, and the iniquities of their fathers.

Neh. 9:13 You came also upon mount Sinai, and spoke with them from heaven, and gave them right *judgments,* and true laws, good *statutes* and *commandments*:
Neh. 9:14 And made known to them your holy *Sabbath,* and commanded them *precepts, statutes, and laws,* by the hand of Moses your servant.

Nehemiah separated the true Israelites from the false. He then restored the Levites and priesthood to their duties. Again, at approximately 444 B. C. the whole Law with the Sabbath is reserved only for true Israelites. At least at this time, every effort was made to *exclude* non-Israelites from joining in with the celebrations and worship services on the Sabbath. If Israel had thought that the Sabbath was also for other nations, then it would have encouraged those outside its covenant to worship with them on the Sabbath.

Neh. 10:31 As for the people of the land who bring wares or any grain on the Sabbath day to sell, we will not buy from them on the Sabbath or a holy day; and we will forego the crops the seventh year and the exaction of every debt. NASU

First, Nehemiah forbade any Israelite from buying anything on either the seventh-day Sabbath or the seasonal Sabbath "holy day" which usually did NOT fall on the seventh-day. This would even eliminate paying tolls for travel today. Second, Nehemiah forbade harvesting and tithing crops every seventh-year Sabbath. Yet how many SDA pastors tell their congregations not to bring in their food-tithes every seventh year? Third, Nehemiah equally enforced the Sabbath-year prohibitions against collecting debts. How many SDA leaders follow this Sabbath commandment today? Therefore, since the seventh-day Sabbath and the seventh-year Sabbath have equal validity in the indivisible Old Covenant, then SDAs should be just a vigilant in not farming every seventh-year and in not collecting debts every seventh year.

Neh. 13:19 And it came to pass, that when the gates of Jerusalem began to be dark before the Sabbath, I commanded that the gates should be shut, and charged that they should not be opened until after the Sabbath: and I placed some of my servants at the gates, that there no burden should be brought in on the Sabbath day. (See context 13:15-22.)

Nehemiah would not allow any traffic in or out of the Hebrew community on the Sabbath day. Yet SDA communities do not shut their gates on the Sabbath. They have tremendous traffic as they come and go to their various churches and mission work. Again, although they are "doing good" on the Sabbath, they are also causing "strangers" such as traffic controllers and utility personnel to work on the Sabbath—and this transgresses the precise wording of the Ten Commandments. Does "doing good" on the Sabbath nullify the clear commandments of God to Old Covenant Israel?

CHAPTER NINETEEN

ALL SABBATHS DAYS/YEARS WERE SHADOWS

Seventh-day Adventists teach that God has two different kinds of Sabbaths. The most important one (they teach) is the weekly seventh-day Sabbath of the Ten Commandments which is eternal, moral and an essential part of God's character. This weekly seventh-day Sabbath is for all nations and all races for all eternity. It is, and always has been, more important than any of the other Sabbaths in the Bible. Now discarded, the other, less important Sabbath days and years, were the monthly new moon Sabbath days, the seasonal Sabbath days, every seventh Sabbath-year, and the 50th year Jubilee Sabbath.

The texts in this chapter are used by non-Sabbatarians to demonstrate that the seventh-day Sabbath is not binding on Christians. However, Seventh-day Adventists deny that these texts include the seventh-day Sabbath. They claim that all of the "days," "ordinances," and "shadows" of the Old Covenant which were abolished when Christ died were only "ceremonial," or "ritual" days.

While excluding the seventh-day Sabbath, SDAs at the least correctly teach that all of the other Sabbaths were purely ceremonial statutes, or ordinances, which were only for national Israel. They were temporary "shadows" of Christ and the gospel, and, as such, are no longer valid. Therefore, when they read the texts, they interpret them as only references to the "ceremonial sabbaths."

However, non-Sabbatarians teach that the other Sabbaths were just as important (if not more so) than the seventh-day Sabbath.

Isa. 1:13-14 "Stop bringing meaningless offerings! Your incense is detestable New Moons [monthly], Sabbaths [weekly] and convocations [seasonal]—I cannot bear your evil assemblies. Your New Moon festivals and your appointed feasts my soul hates. They have become a burden to me; I am weary of bearing them." NIV

Lev. 23:2 Speak unto the children of Israel and say to them, Concerning the feasts of the LORD, which you shall proclaim to be holy convocations, even these are my feasts.
Lev. 23:3 (the weekly Sabbath convocation is first on the list)
Lev. 23:4-44 (seasonal Sabbaths and convocations)

After Israel and Judah had for centuries failed to obey their Old Covenant requirements, God declared that He was "weary" of all of their "convocations"—including the weekly Sabbaths (Isa. 1:13-14). This strong rebuke would hardly be appropriate if the weekly Sabbath were "moral" and if the other monthly, seasonal and yearly Sabbaths were merely ritual.

1 Chron.23:31 "…in the sabbaths, in the new moons, and on the set feasts…"
2 Chron.2:4…on the sabbaths, and on the new moons, and on the solemn feasts"
2 Chron.8:13 "…on the sabbaths, and on the new moons, and on the solemn feasts…"
2 Chron. 31:3 "…for the sabbaths, and for the new moons, and for the set feasts"
Neh. 10:33 "…of the sabbaths, of the new moons, for the set feasts…"
Ezek. 5:17 "…in the feasts, and in the new moons, and in the sabbaths…"
Hos. 2:11 "…her feast days, her new moons, and her sabbaths, and all her solemn feasts…"

Weekly	Monthly	Seasonal
sabbaths	new moons	set feasts; solemn feasts; convocations

These texts from Leviticus, Nehemiah, Isaiah, Hosea and Chronicles clearly place all sabbaths (at the least) on the same level of importance. All of the Sabbaths were the focus of Israel's worship week, month, season and yearly cycles. It is impossible to sever the linkage (as SDAs do) between the weekly sabbaths and its companion non-weekly sabbaths. Transgressing any Sabbath was a sin! All Sabbaths were important and equally condemned when Israel sinned.

God commanded Israel to stop bringing vain offerings during all three kinds of Sabbaths (weekly, monthly and seasonal). "Bring no more vain oblations; incense is an abomination unto me; the *new moons* [monthly] and *sabbaths* [weekly], the calling of *assemblies* [seasonal], I cannot endure it; it is iniquity, even the solemn meeting" (Isa. 1:13). As punishment for her sin, Israel's joy was to cease, even on the seventh-day Sabbath. "I will also cause all her mirth to cease, her *feast days*, her *new moons*, and her *sabbaths*, and all her solemn feasts" (Hos. 2:11). This must include the weekly Sabbath day.

Col. 2:14 Blotting out the handwriting of *ordinances* [Greek: *dogma*] that was against us, which was contrary to us, and took it out of the way—nailing it to his cross;
Col. 2:15 And having spoiled principalities and powers, he made a show of them openly, triumphing over them in it.
Col. 2:16 Let no man therefore judge you in food, or in drink, or in respect of an holyday [seasonal], or of the new moon [monthly], or of the *sabbath days* [weekly]:
Col. 2:17 Which are a *shadow of things to come*; but the body is of Christ.

Heb. 10:1 For the law having *a shadow of good things to come*, and not the very image of the things, can never with those sacrifices which they offered year by year continually make the comers thereunto perfect.

Gal. 4:9 But now, after that you have known God, or rather are known of God, how turn you again to *the weak and beggarly elements*, whereunto you desire again to be in bondage?
Gal. 4:10 You observe days [weekly], and months [monthly], and times [seasonal], and years [yearly].
Gal. 4:11 I am afraid of you, lest I have bestowed upon you labor in vain.

	Weekly	Monthly	Seasonal	Years, Jubilee
Col. 2:16	sabbath days	new moon	holy day	—
Gal. 4:9-10	days	months	times	years
Lev. 23, 25	23:1-2	—	23:1, 4-44	25:2-7, 8-17

When Colossians 2:16 and Galatians 4:9-10 are compared with the nine sets of Old Covenant texts previously discussed, it is clear that (1) Paul was referring to the unity of those texts and (2) that the seventh-day Sabbath was included among those holy days which had been discarded along with all of the other holy days of the Mosaic Law.

Heb 4:3 *For we who have believed do enter that rest*, as He has said: "So I swore in My wrath, They shall not enter My rest," although the works were finished from the foundation of the world.
Heb 4:4 For He has spoken *in a certain place of the seventh day* in this way: "And God rested on the seventh day from all His works";

Heb 4:5 and again in this place: "They shall not enter My rest."
Heb 4:6 Since therefore *it remains that some must enter it,* and those to whom it was first preached did not enter because of disobedience.
Heb 4:11 Let us therefore be diligent to enter that rest, lest anyone fall according to the same example of disobedience. NKJV

Before he transgressed Adam enjoyed sinless rest twenty-four hours a day *every day.* In Christ all believers also have sinless rest twenty-four hours a day *every day.* Hebrews, chapters 3 and 4 leave no doubt that the creation sabbath rest also was a shadow of the future every-day rest to be found in the gospel. "Rest" occurs eleven times in Hebrews 3:11, 18; 4:1, 3, 4, 5, 8, 9, 10 and 11. The seventh-day Sabbath "rest" was not the ultimate rest God wanted for his people. After listing failed efforts of Israel to enter into God's true rest, they never achieved it. Now, the new covenant shouts, *"we who have believed do enter into rest"*—signifying that God's true rest is achieved *by faith in Jesus Christ.* All believers, both Jew and Gentile, presently rest in Christ twenty-four hours a day seven days a week!

There is actually a subtle downgrading of the seventh-day Sabbath in Hebrews, chapter four. The two phrases, **"the works were finished from the foundation of the world"** (4:3) and **"God rested on the seventh day from all His works,"** (4:4) clearly refer to the creation Sabbath. Yet the creation Sabbath is de-emphasized by **"for He has spoken *in a certain place* of the seventh day."** How? It seems discourteous to speak of the Sabbath by saying "in a certain place," "somewhere" (NAS, RSV, NIV) when every Jew knew exactly where these statements were found in God's Word.

Although Israel had been observing the Sabbath day for almost forty years in the wilderness, God made it clear that Sabbath day rest was inferior to every day Canaan rest. "For you are not as yet come to the rest and to the inheritance, which the LORD your God will give you" (Deut. 12:9). The writer of Hebrews went even farther in pointing out that Canaan rest was still not the final rest God desired for His people. Compare Deuteronomy 24:19 and Joshua 21:44; 22:4. The phrase **"They shall not enter My rest"** probably refers to texts like Deuteronomy 28:65 located in the curses of disobedient Israel. God's true rest was not to be found under the terms of the Mosaic Covenant.

The phrases *"it remains that some must enter it"* and *"let us therefore be diligent to enter that rest"* give one more reminder that God's true rest comes, not to the Old Covenant Israelite Sabbath-keeper, but to every New Covenant believer—*"For we who have believed do enter that rest"*—restored to Adam's pre-sin *every day* rest!

Luke 4:18 The Spirit of the Lord is upon me, because he has anointed me to preach the gospel to the poor; he has sent me to heal the brokenhearted, to preach deliverance to the captives, and recovering of sight to the blind, to set at liberty them that are bruised,
Luke 4:19 To preach the acceptable *year* of the Lord.
Luke 4:20 And he closed the book, and he gave it again to the minister, and sat down. And the eyes of all them that were in the synagogue were fastened on him.
Luke 4:21 And he began to say to them, This day is this scripture fulfilled in your ears.

Jesus introduced Himself in Nazareth by comparing His ministry, not to the weekly "rest" of the seventh-day Sabbath, but to the every-day "rest" of the 50th Jubilee year. The Sabbath cycle of weekly, monthly, seasonal and yearly rests culminated in the grandest Sabbath rest of all—the 50th year Jubilee Sabbath. Leviticus 25:8-17 describes the Jubilee Sabbath year in terms that more than combine all of the other Sabbaths together! The land, the Israelites, their servants, and even strangers in Israel were all to rest. Those who had sold themselves into slavery were to be restored. Lost land was to be restored. Broken family ties were to be mended. All debts were to be forgiven. Forfeited possessions were to be returned. And all oppression was to end. Isaiah used the imagery of the Jubilee Sabbath year to describe the every-day Messianic blessedness which would fall on national Israel when the Holy Spirit came via the Messiah (Isa. 61:1-2).

Significantly, it is *this* every-day Sabbath rest, the rest of the Jubilee Sabbath year, not the seventh-day Sabbath that Jesus announced was fulfilled when He began His ministry in Luke 4:16-18!!! In fact, the "Christ event," His birth, life, death, resurrection and ascension "fulfilled" the "rest" of the weekly Sabbath day, the "rests" of the seasonal Sabbath days, the "rests" of the seventh year Sabbaths of the land and especially "fulfilled" the 50th year Sabbath rest for the land and for the poor. The poor, the slaves, and those burdened by debt especially looked forward, not to the weekly, monthly, and yearly Sabbaths, but to the Jubilee 50th year Sabbath for their new start in life. The Jubilee Year was "the acceptable YEAR of the Lord." In Christ all sin debt is forgiven and the believer rests in a new creation every day.

In fact, the Jubilee sabbath was the pinnacle of all sabbaths, with the weekly sabbath at the very bottom of this crescendo of Sabbaths. It is no wonder that the very first words spoken by Jesus to describe His ministry in Luke 4:16-21 compare it to the greatest of all Sabbaths—the Jubilee Sabbath Year! Again, it is evident that each Sabbath was arranged in an ascending order, building upon the previous Sabbath in revealing God's truth to Israel.

Weekly, Seasonal and Yearly Sabbaths

Pre-Sin Rest	every day until Adam sinned
Post-Sin Rest	no mention until Exodus 16
Weekly: Ex. 20	one day a week to remind of lost creation rest
Deu. 5	one day a week to remind of every day rest from slavery
Passover	every day rest of justification
Pentecost	every day rest of sanctification; receipt of the Law and harvest
Day of Atonement	every day rest of Canaan rest; return to pre-sin Eden
Seventh-year	every day rest of farms for one year
Jubilee Year	every day rest, forgiveness and restoration; return to pre-sin Eden

SUMMARY:

ONE: As discussed in a previous chapter, the creation Sabbath day was a memorial, NOT of creation, but of the *every day* sinless "rest" of creation until sin entered! Therefore, as a memorial of the "rest" of creation when sinless Adam walked *every day* in perfect harmony with God, it is also a "shadow" of the *every day* "rest" of the re-creation of the new birth when believers walk in harmony through the blood of Jesus Christ. Just as Adam lived *every day* sinlessly at rest with God before he sinned, even so believers now live *every day* in the sinless righteousness of Christ and in his fulfilled Sabbath rest (Heb. 4:1-9; 2 Cor. 5:17).

The SDA objection that the seventh-day Sabbath was primarily a memorial of the seventh creation day is in error and ignores the more important wording of the Ten Commandments found in Deuteronomy. While the exact wording of the seventh-day Sabbath in Exodus 20:8-11 points backward to the "rest" of creation in Genesis 2:3, the final wording of the seventh-day Sabbath in Deuteronomy 5:14-15 only points backward to the every day "rest" from Egyptian bondage and slavery. The Sabbaths of the festival seasons, seventh-year and Jubilee year point both backward to *every day* "rest" from Egyptian bondage and also forward to the Messianic age. This is especially seen in the Feast of Tabernacles which points both backward to Egyptian slavery and forward to the Messianic age (Lev. 23:39-43).

TWO: There is no biblical indication that a seventh-day Sabbath was ever observed from Genesis 4 until Exodus 16 (at least 2500 years). When the Sabbath was specially revealed by God in Exodus 16:23, it was only given to national Israel as a sign of the old covenant between Himself and them (Ex. 31:13-17; 20:2; Deut. 5:6). The SDA argument that God intended for all mankind to observe the Sabbath is illogical because God did not give the Sabbath to anybody else; neither did He command Israel to give it to anybody else. In fact, Israel was commanded NOT to share any of its covenant (including the Sabbath) with other nations. Exodus 23:32 "Make no covenant with them, nor with their gods." See also Exodus 34:12, 15; Deut. 7:2.

THREE: The seventh-day Sabbath was not more important than the other Sabbaths. In fact, the first Sabbath days given to Israel were NOT the seventh-day weekly Sabbath days. Instead, they were the first and seventh days of the first month set apart for the Passover. "And in the first day there shall be an holy convocation, and in the seventh day there shall be an holy convocation to you; no manner of work shall be done in them, except that which every man must eat, that only may be done of you" (Ex. 12:16; also Lev. 23:7-8). Since violation of the Passover Sabbath days also caused one to be "cut off" from Israel, it is evident that those Sabbath days were at least as important as the seventh-day Sabbath (see Numb. 9:13).

FOUR: SDAs are wrong to define the Ten Commandments as entirely "moral law" and to proceed as if transgression of everything else in the law (except food restrictions) were non-moral. Not only is the eternal "moral law" woven throughout the Ten Commandments, but it is also woven throughout the statutes, judgments and prophets. *Transgression of any of the law was sin!* For example, when Jesus was asked "Which is the great commandment in the law?" (Mt. 22:36), He quoted Deuteronomy 10:12 (or 30:6) and Leviticus 19:18 instead of the Ten Commandments. Thus Jesus did not limit sin to transgression of the Ten Commandments.

FIVE: Even the Ten Commandments are not completely "moral" because they also contain specific elements meant only for national Israel. The Sabbath day is the most obvious of these limited cultic elements. For example, Exodus 20:12 and Deuteronomy 5:14 mention "the land" (Hebrew: 'eretz) of Israel and Exodus 20:10 and Deuteronomy 5:14 imply slave ownership when describing how the Sabbath should be observed. It is inconceivable to think that an eternal moral transcript of God's character pre-existing the creation of man and the entrance of sin would read as do the Ten Commandments. Not even

Seventh-day Adventists would dare teach the "slave" portion of the Sabbath commandment as evidence that is it 'moral" to own slaves today. Yet SDAs do have mostly segregated black churches and black colleges! Lastly, the best description of the character, or "glory," of God is found, not in the Ten Commandments, but in Exodus 34:6-7!

SIX: The only early Christians who interpreted the Sabbath as binding did so because they also interpreted ALL of the Mosaic Law as binding. We see this in the book of Acts among the Jewish Christians and their "God-fearing" Gentile co-worshipers. When the Pharisaic Christians in Jerusalem tried to impose their morality on Gentile Christians (including circumcision and Sabbath-keeping), after hearing Paul and Peter's testimony, James declared, **"Therefore my sentence is, that we trouble not them, which from among the Gentiles are turned to God: But that we write unto them, that they abstain from pollutions of idols, and from fornication, and from things strangled, and from blood"** (Acts 15:19-20).

Yet, if the Sabbath had been a moral imperative, it would have certainly been included in Paul's and James's instructions to Gentile believers. However, after Paul left in Acts 15, it is clear from Acts 21 and Hebrews that the Jerusalem church eventually yielded to the legalizing influence of its Pharisaic Christians. They also continued to worship at the Jerusalem Temple on the Sabbaths with their tithes and offerings.

On the other hand, the book of Acts shows that Paul worshiped "daily" after being kicked out of the synagogues. Paul's statement in First Corinthians 9:19-22 shows his pattern of setting aside Jewish peculiarities while witnessing solely to Gentiles. If the Sabbath had been an eternal moral issue, then history would have shown consistent Sabbath-keeping by Gentile Christians through-out the Roman Empire.

SEVEN: Paul included the seventh-day sabbath in his list of things which were abolished as "shadows of things to come." In Colossians 2:16 he wrote "Let no man therefore judge you in" and clearly progressed from (seasonal sabbath) "holydays" to (monthly sabbath) "new moons" to *(weekly seventh-day) "sab-bath days."* In Galatians 4:9-10 he reversed the order of "the weak and beggarly elements": *(weekly seventh-day sabbath) "days"*, "monthly" (Sabbath days), (seasonal sabbath) "times," and (sabbath) "years." This four-step sequence of "weekly," "monthly," "seasonal" and "yearly" clearly includes the weekly. The seventh-day Sabbath is given no preference, or exclusion, among holy days which are no longer observed.

EIGHT: Leviticus 23 and 25 reveals all of the Sabbaths together for comparison. They were ALL equally commanded (required) rest days, festivals, and assemblies essential for the national identity of Israel. They all required rest and holiness.

In fact, when comparing the required sacrifices of the various Sabbath days, the weekly seventh-day Sabbath required the LEAST. Each successive seasonal and yearly Sabbath also built upon the meaning of the preceding one until a crescendo was reached by the 50th year Jubilee Sabbath year. Therefore, it is difficult to understand why God would abolish the more important Sabbaths and retain (according to SDAs) the one which required the *least* effort to observe.

Rom. 1:19-20 Because that which may be known of God is manifest in them; for God has shown it to them. For the invisible things of him from the creation of the world are clearly seen, being understood by the things that are made, even his eternal power and Godhead; so that they are without excuse.

Rom. 2:14-15 For when the Gentiles, which have not the law, do by nature the things contained in the law, these, having not the law, are a law unto themselves: Which show the work of the law written in their hearts, their conscience also bearing witness, and their thoughts the meanwhile accusing or else excusing one another.

NINE: Those who have never heard the gospel nevertheless die because they are separated from God and commit sins. Yet, while even the most remote tribes on earth have moral codes forbidding most of the Ten Commandments (at least among their peers), they have no inner knowledge of which day of the week to set aside for worship.

Since there is not a specific day of the week written inside man, then the seventh-day Sabbath cannot be an eternal "moral" obligation or expectation from God (see Romans 1:20 and 2:14-15 above). The seventh-day Sabbath was given only through direct revelation of God and was only given to one nation under the treaty stipulations of the Old Covenant. Ancient cultures in Sumeria, Babylon, Egypt and Greece were more likely to identify a new moon or full moon holy day.

TEN: The Sabbath forbad Israelites from performing any work or even causing anybody else to perform any work. Unless one lives in total seclusion in a temperate climate, does not require protection, does not travel and does not use utilities, this is literally impossible even in today's modern culture.

ELEVEN: The Sabbath cannot be observed on a round Earth. The long days and nights at the north and south poles make this impossible without sunrise and sunset. No fires could be kindled on the Sabbath at the poles. Also, the International Date Line and Time Zones are inventions of man for man's convenience. God did not leave instructions for Sabbath observance when crossing them. Astronauts could travel at the same speed as the rotation of the earth and never experience a sunset or sunrise to change days.

CHAPTER TWENTY

GREATER AND LESSER SABBATHS

This chapter demonstrates that the more important Sabbaths required more sacrifices. It is also important to note that, except for the weekly Sabbath, all other Sabbaths were determined by the new moon and could fall on any day of the week! Also, each greater Sabbath provided more rest, more release and more restoration.

Again, the seasonal Sabbath days were determined, not by the weekly cycle, but by the moon. In addition to the first day of each month being a Sabbath day, all of the seasonal Hebrew feasts and Sabbath days were determined by counting from the first of the month.

Although Seventh-day Adventists disagree, the monthly and seasonal Sabbath days were equally commanded by God. A Hebrew man was to be "cut off" from Israel for failure to comply to expected attendance on many of these days.

Ex. 12:16 And in the first day [of the third month] there shall be a holy con-vocation, and in the seventh day [of the third month] there shall be a holy convocation to you; no manner of work shall be done in them, except that which every man must eat, that only may be done of you.

Ex. 13:9 And it [the Passover] shall be for a *sign* unto thee upon thine hand, and for a *memorial* between thine eyes, that the LORD's law may be in thy mouth: for with a strong hand hath the LORD brought thee out of Egypt.

Lest too much significance be placed on the seventh-day Sabbath, the first two Sabbath days given to Israel were associated with the Passover, and not the end of the week! Failure to observe the Passover also resulted in being "cut off" from Israel (12:15, 19). Preceding the seventh-day Sabbath, but like the sev-enth-day Sabbath, the Passover was also a "sign" and a "memorial" only to national Israel as a reminder of their every-day rest from Egyptian slavery.

Lev. 23:2 Speak to the children of Israel, and say to them, Concerning the feasts of the LORD, which you shall proclaim to be holy convocations, even these are my feasts.

Leviticus 23 is a discussion of all Sabbath days except those of the new moon. They are all called "feasts," or "festivals," with their holy "convocations." In comparison, these are even greater Sabbath days than the weekly Sabbath, thus requiring more sacrifices with the seventh-day weekly Sabbath at the *bottom* and the greatest Jubilee Sabbath at the top.

DAILY ANIMAL SACRIFICES: NUMBERS 28:3

Numb. 28:3 This is the offering made by fire which you shall offer to the LORD—*two lambs* of the first year without spot *day by day, for a continual burnt offering.*

Although this is not specifically a Sabbath text, it is foundational to all of the required Sabbath animal sacrifices. It also provides context for the "evening-morning," or "continual," sacrifices so prominent in discussions of Daniel 8:14.

THE WEEKLY SABBATH DAY

Lev. 23:3 Six days shall work be done, but the seventh day is the Sabbath of rest, a holy convocation; you shall do no work therein; it is the Sabbath of the LORD in all your dwellings.
....
Numb. 28:9 And on the *Sabbath day two lambs* of the first year without spot.....
Numb. 28:10 This is the burnt offering of every Sabbath, in addition to the continual burnt offering, and his drink offering.

While Numbers 28 and 29 seem unimportant to most, the SDA contention that the seventh-day Sabbath was more important than the other Sabbaths becomes very questionable because its required animal sacrifices were *less* than the other Sabbath days. The daily two lambs were the only required sacrifices of the Hebrew year that were less than those of the Sabbath day!

THE MONTHLY NEW MOON SABBATH DAY

Numb. 28:11 And in the beginnings of your months you shall offer a burnt offering to the LORD; two young bulls, and one ram, seven lambs of the first year without spot.
....
Numb. 28:15 And one kid of the goats for a sin offering to the LORD shall be offered, in addition to the continual burnt offering and his drink offering. (See also 10:10.)

DAILY: "continual" 2 lambs burnt offering; Numb. 28:3
SABBATH: WEEKLY: additional 2 lambs burnt offering; Numb. 28:9-10
SABBATH: MONTHLY: additional 2 bulls, 1 ram and 7 lambs for the burnt offering, plus 1 goat for a sin offering; Numb. 28:11-15

The new moon Sabbath days were determined by the first confirmed sighting of the new moon around Jerusalem. In addition to the normal daily burnt offering sacrifices of two lambs, there were added two bullocks, one ram, and seven lambs for burnt offerings, plus one goat for a sin offering. Also, if the new moon fell on a weekly Sabbath, all three sets of sacrifices were required. While the congregational sin offering was made on monthly and seasonal Sabbath days, it was not made on the weekly Sabbath day! Notice that, *as the importance of the Sabbath day increased beyond the weekly Sabbath day, so did the sacrificial offerings.*

SEASONAL SABBATH DAYS

SABBATH: PASSOVER: 3rd month. Calculated from the new moon.
        14th day: add Passover lamb; Numb. 28:16; Lev. 23:5
SABBATH: PASSOVER:
        15th day; Numb. 28:18; Lev. 23:7
                add per day: 2 bulls, 1 ram, 7 lambs; goats; 15th to 21st days;
                Total: 14 bulls, 7 rams, 49 lambs, 7 goats; Numb. 28:17-22
SABBATH: PASSOVER:
        21st day; Numb. 28:25; Lev. 23:8
        22nd day: Lev. 23:11-14 wave sheaf offering; one lamb
....
SABBATH; FEAST OF WEEKS: Calculated from the new moon.
                add 2 bulls, ram, 7 lambs; goat; Numb. 28:26-31; Lev. 23:15-21
....

SABBATH: ATONEMENT: 7th month new moon; Numb. 29:1-38; Lev. 23:25-36
        add 1 bull, 1 ram, 7 lambs; goat; Numb. 29:1-6; Lev. 23:25-27
SABBATH: ATONEMENT: 10TH DAY; YOM KIPPUR; JUDGMENT
        add 2 goats: atonement and scapegoat; Lev. 16
        add 1 bull, 1 ram, 7 lambs; goat; Numb. 29:7-11;Lev. 23:28-32

....

SABBATH: BOOTHS: 15TH DAY   Calculated from the new moon.

15th day (1)	add 13 bulls, 2 rams, 14 lambs; goat; Numb. 29:12-38; Lev. 23
16th day (2)	add 12 bulls, 2 rams, 14 lambs; goat
17th day (3)	add 11 bulls, 2 rams, 14 lambs; goat
18th day (4)	add 10 bulls, 2 rams, 14 lambs; goat
19th day (5)	add 9 bulls, 2 rams, 14 lambs; goat
20th day (6)	add 8 bulls, 2 rams, 14 lambs; goat
21st day (7)	add 7 bulls, 2 rams, 14 lambs; goat
22nd day (8)	add 1 bull, 1 ram, 7 lambs; goat

The Passover Sabbath was on a full moon fourteen (14) days from the new moon of the third month. *It usually did not fall on the seventh-day Sabbath.* Two more Passover Sabbaths on the first and seventh feast days were also to be observed as "a statute for ever throughout your generations."

The Feast of Harvest Sabbath, or Pentecost, began on a Sabbath that was not necessarily the seventh-day Sabbath. Its' occurrence fifty days after the first-fruit barley wave sheaf was determined by whatever day the first of the month fell on for the Passover. The seven "sabbaths" preceding it were "weeks" and not actual Sabbath days unless they coincided. Like the seventh-day Sabbath it was a "statute for ever in all your dwellings throughout your generations."

The New Moon Sabbath of the seventh month began the countdown to the Day of Atonement, or Yom Kippur Sabbath. *The Day of Atonement was the most important Sabbath day of the Hebrew year and it was not necessarily on the seventh day of the week either!*

The Feast of Booths contained two Sabbath days: on the 15th and 22nd days of the seventh month. Like all of the other non-weekly Sabbaths, this final yearly Sabbath day was also determined by the new moon and also did not usually fall on the seventh-day Sabbath. It pointed back to the wilderness wanderings and also pointed forward to the Messianic peace in the Promised Land. It lasted eight days and required a total of 71 bullocks, 15 rams, 105 lambs, and 8 goats.

In conclusion, we have seen that the seventh-day weekly Sabbath required the least sacrifices, the smallest congregations, and was but the beginning Sabbath for all of the more important yearly Sabbaths.

SABBATH YEARS

Lev. 25:4 But in the seventh year shall be a Sabbath of rest to the land, a Sabbath for the LORD: you shall neither sow your field, nor prune your vineyard. (See Lev. 25:1-7; Deut. 15:1-11; 31:10-13.)

Every seventh year, during the Feast of Tabernacles, the Sabbath year began. Whereas the weekly, monthly, and yearly Sabbaths gave occasional rest to the people, every seventh year the land rested every day all year along with the people who farmed the land. No sowing, reaping, or pruning was allowed. All ate from whatever grew spontaneously. No tithes were given (or received) every seventh year.

More important, the Sabbath year was a year of "release" for Israelites. Debts were to be either forgotten, or (as some understand) not collected during this year. All in the land were to freely eat in accordance with their daily needs. Special attention was to be given to the poor and needy in the land. *Thus, the Sabbath YEAR, provided far more every-day rest and hope than did the Sabbath DAY.*

JUBILEE: EVERY 50TH YEAR

Lev. 25:10 And you shall hallow the fiftieth year, and *proclaim liberty* throughout all the land to all the inhabitants thereof: it shall be a jubilee to you; and you shall return every man to his possession, and you shall return every man to his family.
Lev. 25:11 A jubilee shall that fiftieth year be to you: you shall not sow, neither reap that which grows of itself in it, nor gather the grapes in it of your vine undressed.
Lev. 25:12 For it is the jubilee; it shall be holy to you: you shall eat the increase thereof out of the field. (See Lev. 25:8-16, 23-55.)
....
Isa. 61:1 The Spirit of the Lord GOD is upon me; because the LORD has anointed me to preach good tidings to the meek; he has sent me to bind up the brokenhearted, to *proclaim liberty* to the captives, and the opening of the prison to them that are bound;

Almost everything connected with the number, "seven," has significance in the Bible, i.e.: the seventh day, the seventh month, the seventh year. Seven times seven weeks (49 weeks) led up to the (50th) Feast of Weeks when the final full harvest began, when the giving of the Law at Mount Sinai was commemorated, and when the Holy Spirit fell on the church at Pentecost. The Bible also uses the number, 70, and 7 x 70, or 490.

However, the crown of all Sabbaths was to be seen in the Jubilee, the 50th YEAR following the seventh Sabbatical year. Like the Sabbath year, the land and its farmers were to have *every day* total rest and live off what was produced without labor.

While it is debated whether or not the Sabbath year required the total release of debts, or merely their temporary non-collection, there is no question about the Jubilee year. All Israelite debts were to be wiped off the books. All land was to revert to its original owners. All Israelites who had sold themselves into slavery were to be released. It was THE year of LIBERTY, of total restoration. And, as such, *the Jubilee Sabbath year provided more every day physical REST than all of the other Sabbaths combined.* This Sabbath year of all Sabbath years was also the Sabbath of all Sabbaths.

CHAPTER TWENTY ONE

JESUS AND THE SABBATH

Seventh-day Adventists teach that, since Jesus honored the Sabbath of the Ten Commandment by worshiping on Saturday, then He is our example, and all Christians should observe the same Saturday-Sabbath which Jesus observed.

An important objection to this logic is Jesus' position under the Mosaic Law. "But when the foulness of time was come, God sent forth his Son, made of a woman, made under the law" (Gal. 4:4). Jesus took on humanity as a Jew, the seed of Abraham. He was "made under the law," that is, under the jurisdiction of the Mosaic Law in order to redeem those under the law. Jesus commanded His Jewish disciples to obey those in authority who were the recognized interpreters of the Law. "The scribes and the Pharisees sit in Moses' seat: All therefore whatsoever they bid you observe, that observe and do; but not after their works: for they say, and do not" (Matt. 23:2, 3). "Leave there your gift before the altar, and go your way; first be reconciled to your brother, and then come and offer your gift" (Matt. 5:24). Jesus instructed the Jews whom He had healed (not the Gentiles) to "show yourself" to the priest, and offer the gift that Moses commanded, for a testimony unto them" (Matt. 8:4). Therefore, if we accept the SDA argument that Jesus' Sabbath-keeping was an example for all Christians to follow, then we must also follow His example and observe ALL of the Law—commandments, statutes and judgments.

Because Jesus was the perfect sinless Law-keeper, He was able to "impute," or account, the righteousness of His law-keeping to the believer who has faith. Since Jesus was a Jew and was obligated to observe the entire Mosaic Law, the righteousness of His law-keeping included the whole Law. Jesus not only observed the weekly Sabbath, but also the monthly and seasonal Sabbaths— *not because he was a human being, but because he was a Jewish human being.* He did not send Gentiles to the priests after healing them.

God's expectations for even Jews to observe the entire Old Covenant has changed. "But **now** the righteousness of God *without the Law* is manifested, being witnessed by the law and the prophets; even the righteousness of God which is by faith of Jesus Christ to all and upon all them that believe; for these is no difference" (Rom. 3:21-22). Although the Gentiles never observed any of the Sabbaths, never brought sacrifices to the Temple, and never stopped eating ceremonially unclean foods, they also are eligible to receive the full righteousness of Christ "without the law," or "apart from the law." See also Acts 15:1-20 and 21:18-28.

"Now" the righteousness of the believer does not reside in the believer's obedience of the law, including the Sabbath; it results from the believer's faith in Jesus (Jn. 16:9). "And be found in him, not having my own righteousness, which is of the law, but that which is through the faith of Christ, the righteousness which is of God by faith" (Phil. 3:9).

The following Sabbath texts are arranged in the order found in a leading harmony of the gospels.

ONE: Luke 4:15-21
Luke 4:18 The Spirit of the Lord is upon me, because he has anointed me to preach the GOSPEL to the poor; he has sent me to heal the brokenhearted, to preach deliverance to the captives, and recovering of sight to the blind, to set at LIBERTY them that are bruised,
Luke 4:19 To preach the acceptable YEAR of the Lord.
Luke 4:20 And he closed the book, and he gave it again to the minister, and sat down. And the eyes of all them that were in the synagogue were fastened on him.
Luke 4:21 And he began to say to them, This day is this scripture fulfilled in your ears.

As previously discussed, Jesus began His ministry on a Sabbath DAY by proclaiming that He was the fulfillment of the Jubilee Sabbath YEAR—the every day greatest Sabbath of all Sabbaths! After quoting Isaiah 61:1-2, He declared concerning the acceptable year of the Lord,' "This day is this scripture fulfilled in your ears" (Luke 4:21).

Jubilee: The fiftieth year Jubilee Sabbath was the crowning glory of all other Sabbaths (compare Leviticus 23, 25 and 27). First, every seventh DAY Israel rested for one day. Second, every seventh YEAR the farmers and the land rested every day. Third, every day of the fiftieth JUBILEE year the farmers rested, the land rested, and all oppressed people rested and experienced release from debts and slavery. Thus Jesus used the Jubilee Sabbath year as a greater type of his liberating ministry than the weekly Sabbath. Jesus' presence and ministry fulfilled the Jubilee Sabbath.

TWO: John 5:1-18: Because he had healed a man on the Sabbath, Jesus was accused of breaking the law. Next, after He called God His Father, they used both the healing and the statement as reasons to plot His death.

THREE: Matthew 12:1-14; Mark 2:23 to 3:6, Luke 6:1-11: These passages are the most detailed discussions of Christ's relationship to the Sabbath in Scripture. As His disciples plucked and sifted grain in their hands, they were accused of breaking the Sabbath by harvesting. Actually such gleaning was allowed in the Law as provision for the poor (Lev. 19:10).

However Jesus did not use the legitimate "gleaning" defense. He wanted to teach a greater truth. As He began to answer the accusation, Jesus gave two Scriptural illustrations. The first was David, God's anointed king, who had once entered into the Holy Place of the sanctuary and ate the sacred show-bread without being accused of being guilty of sin! Thus, in times of necessity, King David violated a statute/ordinance of the law without guilt (Mt. 12:3-4). Jesus' second illustration was the priests: they must "violate" every Sabbath by carrying out daily duties of sacrifice (Mt. 12:5-6). Finally, Jesus gave the example of ordinary citizens who rescue animals who had fallen in the ditch on the Sabbath (Mt. 12:11).

Jesus then said "But if you had known what this means, I will have mercy and not sacrifice, you would not have condemned the guiltless" (Mt. 12:7). Jesus thus used non-Law teachings to explain the real meaning of the Sabbath commandment (Isa. 1:11-17; Hos. 6:6; Mic. 6:6-8). Again, as in Matthew 23:23, "mercy" is a more important part of the law, "a weightier matter"; yet the Ten Commandments say nothing about showing mercy to law breakers. Jesus wanted his listeners to understand that the Sabbath was primarily to be a day of showing mercy. If His accusers had been merciful, they would have provided food for his disciples on the Sabbath, and the disciples would not have been forced to glean.

FOUR:
Mark 2:27 **The sabbath was made for man, and not man for the sabbath.**
Mark 2:27 (Greek) *Ta sabaton dia ton anthropon egeneto, kai ouch ho anthropos dia ton sabbaton.* (Literally) **The sabbath for the man (singular) came to be, and not the man (singular) for the sabbath.**

There are three different ways to interpret Mark 2:27. Seventh-day Adventists insist that "man" means "man in general," "all men" or "mankind." Therefore, (to SDAs) the text means, "The Sabbath was made for all mankind, not all mankind for the Sabbath." God expects all mankind to observe the seventh-day Sabbath, or Saturday, as holy.

However, there are several things wrong with such logic. **First,** when *anthropos* is generically translated as "man," "mankind" or "flesh," then no specific article "the" is required in Greek. With the article, one specific man is usually intended. Texts where "man in general" is meant do not include the definite article in the Greek (compare Mt. 4:4; Rom. 1:18; 5:12). (2) "*Anthropos,*" an extremely common New Testament word, is *never* translated as "mankind" in the King James Version. A different Greek word, *phusei,* is translated "race," "species" or "mankind" in James 3:7.

God gave the Sabbath to national Israel as a sign of their Old Covenant relationship, "It is a sign between me and the children of Israel for ever" (Ex. 31:13, 17). *At the same time God commanded Israel not to share their covenant and Sabbath with other nations (Ex. 23:32; Deut. 7:1-6).* This is why Jesus did not command the non Israelites whom he healed to observe the Sabbath and the rest of the Law. This is also why the Jewish Christians at the first church council did not require Gentile Christians to observe the Law (Acts 15:1-20; 21:18-28). Therefore, the seventh day weekly Sabbath was not given to all mankind (Ex. 19:5, 6; 20:2; 31:13-18; Deut. 5:12-15).

A **second** possible meaning of Mark 2:27 refers to the question it answers. The Pharisees asked, "Why do they [Jesus' disciples] on the Sabbath day do that which is not lawful?" (Mk. 2:24; Lk. 6:2). Jesus, in turn, asked the Pharisees, "Is it lawful on the Sabbath days to do good or to do evil? to save life? Or to destroy it?" (Lk. 6:9). Since "they" were Jews, then, the question concerned only the *Hebrew* man who is *under the Law!* The Pharisees would not have asked Jesus this question if "they" were Gentiles who were not under the Law! If this is the correct logic, then the answer would be: "The sabbath was made for *the Hebrew man* [who is under the law], and *the Hebrew man* was not made for the Sabbath." This answer would be honest both to the question and to the Greek syntax. Whether of not the Sabbath day was a day of rest since the creation is irrelevant because it had been forgotten. Beginning in Exodus 16, God clearly pointed out the day only for the observance of the Hebrews.

A **third** possible interpretation of Mark 2:27 is that "the man" refers neither to mankind in general, nor to the Hebrews under the Law, but to **Jesus Himself!** When the Greek article "the" (Strong's 3588) and "man" (Strong's 444) are combined in a word search, 13 of 21 times in Mark it refers to Jesus Christ as "the Son of THE man." There is an article in front of *anthropos.* Jesus was THE Second Adam (which means man), THE Messiah, and THE Representative Man. He was the One who first rested on the first Sabbath and all things were created by Him and FOR Him (Col. 1:16). This would make

Mark 2:27 say "The Sabbath came into existence for THE MAN [Jesus Christ] and [Jesus Christ] THE MAN did not come into existence [as a man] for the Sabbath."

Fourth, perhaps Jesus' concluding statement, recorded in Matthew, Mark, and Luke holds the key to the correct understanding of Mark 2:27. Matthew 12:8 concludes, "For the Son of man is Lord {even} of the sabbath day." Mark 2:28 and Luke 6:5 conclude, "Therefore, the Son of man is Lord ALSO of the sabbath" with the additional Greek word for "also."

The Greek word for "made," is *egeneto*, the passive form of "to be" and is better translated as "was being" or "came into being." Keeping this in mind, we compare the four possible interpretations:

"Because the Sabbath was made for *all mankind*....

"Because the Sabbath was made for *THE Hebrew man* who is under the law...

"Because the Sabbath was made for *THE MAN, Jesus Christ*...

...THEREFORE, the Son of man is Lord also of the Sabbath!"

Since the days of Ezekiel, the phrase, "the Son of man," had been an extremely common apocalyptic phrase for the Messiah, the second Adam, which Christ applied to Himself. From Jesus' three previous illustrations, God's anointed King, priests, and even ordinary Hebrews could over-ride the letter of the law when performing acts of mercy on the Sabbath. Since this is true, then Jesus, the Son of man, the Messiah, could certainly do the same thing on the Sabbath. He had already declared Himself greater than the temple (Mt. 12:6) and now he declared himself greater than the Sabbath!!!

However, none of the alternative interpretations of Mark 2:27 would be acceptable to Seventh-day Adventists. All destroy their claim that Jesus was teaching that the Sabbath was made for all mankind to observe. While ministering under the jurisdiction of the Mosaic Law, Jesus performed many of His notable miracles on the Sabbath Day. In so doing, He demonstrated that He was Lord of that day, just as He was Lord of every other day (Mark 2:28). Again, the Sabbath which he chose to illustrate his gospel deliverance was the Jubilee sabbath year, and not the seventh-day Sabbath.

FIVE: John 7:21-24: During the Feast of Tabernacles Jesus came alone into the temple and began teaching (7:2, 10, 14, 15). "If a man on the sabbath receives circumcision, that the law of Moses should not be broken; are you angry at me, because I have made a man completely well on the sabbath day?" (7:23). Thus He pointed out their hypocrisy in Sabbath-keeping.

SIX: Luke 13:10-17: While teaching in a synagogue Jesus healed a woman on the Sabbath. The ruler of the synagogue accused Him of working on the Sabbath because He had healed. The ruler said that healing should be done only on the other six days of the week. Jesus called him a hypocrite and reminded all of them that they untied animals to water them on the Sabbath.

SEVEN: John 9:1-16: On the Sabbath, Jesus healed a man who had been blind from birth (9:1-7, 14). The Pharisees said that Jesus was "not of God because he does not keep the sabbath day" (9:16).

EIGHT: Luke 14:1-5: Jesus was eating in the house of a Pharisee on the Sabbath day when a man sick with dropsy appeared. He then asked the scribes and Pharisees, "Is it lawful to heal on the sabbath day?" When they refused to reply, Jesus healed the man. Next, after asking if they would free their ox from a ditch on the sabbath, "they could not answer."

NINE: Matthew 24:20: "But pray that your flight is not in the winter, neither on the sabbath day." Seventh-day Adventists use this text to prove that the true church (SDAs) will still be keeping the Sabbath when Jesus returns. They see themselves as the only true remnant of Christians who will safely go through the wrath of God in the book of Revelation. Therefore, they apply this text prophetically to themselves as the only true church because they keep the Sabbath.

Actually, this text has a two-fold prophetic meaning. Most importantly, the immediate context of Matthew 24, Mark 13, and Luke 21 refers to Jewish Christians within Jerusalem, and not to the church at large. The Epistle of Hebrews was probably written to address the problem of Jewish Christians who refused to remove themselves from all ties to the Temple and its laws. In A.D. 70 unbelieving Israel was destroyed by Roman armies. Before the final battle, a brief interlude allowed Christians to escape the city. *Because of severe Sabbath restrictions, escape on that day would have been more difficult.* Therefore this does not refer to worship on that day, but, instead, to escape on that day.

Dispensational futurists believe that a second greater fulfillment of Matthew 24:20 will occur in Revelation 11, 12, 13, and 17. The 144,000 are national Israelites (not sinless SDAs) who have accepted Christ and will be preaching to the rest of Israel and other nations. Antichrist will forcibly take over Jerusalem. In this context, the Jews still have their misunderstood Sabbath restrictions. And, in this context, such restrictions will still impose hardships on those fleeing in Revelation 11 and 12. Once again Matthew 24:20 is not an endorsement of Sabbath sacredness for Christians. It is merely a description of hardships caused by strict Jewish Sabbath observance.

TEN: Mt 27:52 to 28:1; Mk 15:42 to 16:1; Lk 23:54 to 24:1; Jn 19:31 to 20:1. Seventh-day Adventists use these Calvary texts to prove that the Sabbath was honored by the disciples even after Christ's death.

Actually, (1) most Jewish Christians at that time did not realize that the veil in the temple had been destroyed when Christ died. (2) Even if they had known about the veil, they still would not have immediately realized that the Old Covenant had ended. (3) They did not immediately understand what Christ had meant about the New Covenant at the last supper. (4) It was much too early to analyze their new relationship as opposed to the Mosaic Law. Therefore, they were still habitually responding under the terms and jurisdiction of the Old Covenant Sabbath which had controlled their entire life up until that point.

It would take many years (even centuries) to fully grasp the truth of what Calvary meant. Jewish Christians had more difficulties than did Gentile Christians because they needed to first disassociate themselves from strictly Old Covenant practices. Again, the Epistle of Hebrews was needed for exactly this kind of problem among Jewish Christians. They were still going to the temple, still honoring the high priest, still offering sacrifices, still keeping the Sabbath, and still paying tithes. Unless this pattern were soon broken, their spirits would be utterly devastated when the temple was soon destroyed and temple worship made impossible. Yet this confusion about the status of the entire Law was still causing problems many years later in Acts 15, Acts 21, Romans, Galatians, Ephesians, Colossians and the Epistle of Hebrews.

Summary: Since the Old Covenant was in full force during the life of Christ, the Sabbath laws were also in full force. Unfortunately, as we have just surveyed, the Sabbath was always a point of contention. Because of the open forum to Jewish men, Jesus wisely used every opportunity to enter the synagogue and teach on the Sabbath. But when he healed and proclaimed Himself equal to God, He was quickly ejected from the synagogues for breaking the Sabbath.

At Calvary the Old Covenant ended (Heb. 8:7, 13). The weekly Sabbath sign of the Old Covenant, according to Exodus 31:13-18, became meaningless. The decline of Sabbath importance is evident. In Matthew to John, under the Old Covenant period before Pentecost, it is mentioned 50 times. In the book of Acts it is only mentioned 9 times when Paul went into the synagogues to preach to the Jews and their proselytes. However, in the 22 epistles there are only 2 direct references to the Sabbath Day—neither positive. Such decline would not be evident for a doctrine that God wanted preserved for His church.

CHAPTER TWENTY TWO

THE SABBATH IN ACTS

Sabbatarians often point to the book of Acts as proof that Paul and the early church faithfully continued to observe the Sabbath of the Law of Moses. The following discussion looks at every Sabbath text in the book of Acts.

FIRST MISSIONARY JOURNEY

CYPRUS: 13:4-12
Acts 13:5 And when they were at Salamis, they preached the word of God in the synagogues of the Jews: and they had also John to their minister.

Throughout the book of Acts, whenever possible, Paul began his preaching in the synagogue. He did this because, as a Jewish man, he had an open pulpit. Just as these actions do not prove that Paul observed all of the Mosaic Law, neither should they be used to prove that he felt a necessity to worship on the Sabbath. However, the church conferences in Acts 15 and 21should prove beyond doubt that neither Paul nor the Jewish church in Jerusalem wanted to place Gentile Christians under any obligation of the Mosaic Law.

ANTIOCH IN PISIDIA: 13:13-51
Acts 13:14 But when they departed from Perga, they came to Antioch in Pisidia, and went into the synagogue on the sabbath day, and sat down.
Acts 13:15 And after the reading of the law and the prophets the rulers of the synagogue sent to them, saying, Men and brethren, if you have any word of exhortation for the people, say on.
Acts 13:16 Then Paul stood up, and beckoning with his hand said, Men of Israel, and you that fear God, give audience.

Again, the primary reason that Paul began his worship on the Sabbath at Antioch in Pisidia is because, as a Jewish man, he had an open pulpit in the Jewish synagogue. The congregation was composed of both Jews and Gentile "God fearers."

Acts 13:39 And through Him everyone who believes is freed from all things, from which you could not be freed through the Law of Moses.

What did Paul mean here? Why did he say it? This is a strong argument that Paul was teaching against the Mosaic Law and was not worshiping on the Sabbath because he thought that the Mosaic Law was still in full force. In fact, in Acts 15 and 21, the Jewish church elders made a divisive compromise when they commanded that Jewish Christians were obligated to observe all of the Mosaic Law, but Gentile Christians were not.

Acts 13:42 As Paul and Barnabas were going out, the people kept begging that these things might be spoken to them the next Sabbath.

The "people," not the leaders of the synagogue, invited Paul to return to their synagogue the next Sabbath to worship again with them. SDAs boast that this proves Paul still felt obligated to worship on Saturday because he did not **change** the day to Sunday. However, Paul's remarks in First Corinthians 9:20-22 and Romans 14: 6 reveal that he was not convicted about **either** day—Saturday nor Sunday!

Acts 13:43 Now when the congregation was broken up, many of the Jews and religious proselytes followed Paul and Barnabas: who, speaking to them, persuaded them to continue in the grace of God.
Acts 13:44 And the next sabbath day came almost the whole city together to hear the word of God.

This is a favorite SDA text used to prove that Paul worshiped on the Sabbath as part of "continuing the grace of God" even after being ejected from the synagogue. However, Paul did not consider it "wrong" to worship on Saturday and "correct" to worship on Sunday (1 Cor. 9:20-22; Rom. 14:6). Actually, he did not prefer any day! He went "**where**" the people were "**when**" the people could be found.

Many Sunday worshipers (Sunday Sabbatarians) believe that Sunday is the moral replacement in the Ten Commandments for the Sabbath. For these, the SDA argument is appropriate because Paul did not tell the crowd to worship on Sunday instead of Saturday.

However, many Sunday worshipers (like myself) believe that the Old Covenant Hebrew-only Sabbath has been abolished. These worship on Sunday merely because they have freely chosen to worship on that day (or any other day). For these the SDA argument has no effect. Paul merely honored the wishes of the people. "Continuing in the grace of God" did not include forcing Gentile Christians to observe any particular day in Acts 15:19-29; Acts 21:19-21 and Galatians 4:10-11.

Acts 13:46 Then Paul and Barnabas became bold, and said, It was necessary that the word of God should first have been spoken to you: but seeing you put it from you, and judge yourselves unworthy of everlasting life, lo, we turn to the Gentiles.

Up until this verse, Paul had been hoping for success with the Jews and God-fearing Gentiles who had been attending the synagogue. He would later write to the Romans, "For I am not ashamed of the gospel of Christ: for it is the power of God unto salvation to every one that believes; **to the Jew first**, and also to the Greek" (Rom. 1:16). However, after this verse Paul evidently left the synagogue and focused primarily on the Gentiles in Antioch in Pisidia. The Sabbath is not mentioned when only Gentiles were involved.

ICONIUM, LYSTRA AND DERBE: 14:1-23
Acts 14:1 And it came to pass in Iconium, that they went both together into the synagogue of the Jews, and so spoke, that a great multitude both of the Jews and also of the Greeks believed.

After this verse Jews from Iconium and Antioch of Pisidia began following Paul to prevent him from using the synagogues on the Sabbath.

FIRST JERUSALEM CHURCH COUNCIL: ACTS 15

Acts 15:1 And certain men which came down from Judaea [TO ANTIOCH IN SYRIA] taught the brethren, and said, Except you become circumcised after the manner of Moses, you cannot be saved.
Acts 15:2 [The problem is brought to the apostles and elders in Jerusalem.]
Acts 15:5 But there arose up certain of the sect of the Pharisees which believed, saying that it was needful to circumcise them, and to command them to keep the law of Moses.

This is an extremely important passage concerning both the Law and the Sabbath. Jewish Pharisee Christians, not Paul, insisted that Gentile Christians observe **all** of the Law of Moses. Note that their definition of the "Law" is not limited to the Ten Commandments. Since the Pharisees emphasized both circumcision and Sabbath-keeping, then this statement must certainly also include a request that the Gentile converts also observe the Sabbath!

Acts 15:6-7 And the apostles and elders came together to consider this matter. And when there had been much disputing....

This conference occurred approximately twenty (20) years after Calvary and the question of Gentile observance of the Law of Moses was still being hotly discussed. Clearly from the nature of the conference, Gentile Christians had not previously been compelled to observe the Sabbath.

Acts 15:10 [Peter said] "Now therefore why do you tempt God, to put a yoke upon the neck of the disciples, which neither our fathers nor we were able to bear?"

The entire Law is being discussed, especially the Pharisees' favorites—circumcision and Sabbath observance.

Acts 15:19 [James the leader said] Wherefore my sentence is, that we do not trouble them which from among the Gentiles are turned to God:
Acts 15:20 But that we write to them that they abstain from pollutions of idols and from fornication and from things strangled and from blood.
Acts 15:21 For Moses of old time has in every city them that preach him, being read in the synagogues every sabbath day.

Notice that Sabbath observance is NOT placed on the Gentile Christians in verse 20!!! Neither was circumcision!!! They could not enter the Temple to worship on the Sabbath as did the Jewish Christians in Acts 21. What is the purpose of verse 21? If Gentile Christians freely choose to be circumcised and submit to the Law, then they could do so and worship with them on the Sabbath as Jewish proselytes. At this early time in Christianity the Jewish-Christians were still considered to be Jews first.

SECOND MISSIONARY JOURNEY

DERBE, LYSTRA AND ICONIUM: 16:1-10
Acts 16:4 And as they went through the cities, they delivered the decrees to keep that were ordained of the apostles and elders which were at Jerusalem.
Acts 16:5 And so were the churches established in the faith and increased in number DAILY.

Paul delivered copies of the letter written by James and the Jerusalem church stating that Gentile Christians were not obligated to observe any of the

Law of Moses. The church "increased in number daily" because the gospel was being preached "daily." However, since the letters (decrees) from the Jerusalem church did not release Jewish Christians from keeping all of the Mosaic Law, we must assume that, at this point in history, many Jewish Christians also kept observing the Sabbath. For Jewish Christians at least, the change from Saturday to Sunday took many years—at least until Paul's explanation of the status of the Law in Romans and Galatians had circulated.

PHILIPPI OF MACEDONIA: 16:11-40
Acts 16:13 And on the sabbath we went out of the city by a riverside where prayer was customarily made and we sat down and spoke to the women which met there.

Once again Paul chose the Sabbath because he knew that Jews could be found worshiping on that day.

Acts 16:17-18 The same [possessed woman] followed Paul and us, and cried, saying, These men are the servants of the most high God, which show to us the way of salvation. And she did this many days......

Note the "many days." Paul was preaching and worshiping every day.

THESSALONICA: 17:1-9
Acts 17:1 Now when they had passed through Amphipolis and Apollonia, they came to Thessalonica, where there was a synagogue of the Jews:
Acts 17:2 And Paul, as his manner was, went in to them and three sabbath days reasoned with them out of the scriptures.

Again, Paul went to "where" the audience was "when" they gathered to worship because, as a Jew, he had an open invitation to speak. And, again, this does not prove that Paul went to the Jewish synagogue to worship on the Sabbath because he thought that it was the only correct day to worship.

BEREA: 17:10-13
Acts 17:10 And the brethren immediately sent away Paul and Silas by night to Berea. When they arrived they went into the synagogue of the Jews
Acts 17:11 These...searched the scriptures DAILY, whether those things were so.

Paul's pattern continued. Upon arriving at Berea, he went first to the Jewish synagogue where he had an open pulpit. However, Paul's preaching and teaching continued "daily" because the Bereans "searched the scriptures daily" as Paul presented his arguments daily.

ATHENS: 17:14-34
Acts 17:17 Therefore he disputed in the synagogue with the Jews and with the devout persons and in the market DAILY with them that met with him.

Being consistent with his convictions as stated in First Corinthians 9:20-22, Paul worshiped with the Jews in the synagogue on the Sabbath and worshiped with the Gentiles in the marketplace every other day of the week.

CORINTH: 18:1-18
Acts 18:4 And he reasoned in the synagogue every sabbath, and persuaded the Jews and the Greeks.

Afterwards (verse 7) Paul left the synagogue and preached in the house of Crispus where many believed and were baptized (verse 8). Paul stayed in Corinth for eighteen months (verse 11).

EPHESUS: 18:19-23
Acts 18:19 And he came to Ephesus and left them there: but he himself entered into the synagogue and reasoned with the Jews.

THIRD MISSIONARY JOURNEY: 18:23-21

GALATIA AND PHRYGIA: 18:23
EPHESUS: 18:23-28 APOLLOS IN EPHESUS
Acts 18:26 And he [Apollos] began to speak boldly in the synagogue.

Apollos wisely used the same pattern as Paul when he took advantage of an open pulpit on the Sabbath in the synagogue.

EPHESUS: 19
Acts 19:8 And he [Paul] went into the synagogue, and spoke boldly for three months disputing and persuading the things concerning the kingdom of God. Acts 19:9 But when some were hardened and did not believe, but spoke evil of that way before the multitude, he departed from them, and separated the disciples, disputing DAILY in the school of one Tyrannus.

When Paul arrived in Ephesus the second time, he found Apollos' disciples who were unaware of Christ and Pentecost. They were allowed to preach for three months in the synagogue on the Sabbath before being ejected. Afterwards Paul preached "daily" outside of the synagogue.

SECOND JERUSALEM CHURCH CONFERENCE: ACTS 21

Acts 21:20 And when they [the Jerusalem church leaders] heard it, they glorified the Lord and said to him [Paul], You see, brother, how many thousands of Jews there are which believe and they are all zealous of the law:
Acts 21:21 And they are informed about you that you teach all the Jews which are among the Gentiles to forsake Moses saying that they ought not to circumcise their children, neither to walk after the customs.

These verses tell a sad story. The date is approximately 25 years after Calvary and the status of the Mosaic Law was still hotly contested among Jewish Christians. Notice that thousands of Jewish Christians around Jerusalem were still observing ALL of the Mosaic Law, including circumcision and Sabbath-keeping. Those Jewish Christians again accused Paul of not requiring *Jewish* (not Gentile) converts to do the same. Whether true, or not, Paul's opponents most likely thought that he had instructed neither Jews nor Gentiles to observe the Sabbath, a favorite doctrine of the Pharisees.

Acts 21:24 Take them and purify yourself with them and pay their expenses that they may shave their heads and all may know that those things whereof they were informed concerning you are nothing; but that you yourself also walk orderly and keep the law.

This verse makes it absolutely clear that Jewish Christians—not Gentile Christians—were still being circumcised, still worshiping at the Temple and still observing the Sabbath of the Mosaic Law.

Acts 21:25 *As touching the Gentiles which believe, we have written and concluded that they observe no such thing,* except that they keep themselves from things offered to idols, and from blood and from strangled and from fornication.

The compromising decisions of the Jerusalem councils in Acts 15 and 21 should be enough proof that Gentile Christians were NOT required to, or expected to, observe the Sabbath. Peter had previously told the first conference, "Now therefore why do you tempt God, to put a yoke upon the neck of the disciples, which neither our fathers nor we were able to bear?" (15:10) and James, the leader, had earlier declared, "Wherefore my sentence is, that we do not trouble them, which from among the Gentiles are turned to God" (15:19) and "Forasmuch as we have heard, that certain which went out from us have troubled you with words, subverting your souls, saying, You must be circumcised, and keep the [whole] law [including its Sabbaths]: *to whom we gave no such commandment*" (15:24).

SDAs who ignore the above texts and insist that the Sabbath was not an issue (because everybody observed it) are also ignoring two of the key teachings of the Pharisees—circumcision and Sabbath-keeping.

CHAPTER TWENTY THREE

CHRISTIAN LIBERTY AND HOLY DAYS

Rom. 14:5 One man regards one day above another, another regards every day alike. Let each man be fully convinced in his own mind.

While many (like myself) claim that all holy days have been abolished, including the seventh-day Sabbath, Seventh-day Adventists dismiss Romans 14:5 as another reference only to the ceremonial holy days. The seventh-day Sabbath, they claim, cannot possibly be included in this text because, as one of the eternal moral principles given by God in the Ten Commandments, it was not negotiable.

On the one hand, Jewish Christians found it very difficult to immediately cease centuries of tradition, the Mosaic Law observance, Temple worship, and Sabbath observance. On the other hand, Paul never encouraged Gentile Christians to observe the Mosaic Law, Temple worship, or any holy day. For Paul, the doctrine of Christian liberty, or freedom, extends also to holy days, whether Saturday, Sunday, Passover (Easter), or Christmas!

First Corinthians, chapters 8 and 9, explain the "freedom," or "liberty," of the believer in Christ. The doctrine of Christian liberty is important regarding "holy days" such as the Seventh-day Sabbath or Sunday. This liberty also involves the difference between the Mosaic Law and the "Law of Christ." Paul's discussion in First Corinthians is also related to his statement in Romans 8:2, **"For the law of the Spirit of life in Christ has made me free from the law of sin and of death."**

Those who do not grasp the concept of Christian liberty are easily offended. "But take heed lest by any means this *liberty* of yours become a stumbling block to them that are weak" (1 Cor. 8:9). "To the weak I became weak, that I might win the weak. I have become all things to all men, that I might by all means save some" (1 Cor. 9:22).

One example of this 'freedom in action' involved food offered to idols. Specifically, because Paul knew that an idol is nothing" (1 Cor. 8:4), it did not offend him personally to eat food which had been offered to idols. "Howbeit there is not that knowledge in all men." Former pagan idolaters who had become Christians were offended by the sight of Jewish Christians eating food purchased at the marketplace of the pagan temple (8:7). Therefore, rather than offend the conscience of a more-sensitive Gentile believer, Paul refused to eat food offered to idols in the presence of these new believers (8:10-13).

A second example of Paul's 'freedom in action' involved payment of wages for preaching. While he was "free" to receive financial help in his ministry, he was also *free to refuse* financial assistance (1 Cor. 9:1-14). As long as it did not offend others, Paul often exercised his 'freedom' by refusing regular financial support most of the time from most churches (Acts 20:33-35). This 'freedom,' or 'liberty,' allowed him to preach the gospel fully and unhindered (1 Cor. 9:15-19).

1 Cor. 9:19 For though I am free from all men, yet I have made myself servant to all that I might gain the more.
1 Cor. 9:20 And to the Jews I became as a Jew that I might gain the Jews. To them that are under the law, as under the law, that I might gain them that are under the law;
1 Cor. 9:21 To them that are without law, as without law (being not without law to God, but under the law to Christ) that I might gain them that are without law.
1 Cor. 9:22 To the weak I became as weak that I might gain the weak. I am made all things to all men that I might by all means save some.
1 Cor. 9:23 And this I do for the gospel's sake that I might be partaker thereof with you.

A third example of 'freedom in action' involves holy days. First, while only with Jews, Paul acted as a Jew, observed the Mosaic Law, including its food laws, temple sacrifices, and its Sabbath days. This explains why he entered into the synagogues on the Sabbath days and tried to explain to those inside the gospel of Jesus Christ (9:20). Next, while only with Gentile Christians, Paul acted as one of them by refusing to eat food offered to idols and by ignoring holy days (9:21). Finally, when Paul was with BOTH groups at the same time, he was very careful not to offend either in order that he might lead both to a knowledge of the gospel (9:22). All of Paul's careful actions were "for the gospel's sake" (8:13; 9:23).

Gal. 5:22-23 But the fruit of the Spirit is love, joy, peace, longsuffering, gentleness, goodness, faith, meekness, temperance—*against such there is no law.*

As long as Paul's "freedom" in Christ did not offend those whom he was try-ing to win, there was no moral code, or law principle, against it. It was a diffi-cult transitional time. While the things Paul did might tempt us to accuse him of being "hypocritical," or "two-faced," his actions were entirely results of the "fruit of the Spirit."

An extension of Paul's freedom in Christ applied to worship days. As seen in the book of Acts, he could worship with Jews on the Sabbath and be free, or else he could worship with Gentiles on other days and still be free. *Paul had the gospel "privilege," "right" or "liberty," to chose ANY day of the week to worship and be free, or else he could consider every day of equal importance and be free.* However, according to Romans 14:5 Paul did hope that each person would thoroughly research the subject and become "fully convinced" personally. Paul did not make "the day of the week" an issue!

The point is that, under the New Covenant, there is absolutely no impor-tance given to any holy day!—whether Saturday or Sunday!—only to a holy person, Jesus Christ! "In Christ" the believer has completion in everything God requires of salvation, both justification and sanctification (1 Cor. 1:30; Col. 2:10). The believer has complete sinless rest "in Him" all day, every day (Heb. 4:3).

Many Christians believe that Sunday has replaced Saturday on the list of Ten Commandments as the new holy day which God commanded all Christians to observe. Both Sunday Sabbatarians and Saturday Sabbatarians teach that Calvary only abolished the judicial and ceremonial aspects of the Law, but not the Ten Commandments. Such reasoning is what led me to become a Seventh-day Adventist many years ago. SDAs have boldly offered $5,000 to anybody who can produce any text which says that God commanded a "change" from Saturday to Sunday. Nobody will ever collect the money because such a text does not exist! The "change" was from Saturday to every-day rest in Christ (Heb. 4:3).

In fact, the New Covenant does not instruct believers to "remember" any "day," to keep it holy! Seventh-day Adventists have a real problem in defining the word, "Law." Their narrow definition of "Law" as the "Ten Commandments" is unscriptural. The Law was an indivisible whole, the Old Covenant, only for national Israel. This is clearly stated many times in the Old Testament. Either ALL of the Law is still valid—commandments, statutes, and judgments—or none of it is (Mt. 5:17-48). Research this for yourself! The examples given by Jesus in Matthew 5:20-48 include all three sections of the Mosaic Law. There is quite a problem encountered when one tries to quote 5:17-19 and limit its scope to the Ten Commandments in order to prove the Sabbath.

Believers who acknowledge Christ's vicarious death, burial, resurrection and ascension are actually dead to all of the Law (John 1:7; Rom. 6:14; 7:4, 6; 8:2-3; 2 Cor. 3:6-11; Gal. 3:19, 23-25; 5:18; Heb. 8:13). That part of God's Law which is eternal and moral is now written in the heart of the believer and obedience is prompted by the indwelling Holy Spirit (Heb. 8:10-13). The Christian obeys God because of the "law of Christ" (Rom. 8:2), the "law of love" (Rom. 13:10; Gal. 5:14), the "law of faith" (Rom 3:27; Gal. 5:22-25) or the "royal law" (Jas. 2:8).

While only the moral parts of God's character are repeated in the terms of the New Covenant, there is no specific holy day repeated. (The inherent Sabbath command to let slaves rest is also gone.) There is no command to switch Saturday to Sunday; there is only evidence that the Sabbath command ended because the Christian is not under any part of the Mosaic Law as a covenant. That means that neither Saturday, nor Sunday are **commanded** holy days! Although most believers have freely chosen to assemble for worship on Sundays (and Wednesdays), **any day is appropriate.** Thus, while Seventh-day Adventists are correct in pointing out that the New Testament does not contain a single text changing Sabbath to Sunday, neither does it contain a single text continuing Saturday worship. Just the opposite is true in Acts 15:5-11, 24; 16:21, 29; Romans 14:5, Colossians 2:16 and Galatians 4:9-11.

Sunday is not a replacement of the Ten Commandment Sabbath. Otherwise, it would of necessity place the believer again under the strict restrictions of the Old Covenant Sabbath, including the death penalty for violation. In order to have corporate worship, early Christians **chose** Sunday. Most believe they did so in honor of the resurrection of Christ.

First Corinthians 16:2 does not command Sunday observance either. "Upon the first day of the week let every one of you lay by him in store as God has prospered him, that there be no gatherings when I come." The context of 16:2, is 16:1, "Now **concerning the collection for the saints.**" Paul was collecting food for famine relief in Judea. The believers were commanded, not to worship, but to **perform physical labor** on Sunday. They were told to "put aside and save" (NAS), "lay by him in store" (KJV) "that no collections be made when I come." This meant physically carrying food-supplies to storage areas to avoid delaying Paul's ship at port. The text does not discuss either holy days or offerings for church salaries and buildings! Although probable, corporate worship is not even mentioned.

Holy days restrict Christian unity and liberty! According to Ephesians 2:10-17 the "law of commandments contained in ordinances" was the "middle wall of partition," or the "enmity" that prohibited Israel from fellow-shipping with other nations. **The weekly and seasonal sabbath holy days were ordi-**

nances which especially separated Israel from the Gentiles. The Pharisee-Christians of Acts 15 wanted to force these holy days on the Gentiles converts. However, **God choose another way**; He chose to abolish all holy days (Acts 15:5-11, 24).

Gal. 4:9-11 "But NOW that you have come to know God, how is it that you turn back again to the weak and worthless elemental things, to which you desire to be enslaved all over again? You observe days [weekly] and months [monthly] and seasons [seasonal] and years. I fear for you, that perhaps I have labored over you in vain."

Col. 2:16-17 "Therefore let no one act as your judge in regard to food or drink or in respect of a festival [seasonal] or a new moon [monthly] or a Sabbath day [weekly], things which are a mere shadow of what is to come; but the substance belongs to Christ."

Returning to a pattern of commanded holy days destroys Christian liberty and places one back under a legalistic approach to sanctification. Galatians 4 is a warning not to replace former PAGAN holy days with so-called CHRISTIAN (or Jewish) holy days. As detailed in another chapter, the sequence of Galatians 4:9-11 and Colossians 2:16-17 is from weekly, to seasonal, to yearly and must include the weekly Sabbath day.

Required "holy days" have no place in the New Covenant because they draw attention away from Christ, our holy all-in-all. Every promise that was signified by holy days is already "yes" in Christ (2 Cor. 1:20). Sunday is merely a non-commanded day that many Christians themselves have freely chosen to assemble for worship. Correctly understood, Sunday is NOT the replacement for the Sabbath day of the Ten Commandments. For believers, every day is a new-creation rest day granted by the sinless atonement of Jesus Christ (Heb. 4:3).

Paul's "fear" in Galatians 4:11 of putting emphasis on holy days and festivals applies also to Christian emphasis of Sunday, Easter and Christmas. Like Seventh-day Sabbath-keepers, too many feel they have met their duty to God by observing "holy days."

CHAPTER TWENTY FOUR

THE UNITED STATES, ROMAN CATHOLICISM AND THE MARK OF THE BEAST

Seventh-day Adventists are taught to fear and distrust the Roman Catholic Church, other Protestants and, especially, the United States government. They are taught by Ellen G. White that, in the last days, the United States will be the false prophet nation of Revelation 13:11-18 which will be foremost in placing them under the death decree of the beast.

GC440: [Ellen G. White] One nation, and only one, meets the specifications of this prophecy [Rev. 13:11-18]; it points unmistakably to the United States of America.

According to EGW, the Roman Catholic Church is the little horn of Daniel 7 and 8, the beast power of Revelation 13:1-10 and Babylon of Revelation 17 and 18. They teach that, since Roman Catholics claim to have used their own authority to change God's Law from Saturday to Sunday, then those who worship on Sunday pay homage to the pope and are the "daughters" of Babylon of Revelation. When apostate Protestantism in the United States controls legislation to enforce Sunday worship in the last days, it will have fulfilled prophecy and will have made an image to the beast.

GC445: "WHEN the leading churches of the United States, uniting in such points of doctrine as are held by them in common, shall influence the state to enforce their decrees and to sustain their institutions, THEN Protestant America will have formed an image to the Roman hierarchy, and the inflictions of civil penalties upon dissenters inevitably result."

GC448-449: "The enforcement of Sunday keeping on the part of the Protestant churches is an enforcement of the worship of the papacy-the beast....hence the enforcement of Sunday keeping in the United States would be an enforcement of the worship of the beast and his image."

The mission of the Seventh-day Adventist Church is to proclaim that God's Law is unchangeable. Up until the very last days, those who have never heard the Sabbath truth can barely be saved through ignorance. However, those who have heard the seventh-day Sabbath message and rejected it will receive the mark of the beast and cannot be saved. Before Jesus returns, every person on earth will hear the Sabbath message and make a decision either to leave the Babylonian Sunday-worshiping churches and join the Seventh-day Adventist Church, or else be killed and forever lost when Jesus returns.

GC449: "But when Sunday observance shall be enforced by law, and the world shall be enlightened concerning the obligation of the true Sabbath, then whoever shall transgress the command of God to obey a precept which has no higher authority than that of Rome, will thereby honor popery above God. He is paying homage to Rome and to the power which embraces the institution ordained by Rome. He is worshiping the beast and his image. As men then reject the institution which God has declared to be the sign of His authority, and honor in its stead that which Rome has chosen as the token of her supremacy, they will thereby accept the sign of allegiance to Rome—'the mark of the beast.' And it is not until this issue is thus plainly set before the people and they are brought to choose between the commandments of God and the commandments of men, that those who continue in transgression will receive "the mark of the beast."

According to SDAs, before Christ returns the entire world will be controlled by the Popish Antichrist and the Roman Catholic Church. A death decree will be imposed on Sabbath-keeping Seventh-day Adventists for causing the last-day great catastrophes. SDAs (144, 000), under God's seal of protection, will boldly teach the Sabbath until every person is fully aware of the choices. As the last days approach and the seals, trumpets and vials of Revelation are occurring, apostate Protestantism in the United States will be Satan's instrument that returns the Roman Catholic Church to its old dominance.

GC573: "In the movements now in progress in the United States to secure for the institutions and usages of the church the support of the state, Protestants are following in the steps of papists. Nay, more they are opening the door for the papacy to regain in Protestant America the supremacy which she has lost in the Old World. And that which gives greater significance to this movement is the fact that the principle object contemplated is the enforcement of Sunday observance—a custom which originated with Rome, and which she claims as the sign of her authority."

The entire world will blame the judgments of Revelation on SDAs because they refuse to worship on Sunday in obedience to the enforced national Sunday laws. Church leaders will encourage their members to hunt down and imprison SDAs for a death sentence.

GC604a: "Fearful is the issue to which the world is to be brought. The powers of earth, uniting to war against the commandments of God, will decree that 'all, both small and great, rich and poor, free and bond' (Revelation 13:16), shall conform to the customs of the church by the observance of the false Sabbath. All who refuse compliance will be visited with civil penalties, and it will finally be declared that they are deserving of death. On the other hand the law of God enjoining the Creator's rest day demands obedience and threatens wrath against all who transgress its precepts...."

GC614: "Those who honor the law of God have been accused of bringing judgments upon the world, and they will be regarded as the cause of the fearful convulsions of nature and the strife and bloodshed among men that are filling the earth with woe."

According to SDAs, the Sabbath, not the gospel, is the great final test to determine who really loves God and who finally will be saved in the final days.

THE MARK OF THE BEAST

GC604b: "...With the issue thus *clearly* brought before him, whoever shall trample upon God's law to obey a human enactment receives *the mark of the beast*; he accepts the sign of allegiance to the power he chooses to obey instead of God."

GC605:"The Sabbath will be the great test of loyalty, for it is the point of truth especially controverted. When the final test shall be brought to bear upon men, then the line of distinction will be drawn between those who serve God and those who serve Him not. While the observance of the false sabbath in compliance with the law of the state, contrary to the fourth commandment, will be an avowal of allegiance to a power that is in opposition to God, the keeping of the true Sabbath, in obedience to God's law, is an evidence of loyalty to the Creator. While one class, by accepting the sign of submission to earthly powers, receive the mark of the beast, the other, choosing the token of allegiance to divine authority, receive the seal of God."

GC615-616: "This argument will appear *conclusive*; and a DECREE will finally be issued against those who hallow the Sabbath of the fourth commandment, denouncing them as deserving of the severest punishment and giving the people liberty, after a certain time, to put them to DEATH. Romanism in the Old World and apostate Protestantism in the New will pursue a similar course toward those who honor all the divine precepts."

Seventh-day Adventists are taught to find a remote place to hide and to store up provisions for the last days per Revelation 12. This is why they should not trust others.

GC626: "As the decree issued by the various rulers of Christendom against commandment keepers shall withdraw the protection of government and abandon them to those who desire their destruction, the people of God will flee from the cities and villages and associate toget6her in companies, dwelling in the most desolate and solitary places."

COMMENTS:
    All of the preceding theory is built upon a series of assumptions which must ALL be true in order for the total scenario to be true. (1) That the seventh-day Sabbath is binding on all nations; (2) that the Sabbath is the great test in the last days for salvation; (3) that the remnant in Revelation refers only to the Seventh-day Adventist Church; (4) that Ellen G. White is the final fulfillment of Revelation 19:10; (5) that Revelation 13 is unfulfilled future prophecy; (6) that the beast of Daniel and Revelation is the Roman Catholic Church; (7) that the beast in Revelation 13:11-18 is the United States of America; (8) that the U. S. A. will become a totalitarian religious state and enforce Sunday worship; (9) that a death decree will be issued by the U. S. government against SDAs for not worshiping on Sunday and for causing worldwide devastation; (10) that the seventh-day Sabbath is the seal of God and (11) that Sunday is the mark of the beast.
    Yet, after all this, SDAs insist in their pamphlet, *Who are the Seventh-day Adventists?*, page 6, "So who are [we] really? Are [we] some **strange group with weird ideas**? Do [our] leaders make **bizarre predictions about the future?**" "Yes" and "Yes" again! SDAs want others to see them as normal lovable

Christians whose main difference is that they worship on Saturday instead of Sunday.

It is my personal opinion that this Seventh-day Adventist doctrine [the Mark of the Beast] makes them untrustworthy as U. S. legislators, soldiers or as persons in responsible government positions.

CHAPTER TWENTY FIVE

TWO DIFFERENT THREE ANGELS' MESSAGES

[1ST ANGEL'S MESSAGE]

Rev. 14:6 And I saw another angel fly in the midst of heaven, having the everlasting gospel to preach to them that dwell on the earth, and to every nation, and kindred, and tongue, and people.

Rev. 14:7 Saying with a loud voice, Fear God, and give glory to Him; for the hour of His judgment is come; and worship Him that made heaven, the earth, and the sea, and the fountains of water.

[2ND ANGEL'S MESSAGE]

Rev. 14:8 And there followed another angel saying, Babylon is fallen, is fallen, that great city, because she made all the nations drink of the wine of her fornication.

[3RD ANGEL'S MESSAGE]

Rev. 14:9 And the third angel followed them, saying with a loud voice, If any man worship the beast and his image, and receive his mark in his forehead, or in his hand,

Rev. 14:10 The same shall drink of the wine of the wrath of God, which is poured out without mixture into the cup of his indignation; and he shall be tormented with fire and brimstone in the presence of the holy angels, and in the presence of the Lamb;

Rev. 14:11 And the smoke of their torment ascends up for ever and ever: and they have no rest day nor night, who worship the beast and his image, and whosoever receives the mark of his name.

Rev. 14:12 Here is the patience of the saints; here are they that keep the commandments of God and the faith of Jesus.

The "Three Angels," not the Seventh-day Sabbath, are the "symbol" of Seventh-day Adventism. The sign in front of each church depicts the three angels of Revelation 14:6-12. SDAs trace their existence and their calling to their unique interpretation of the Three Angels' Messages.

However, once again SDAs are inconsistent with their interpretation of Scripture. Although trying to display continuity between early Adventists under William Miller from 1818 until 1844 and later (Seventh-day) Adventists, they actually have completely changed the message delivered from Revelation 14 by the Millerites.

Two Different First Angel's Messages

14:7 Fear God and give glory to Him for the hour of His judgment is come

Miller's Interpretation: From 1818 until 1844, William Miller taught that this referred to the second coming of Christ to rescue true believers and to judge the earth with fiery destruction. This is also what Ellen G. White and early Adventists believed before October 22, 1844.

Ellen G. White's Endorsement of William Miller: Although Miller was completely wrong when he predicted that Jesus would return to earth in 1843 and (twice in) 1844, he still received the most glowing endorsement from Ellen White.
GC320: "*Endeavoring to lay aside all pre-conceived opinions...*
COMMENT: Miller was uneducated; he used the KJV and a small concordance. He valued the KJV over the Hebrew used by his detractors.
GC324-325: "Miller *accepted the generally received view* that in the Christian age the earth is the sanctuary...
COMMENT: This partially contradicts the previous statement.
GC 328-329: "Miller and his associates at first believed that the 2300 days would terminate in the *spring* of 1844, whereas *the prophecy refers to the autumn of that year*."
COMMENT: For 25 years Miller taught 1843. Regardless, all three dates were wrong.
GC 331: "*As Elisha was called...so was William Miller called...*
COMMENT: EGW incorrectly compares Miller's calling to Elisha's calling.
GC335: "William Miller possessed...*the wisdom of heaven*.... enabled him to *refute error and expose falsehood*."
GC339: [God] sent *chosen messengers* to make known the *nearness of the final judgment*.
COMMENT: Miller could not refute error because he did not know the truth.
Chapter 19, *Light Through Darkness* **(William Miller), 343-354**
GC352-353: "*Those* [Millerites] *who proclaimed this warning [Rev 14:7] gave the right message at the right time.*

COMMENT: How could it have been "the right message at the right time" if Miller always preached the second coming of Christ and never the Investigative Judgment?

GC354: "When called to endure the scoffs and reproach of the world, and the test of delay and disappointment [that Christ did not come in the spring of 1844], would they renounce the faith? Because they did not immediately understand the dealings of God with them, would they *cast aside truths sustained by the clearest testimony of His word*?

COMMENT: How can they be "truths sustained by the clearest testimony of His word" if Miller was wrong about the sanctuary being earth and the cleansing being the second coming with fire?

GC353: "Yet God accomplished His own beneficent purpose in *permitting* the [spring 1844] warning of the judgment to be given *just as it was.*

COMMENT: EGW says that God endorsed Miller's false message of the second coming of Christ "just as it was."

GC354: "This test [Christ failing to return in spring 1844] would reveal the strength of those who with real faith had obeyed what they believed to be the teachings of the word and the Spirit of God. It would teach them, as only such an experience could, *the danger of accepting the theories and interpretations of men*, instead of making the Bible its own interpreter."

COMMENT: One must read the previous paragraph on page 354. How can believing Miller's error teach "the danger of accepting the theories and interpretations" of those who disagreed with Miller?

SDA Post-1844 Different Interpretation of 14:7: Now, instead of the second coming to earth with fire, this refers to the Investigative Judgment which began in heaven on October 22, 1844. The phrase **"worship Him that made"** now refers to the Sabbath Day because it is the commandment which refers to God as the Creator.

The Problem: Although these are completely different interpretations, SDAs still teach that William Miller taught the truth from God. Yet Miller did not accept the SDA post-1844 interpretation.

Two Different Second Angel's Messages

14:8 Babylon is fallen, is fallen

Miller's Interpretation: "Babylon" represents all of the churches which refused to believe that Christ was coming back on October 22, 1844. After the failure of the spring 1844 date-setting many of his followers returned to their former churches and ridiculed Miller. "Babylon is fallen" was Miller's rebuke to his former followers and to other churches.

Ellen G. White's Endorsement of Miller's Errors:
Chapter 21, *A Warning Rejected* **[All Non-Adventists are Babylon], 375-390**
This chapter explains that the failed prediction of a second coming in the spring of 1844 and the resulting ridicule in the summer and fall of 1844 were not Miller's fault, but God's design.
GC373-374: "God *designed* to prove his people. *His hand covered a mistake* in the reckoning of the prophetic periods [autumn 1844 instead of spring 1844]. Adventists did not discover the error."
COMMENT: EGW blamed Miller's false prophecy on God. God intended for Miller to preach error about the second coming in the fall of 1843 and the spring of 1844.
GC375: "In preaching *the doctrine of the second advent,* William Miller and his associates had labored with the sole purpose of arousing men to a preparation for the judgment."
COMMENT: EGW justified Miller's error of date-setting for the second coming.
GC376: "Those [non-Millerites] who sought to shut out the testimony of God's word they [Millerites] could not regard as constituting the church of Christ, *'the pillar and ground of the truth.'* Hence they felt themselves justified in separating from their former connection. In the *summer of 1844* about fifty thousand withdrew from the churches."
COMMENT: EGW condemned those who left the Millerite movement after two failed predictions for Christ's second coming. She called Miller's false teachings "the testimony of God's Word." Fifty thousand accepted the false doctrine.
GC379: "The first angel's message of Revelation 14 [the false message preached by Miller] *was designed* to separate the professed people of God from the corrupting influences of the world.... Had they [non-Millerites] received the *message from heaven...*
COMMENT: EGW called Miller's false prophecy before October 22, 1844 "the message from heaven."
GC380: "In refusing the warning of the first angel [Miller himself], they rejected the means which heaven had provided for their *restoration.* They spurned the gracious messenger [Miller] that would have *corrected* the evils which separated them from God...."
COMMENT: After October 22, 1844 SDAs themselves rejected Miller's false message and totally replaced it with another false doctrine. How can Miller be

God's messenger who preached the first angel's message if he was wrong? How can believing a lie provide "restoration"?

GC389: "*The second angel's message of Revelation 14 was first preached in the summer of 1844.*

COMMENT: EGW calls Miller the second angel. Again, how can Miller preach the second angel's message if he was wrong? In the summer of 1844 Miller still preached the second coming, not the Investigative Judgment. To Miller, "Babylon" was the mass who disagreed with him. Yet after October 22, 1844 the SDAs disagreed themselves with Miller (and became the Babylon of Miller's viewpoint).

Chapter 22, Prophecies Fulfilled [Explains Why Jesus Did Not Return in the Spring of 1844, but Would Return to Earth in October 1844], 391-408

Tarrying Time of **Second Coming** from Spring to Fall of 1844.

GC391 "When the time passed in which the Lord's coming was first expected—in the spring of 1844—those who had looked in faith for his appearing were for a season involved in doubt and uncertainty."

GC391 "Signs which could not be mistaken pointed to the [second] coming of Christ as near."

COMMENT: These signs included the 1755 Lisbon earthquake, the 1833 meteor shower in New England, and the 1840 treaty with Turkey. EGW says that the signs were for the soon second coming and not the Investigative Judgment.

GC393 Matthew 25:1-12 parable of ten virgins teaches a delay.

GC396: "William Miller had no sympathy with those influences that led to fanaticism."

GC398 "It was not the proclamation of the second advent that caused fanaticism and division. These [fanatics] appeared in the **summer of 1844**, when Adventists were in a state of doubt and perplexity concerning their real position. The preaching of the first angel's message and the 'midnight cry' tended directly to *repress fanaticism* and dissension."

COMMENT: These statements are in the context of why Jesus did not come in the spring of 1844. They have no relevance to the fall of 1844 or the Investigative Judgment. The real Babylonians were those who believed Miller's next prediction that Jesus would return in October 1844.

GC400: "Like a tidal wave the movement [with its revised October 22, 1844 **second coming** date] swept over the land....*Fanaticism disappeared* before this proclamation.... Believers saw their doubt and perplexity removed, and hope and courage animated their hearts. The work was *free from those extremes* which are ever manifested when there is human excitement without the *controlling influence of the word and Spirit of God*."

COMMENT: The summer of 1844 context of the statement makes it evidently ridiculous.

GC401: "Of all the great religious movements since the days of the apostles, none have been more free from human imperfection and the wiles of Satan than was that of the autumn of 1844."

COMMENT: This is one of the most bizarre statements ever written by Ellen G. White! William Miller was still preaching that Jesus would return to earth on October 22, 1844!

GC402: "At the call, 'the Bridegroom cometh, go ye out to meet Him,' 'the waiting ones arose and trimmed their lamps;' they studied the Word of God with an intensity of interest before unknown. *Angels were sent* from heaven to arouse those who had become discouraged and prepare them *to receive the message.* The work did not stand in the wisdom and learning of men, but in *the power of God.* It was not the most talented, but *the most humble and devoted* who were the first to hear and obey the call. Farmers left their crops standing in the fields; mechanics laid down their tools, and with tears and rejoicing went out to give the warning. Those who had formerly led in the cause were among the last to join this movement. The churches in general closed their doors against *this message,* and a large company of those who received it withdrew from their connection. In the *providence of God* this proclamation untied with the second angel's message and gave power to that work. The message, *'Behold the bridegroom cometh'* was not so much a matter of argument, though *the Scripture proof was clear and conclusive."*

COMMENT: Read this again slowly for its full effect! It is still referring to Miller's second coming message which was preached in the summer of 1844.

GC407: "God did not forsake his people; His Spirit still abode with those who did not *rashly* deny the light which they had received, and denounce the advent movement."

COMMENT: EGW again condemns those who left the 1844-second-coming Millerite movement in the summer of 1844 as "rashly denying the light."

SDA Post-1844 Different Interpretation: Instead of being those who rejected Miller's second coming in the summer of 1844, "Babylon" now represents all churches who reject the special truths given to the SDA church—beginning with the Investigative Judgment and including the Sabbath, non-immortality of the soul, unclean food restrictions, etc.

The Problems: (1) Miller was wrong. (2) Miller was a false prophet. (3) Miller's teachings caused fanaticism. (4) God did not deliberately design the great lie that Jesus would come back in the spring of 1844. (5) Ellen White's many comments about God's truth are all wrong because Miller taught the second coming of Christ. (6) Even SDAs later rejected Miller's teachings and condemned him as a Babylonian for not accepting the Investigative Judgment.

The pre-1844 and post-1844 explanations are completely different. SDAs and Miller condemn each other! Since SDAs rejected Miller's second coming doctrine, then SDAs are included in Miller's definition of "Babylon is fallen." And, since Miller rejected the SDA Investigative Judgment doctrine, then Miller is included in the later SDA "Babylon is fallen" condemnation.

Two Different Third Angel's Messages

14:8 If any man worships the beast and his image and receive his mark…

Miller's Interpretation: Referred to the rejection of the everlasting gospel which included the doctrine of the second coming of Christ. Miller definitely had no connection with the Investigative Judgment and the Sabbath Day doctrines.

Ellen White Finally Condemned William Miller:
Chapter 23, *What is the Sanctuary,* 409-422 [Why Miller was Wrong]
GC409: "Many *rashly* cut the knot of difficulty by denying that the 2300 days ended in 1844."
COMMENT: They had been embarrassed by three false dates for the second coming of Christ (1843; spring 1844; autumn 1844). There was nothing *rash* about admitting error. The overwhelming majority of William Miller's followers, including himself, admitted error.
GC410: "To deny that the days [of Daniel 8:14] ended at that time [October 22, 1844] was to involve the whole question in confusion, and to renounce positions which had been established by *unmistakable fulfillment* of prophecy."
COMMENT: The confusion was in refusing to admit that Miller was wrong and inventing the Investigative Judgment doctrine.
GC411: "…they found in the Bible a full explanation of the subject of the sanctuary, its nature, location, and services; the testimony of the sacred writer being so clear and simple as to *place the matter beyond all question.*"
COMMENT: *"The matter"* of the sanctuary is indeed *"beyond all question."* It is clear to all except SDAs that the types, shadows, examples, and patterns were all fulfilled at Calvary. Yet, for SDAs, it is truly *"the matter beyond all question"* because the prophetess has written it.
GC417 "Thus the prophecy [quotes Dan. 8:14] *unquestionably* refers to the sanctuary in heaven."

COMMENT: Only SDAs say this.

GC422: "Thus those who followed in *the light of prophetic word* saw that, instead of coming to the earth at the termination of the 2300 days in 1844, Christ then entered the MOST HOLY PLACE of the heavenly sanctuary to perform the closing work of atonement preparatory to his coming."

COMMENT: This is completely new and completely contradicts Miller.

Chapter 24, *In the Holy of Holies* (Investigative Judgment), 423-432

GC423: "The subject of the sanctuary was the key which unlocked the mystery of the disappointment of 1844. It opened to view a *complete system of truth*, connected and harmonious, showing that *God's hand* had directed the great advent movement and revealing present duty as it brought to light the position and work of his people."

COMMENT: It really opened a pandora's box of other false doctrines used to justify their error. First among these is that sacrificial blood defiles God's Most Holy Place in heaven. Second is the doctrine of the non-immortality of the soul.

GC423 "Now in the holy of holies they again beheld him, their compassionate High Priest, *soon* to appear as their king and deliverer."

COMMENT: Even with the Investigative Judgment message, early Adventists still expected a "soon" return of Christ to earth. They thought that the investigation would be very short.

GC424 "The *mistake* had not been in the reckoning of the prophetic periods, but in the *event* to take place at the end of the 2300 days. Through this *error* the believers had suffered disappointment, *yet all that was foretold by the prophecy and all that they had any Scripture warrant to expect, had been accomplished.*"

COMMENT: This conclusion about the Millerites' expectations is simply wrong.

GC426: "In the summer and autumn of 1844 the proclamation, 'Behold the bridegroom cometh' was given."

COMMENT: Miller preached that, per Matthew 25, Jesus has only delayed his second coming, but was still coming on October 22, 1844. This is still not a reference to the Investigative Judgment.

GC428: "In the parable of Matthew 22 the same figure of the marriage is introduced, and *the investigative judgment is clearly represented* as taking place before the marriage...." [Matthew 22:1-13]

COMMENT: The discussion has changed from the second coming to the Investigative Judgment.

GC430: "It is those who by faith follow Jesus in the great work of the atonement who receive the benefits of his mediation in their behalf, WHILE those who reject the light which brings to view this work of ministration are not benefitted thereby."

COMMENT: Once again, EGW clearly says that only those who follow SDAs in accepting the Investigative Judgment message will "benefit" from it. Therefore, even William Miller forfeited his salvation!

SDA Post-1844 Different Interpretation of the Third Angel's Message

SDAs teach that Miller was deliberately misled by God because many special truths still needed to be presented to the world by the true remnant SDA Church. This especially refers to the Sabbath and the non-immortality of the soul doctrines which Miller did not teach.

Chapter 26, A Work of Reform (Sabbath Reform), 433-450

Chapter 27, (Satanic) Modern Revivals, 461-478

Chapter 28, Facing Life's Record (The Investigative Judgment), 479-491

Chapter 29, *The Origin of Evil* (Soul Sleep), 492-504

Chapter 31, *Agency of Evil Spirits* (Soul Sleep), 511-517

Chapter 32, *Snares of Satan* (Soul Sleep), 518-530

Chapter 33, *The First Great Deception* (Soul Sleep), 531-550

Chapter 34, *Can Our Dead Speak to Us* (Soul Sleep), 551-562

Compared to what Miller taught, Babylon changed to the Roman Catholic Church. Her daughters changed to all Protestantism other than themselves. The "mark" changed to Sunday worship. And the last day conflict changed to center around the Sabbath.

The Problem: The completely changed First, Second, and Third Angels' messages are not what the Millerites and early Adventists taught and believed from 1818 until October 22, 1844. The continuity they claim is simply not there! In fact, in GC430, William Miller is included among those who will not be saved because he rejected the Investigative Judgment interpretation of Daniel 8:14.

Conclusion: It is strange to see present SDA hospitals merging with "Babylonian" denominations whom they denounce as anti-Christ. Church members are taught to suspect others as last-day oppressors. While pretending to join the evangelical ranks and even join ministerial associations, SDA ministers consider all others as "Babylon" or her "harlot" false offspring churches (Rev 17:5). GC355-408.

The third angel's message teaches that Roman Catholicism (Rev 13:1-10) and "apostate Protestantism" (Rev. 17:5) will join the United States (the false prophet nation of Rev 13:11-18) in imposing universal forced Sunday observance (Rev. 13:16-18). Anti-Christ and Satan himself will control all churches and political forces other than their own. To SDAs, the beast is the Pope and the "mark of the beast" IS "Sunday-worship." They have created a paranoia that Sunday-keeping friends and relatives will eventually turn them over to the authorities for refusing to worship on Sunday (Rev 13:15-17; 12:14-16). Many of them live in constant mistrust of non-SDAs. See *The Great Controversy,* chapters 36-40.

SDAs are totally consumed with Sabbath issues. The average non-SDA has absolutely no idea how different they are. Therefore most of us tend to accept them as normal Christians and ignore their strange doctrines. To SDAs, those who "keep the commandments of God and have the testimony of Jesus" (Rev 12:17:19:10) perfectly describes ONLY themselves. They claim to keep ALL the Ten Commandments, especially the Sabbath; they claim to have the "Spirit of Prophecy" in the writings of Ellen While, which, to them, means "the testimony of Jesus" (Rev 19:10). To them, Christ will not return until there are 144,000 **sinless** Seventh-day Adventists who prove to all mankind that the Ten Commandments can be kept perfectly (14:5). GC582-678.

DANIEL 8:14 AND REVELATION 14:6-12

William Miller	Seventh-day Adventists
sanctuary was earth	sanctuary is God's in heaven
cleansing fire destroys earth	cleansing removes sins of saints from heaven
hour of judgment was 1843/1844	hour of judgment begins 1844
second coming	Investigative Judgment
Babylon: those who rejected second coming message	Babylon: those who reject SDA doctrines
mark on those who reject his message	mark of beast is Sunday worship

Rev. 14:10 The same shall drink of the wine of the wrath of God, which is poured out without mixture into the cup of his indignation; and he shall be tormented with fire and brimstone in the presence of the holy angels, and in the presence of the Lamb:
Rev. 14:11 And the smoke of their torment ascends up for ever and ever: and they have no rest day nor night, who worship the beast and his image, and whosoever receives the mark of his name.

Oddly, the third angel's message concludes with what is perhaps the longest description in God's Word of Gehenna, the Lake of Fire. Yet SDAs teach that these fires are very soon extinguished because they deny the doctrine of the immortality of the soul.

APPENDIX 1

SHEOL AND THE SOUL

1. INTRODUCTION AND PURPOSE:

Sheol is one of the most mysterious words in all of the Bible. It conjures up such Old Testament companion words as the "rephaim," or "spirits of the dead," "the nether world," "shadows," "the bottoms of the mountains," and *Abaddon*. However, it is unfortunate that most of us have never noticed *Sheol* in our Bibles because it is usually translated into words such as "grave," "pit" and "Hell."

What happens to the soul at death? Does the soul immediately enter its full reward or punishment before the resurrection of the body? Does the soul enter only a partial reward or punishment and await its full reward or punishment after resurrection? Does the soul cease to exist entirely until the resurrection for one judgment of both body and soul? Do only the souls of the righteous survive death and the souls of the wicked cease to exist without any punishment? All of these views are current within Christianity today.

I have been a member of churches which advocated the first (Baptist) and third (Seventh-day Adventist) views which have used the King James Version to validate both doctrines. It will be shown that a proper understanding of *Sheol* is one of the most important keys in researching this mystery.

The greatest difficulty in understanding the intermediate state of the soul is caused by the different ways that the word *Sheol* is translated in some of the most accepted Bible versions. *Sheol* is the Hebrew word for *Hades*. The most accepted versions widely disagree concerning their translation of *Sheol*. For example, the King James Version translates it as "Hell" 31 times, "grave" 30 times and "pit" 3 times. The New King James revisers left *Sheol* as "Hell" 18 of the 31 occurrences; however, it changed "Hell" to *Sheol* 13 times, "grave" to *Sheol* 4 times, "pit" to *Sheol* once and "grave" to "Hell" once. Unfortunately, the New International Version *never* uses the word "Hell" in the Old Testament! It translates *Sheol* as "grave" in 56 of its 64 occurrences; "death" is used 6 times and "depths" once. Only in Deuteronomy 32:22 does the NIV approach the truth with "the realm of death below." However, in contrast to these, the New American Standard Version and the Revised Standard Versions wisely avoid interpretation and conjecture by simply leaving the word as *Sheol* in all occurrences. A comparative chart is supplied at the end of this article.

Therefore, on the one hand, those Christians who deny the doctrine of the intermediate conscious state of souls between death and the resurrection quote the KJV and NIV for textual support and avoid the NAS and RSV. On the other hand, Christians who believe that souls continue to exist in a conscious intermediate state prefer the NAS and RSV.

Something has gone seriously wrong within the realm of Bible translations when versions differ this much! While claiming to be written for contemporary man's clear comprehension of God's Word, at least here inaccurate translations have actually lessened our understanding of how the men and women of the Bible perceived life and death.

Some Christians believe the Bible teaches that there is not an independent "soul" which survives the death of the body in a conscious intermediate state. Prominent among these are Jehovah's Witnesses and Seventh-day Adventists. Jehovah's Witnesses teach that physical death is the absolute end for the unbeliever. They deny a resurrection of unbelievers, a final judgment of them and any kind of after-life punishment, whether it is in *Sheol*, Hell, *Hades, Gehenna* or the lake of fire.

Seventh-day Adventists, like Jehovah's Witnesses, teach that the soul does not exist apart from the body, and, therefore, both the righteous and unrighteous actually cease to exist at death. Although SDAs soften this by calling it "soul-sleep," it is really a doctrine of "non-existence," or "annihilation." Only after an after-death judgment (which began in 1844) and re-creation, they teach, will the righteous enter the presence of God. The wicked will then be judged and finally completely destroyed soon after they are cast into the lake of fire. In recent years similar views to this have gained proponents in almost every major liberal denomination.

Other Christians, especially conservatives, accept the traditional position. These believe the Bible teaches that, for mankind, life and death are both physical and spiritual. The physical part ends when the body dies. On the other hand, at the moment of death, man's spiritual being continues a conscious existence in another place. The Old Testament name for the place of both bodies and souls is *Sheol*.

Many of these believe that, before the resurrection of Christ, the souls of both the righteous and the wicked went into one of several regions of *Sheol*, the New Testament *Hades*. At Christ's ascension, he transplanted the upper Paradise portion of *Sheol* containing the souls of the righteous to heaven itself, into the presence of God. They believe that this is a conscious existence, an intermediate state, between the death of the body and the resurrection of the body. The souls of the wicked remain in conscious, or semi-conscious, torment in *Sheol*, or *Hades*.

Which view is correct? The doctrine of *Sheol* is very important in deciding the answer to this question. Is *Sheol* equal to the grave and only a storage place for the body because souls have ceased any conscious existence? Or did O. T. *Sheol* contain both dead bodies and conscious souls? Or is the truth somewhere in between? It is extremely difficult to comprehend Old Testament man's understanding of the afterlife without proper discernment of the word *Sheol*.

As previously stated, these differing doctrines about the intermediate state result partially from the understanding and definition of *Sheol* and *Hades*. Both Seventh-day Adventists and Jehovah's Witnesses claim that *Sheol/Hades* and "the grave" are wholly identical Bible terms which refer only to the body between death and the resurrection. They support their doctrine by quoting many texts which incorrectly translate *Sheol* as "grave."

However, a thorough Old Testament study of *Sheol* reveals that it must mean much more than only the "grave." Anyone who earnestly wants to know the truth about the subject should begin with an exhaustive study of every Old Testament reference to *Sheol*. Rather than limiting the study to inconclusive discussions about "immortality" and the meaning of "spirit" and "soul," try to discover the mind-set of Old Testament writers. Try to discover what they actually thought about the afterlife as shown by their actions.

Again, the King James Version, New International Version, and many popular modern versions have contributed much to the confusion by translating the Hebrew word, *Sheol* as "grave" instead of leaving it accurately as *Sheol* as does both the New American

Standard and the Revised Standard Versions. Moreover, because many Christians confuse *Sheol*, Hell and *Hades* with the "lake of fire" (*Gehenna*), then translating *Sheol* as "Hell" also contributes to the confusion. *Sheol* is the better word because it does not interpret itself by theological speculation; if misunderstood, it at the least stimulates inquiry.

It is my purpose to demonstrate that *Sheol* should be left untranslated. The integrity of God's Word and the clear understanding of Bible doctrine depends on translations which retain unchangeable truth.

2. *SHEOL*: CONFUSING DEFINITIONS

The following are direct quotations, though excerpts, from several leading source materials. Oddly, several insist on using the word "grave" for *Sheol*, but their extended definitions reveal that their use of "grave" includes the concepts of "soul," "body," "death," and "the pit." This is confusing, at the least, because contemporary usage of the word "grave" has mostly changed from usage over the centuries.

International Standard Bible Encyclopedia: Sheol
This word is often translated in the King James Version "grave".... It means *really* the unseen world, *the state or abode of the dead*.... The English Revisers have acted somewhat inconsistently in leaving "grave" or "pit" in the historical books and putting *Sheol* in the margin, while substituting *Sheol* in the poetical writings, and putting "grave" in the margin....

Not a state of unconsciousness: Yet it would be a mistake to infer, because of these strong and sometimes poetically heightened contrasts to the world of the living, that *Sheol* was conceived of as absolutely a place without consciousness, or some dim remembrance of the world above. This is not the case. **Necromancy** rested on the idea that there was some communication between the world above and the world below.

Post-canonical Period: There is no doubt, at all events, that in the post-canonical Jewish literature (the Apocrypha and apocalyptic writings) a very considerable development is manifest in the idea of *Sheol*. Distinction between good and bad in Israel is emphasized; *Sheol* becomes for certain classes an intermediate state between death and resurrection; for the wicked and for Gentiles it is nearly a synonym for *Gehenna* (Hell).

Nelson's Bible Dictionary: Sheol
The abode of the dead. *Sheol* is the Hebrew equivalent of the Greek *Hades*, which means "the unseen world."

Sheol was regarded as an underground region, shadowy and gloomy, where disembodied souls had a conscious but dull and inactive existence. The Hebrew people regarded *Sheol* as a place to which both the righteous and unrighteous go at death, a place where punishment is received and rewards are enjoyed. *Sheol* is pictured as having an insatiable appetite.

However, God is present in *Sheol*. It is open and known to Him. This suggests that in death God's people remain under His care, and the wicked never escape His judgment. *Sheol* gives meaning to Psalm 16:10. Peter saw the fulfillment of this messianic psalm in Jesus' resurrection.

Oxford Companion to the Bible: "Hell"

Both *Sheol* and *Hades* refer to *a general dwelling place of souls after death.* It was also called "the pit," "the abyss," and "the lower parts."…There was a general conviction that existence continued in some way after its separation from earthly life. The wicked dwell in a deeper section than those of the righteous.…From a neutral viewpoint, *Sheol* was regarded as the dwelling place of all the dead. When ethical viewpoints are involved, however, *Sheol* is said to be a place of punishment.

Seventh-Day Adventist Bible Dictionary, 1960: "Grave"

The Hebrew *Sheol,* a poetic expression for the *grave,* is difficult to translate. In poetic sections of the Bible it frequently appears in parallel constructions with "death" and "pit," a poetic word for grave. Because of the theological implications of "Hell" (not inherent in the Hebrew word), this rendering is less desirable than grave.

Smith's Bible Dictionary: "Hell"

It would perhaps have been better to retain the Hebrew word, *Sheol,* or else render it always by "the grave" or "the pit." It is deep and dark in the center of the earth, having within it depths on depths, and fashioned with gates and bars. In this cavernous realm are *souls of dead men,* the Rephaim and ill spirits. It is clear that in many passages the O.T. *Sheol* can only mean the grave.

New Unger's Bible Dictionary: Sheol

The world of the dead.… There seems to be an allusion to the belief that there is a dark and deep abyss beneath the center of the earth, inhabited by departed spirits, but not necessarily a place of torment.… In the great majority of cases in the OT, *Sheol* is used to signify the grave.…

Vine's Expository Dictionary: Sheol

First, the word means *the state of death….* It is the final resting place of all men.… *Sheol* is parallel to Hebrew words for "pit" or "Hell," "corruption" or "decay," and "destruction."

Second, *Sheol* is used of *a place of conscious existence* after death.… It is an undesirable place for the wicked and a refuge for the righteous. Thus *Sheol* is also a place of reward for the righteous.…

3. *SHEOL*: A COMPREHENSIVE DEFINITION

Sheol is the proper place-name for "death," "the pit," and "the realm of the dead." Although it includes the place for both the conscious "soul" and the "grave" for the body, *it never stands for either of them alone.* While *Sheol* is the place-name, "death" is the general description, and "the pit" is the geographical description. All three terms *contain* souls and graves.

It is my purpose to demonstrate that the preceding definition of *Sheol*, at least as far as the Old Testament is concerned, is correct. This definition has been derived as the result of several years of pondering a definition that is consistent with every Bible usage of the word *Sheol*.

Accordingly, the Old Testament doctrine of the intermediate state as used in this thesis is as follows:

One: *Sheol*, "death" and "the pit" are all-inclusive and inter-changeable terms.

Two: *Sheol* is the proper "place-name" which includes "death" and "the pit." It most often focuses on the "soul."

Three: "Death" is the "general descriptive term" which includes *Sheol* and "the pit." It also can be a personification.

Four: "The pit" is the "geographical description" of *Sheol* and "death." The pit is a very deep multi-chambered chasm in the earth with caves, or recesses. It contains both the graves and the souls of the dead.

Five: In *Sheol*, "souls" are in a conscious, or semi-conscious, dull and dark condition. They can become aroused, become excited, see, speak and hear.

Six: Before the resurrection of Christ, the souls of the righteous were also in *Sheol* at rest and peace.

Seven: The souls of the wicked in *Sheol* receive some kind of torment and suffering.

Eight: "Souls" are located in the deeper and deepest parts of *Sheol*, death and the pit.

Nine: "Graves" are only one part of *Sheol*, death and the pit. They are usually located in the upper parts around its mouth.

Ten: "Grave" is NOT "equivalent" to *Sheol*, death and the pit. It is only a part of them.

4. *SHEOL* AND "GRAVE" ARE NOT IDENTICAL

The following word comparisons are crucial to a proper understanding of this subject. The word counts are from the King James Version of the Bible as listed in *Strong's Exhaustive Concordance of the Bible.*

One: *Sheol* (Strong's #7585) occurs in the Hebrew Old Testament 64 times. It is a singular place name. As previously stated, in the King James Version it is translated 31 times as "Hell," 30 times as "grave" and 3 times as "pit." *Sheol* is identical to the Hebrew concept of *Hades* (not the Greek), but is not the same as the Hebrew or Greek concept of *Gehenna*, or the lake of fire. Significantly, while the KJV usually translates it as "grave," it is *never* translated as "tomb" or "sepulcher." Therefore, since "sepulcher" and "tomb" are equal, because of the common connection between "grave" and "tomb," it only confuses correct doctrinal study to translate *Sheol* as "grave."

Two: *Qabar* (#6912) is the verb root of *qeber* and *qeburah*. It means "to bury" and occurs 132 times. Very significantly, the "soul" is *never* said to be buried, only the body.

Three: *Qeber* (#6913), a masculine noun, occurs 70 times: 35 times "grave," 28 times "sepulcher," 7 times "burying-place," *but never* as "Hell." It is significant to note, that, while the KJV translators often translated *Sheol* as "grave," they never translated *qeber* as "Hell."

Four: *Qeburah* (#6900), a feminine noun, occurs 15 times: 5 times "grave," 5 times "sepulcher" and 5 times "burial," *but never* as "Hell." When combined, *qabar, qeber,* and *qeburah* occur 275 times. While often being translated as "grave," they are *never* translated as "Hell/*Sheol*." The only logical conclusion is that the translators recognized that *Sheol* means much more than the present use of "grave."

Five: *Bor* (#953) occurs 75 times: 33 times "pit," 23 times "well," 14 times "dungeon," 4 times "cistern," once "fountain," but *never* as "Hell." The "pit" contains tombs and also the upper and lower chambers of *Sheol, bor **parallels Sheol*** and death and *contains* graves and souls.

Six: *Shachat* (#7845) occurs 23 times: 12 times "pit," 4 times "corruption," 3 times "grave," 2 times "ditch" and 2 times "destruction." It is a snare, or trap. The KJV never translates it as "tomb" or "sepulcher." As "pit," it includes the concept of *Sheol* (See Ps. 16:10 and Isaiah 38:17,18).

Seven: *Abaddon* (#11) occurs 6 times in the Old Testament as "destruction" and once in Revelation 9:11 as *Abaddon,* the angel of the bottomless pit. It is neither translated *Sheol* nor the grave.

Eight: *Pachat* (#6354) occurs 11 times: 9 times "pit," once "snare" and once "hole." It is neither translated *Sheol* nor the grave.

Nine: *Gadiysh* (#1430) occurs 4 times: it is a pile, heap or stack and is identical with *qeber* as "tomb" in Job 21:32. It probably refers to an above-ground sepulcher.

For the following linguistic reasons, *Sheol* should never be translated as "grave."

One: Old Testament translators concede that *Sheol* is the only word permissible for the Greek *Hades.*

Two: In contrast to *qeber* and *qeburah,* which are often plural, *Sheol* is always a singular place name.

Three: While *Sheol* is never translated as "tomb," "sepulcher," or "burying place," *qeber* and *qeburah* are the commonly accepted words for "grave."

Four: Since other very common words were in use for "grave" and "tomb," *Sheol* must have been deliberately chosen through inspiration to indicate something other than the grave.

Five: Since *Sheol* is *never* "tomb," and *qeber* and *qeburah* are *never Sheol* or *Hades*/Hell, then *Sheol* should *never* be translated as "grave."

Six: Scripture consistently states that the soul goes to *Sheol* or the pit at death, never to *qeber* or *qeburah.*

[Note: For the sake of clarity, the New American Standard Version will be used as the main text.]

5. *SHEOL* IS AN ANCIENT CONCEPT

JOB AND *SHEOL*

Job 7:9 When a cloud vanishes, it is gone, so he who goes down to *Sheol* does not come up.

Job 11:8 {They are} high as the heavens, what can you do? Deeper than *Sheol*, what can you know?

Job 14:13 Oh that Thou wouldst hide me in *Sheol*, that Thou wouldst conceal me until Thy wrath returns {to Thee,} that Thou wouldst set a limit for me and remember me!

Job 17:13 If I look for *Sheol* as my home, I make my bed in the darkness.

Job 17:16 Will it go down with me to *Sheol*? Shall we together go down into the dust?

Job 21:13 They spend their days in prosperity, and suddenly they go down to *Sheol*.

Job 24:19 Drought and heat consume the snow waters, {so does} *Sheol* {those who} have sinned.

Job 26:6 Naked is *Sheol* before Him and *Abaddon* has no covering.

Since Job does not mention any of the patriarchs or the Mosaic Law, the events described probably preceded that era. Conservative theologians consider Job to be the earliest book in the Bible, therefore, its discursion about what Old Testament man believed happened at death demonstrates that the Biblical concept of *Sheol* is very ancient indeed.

The word, *Sheol*, occurs eight times in Job, but is usually undetectable because it is not translated as *Sheol* in most versions. In the KJV, *Sheol* is translated "grave" five times, "Hell" twice and "pit" once. However, significantly, it is never translated as "sepulcher" or "tomb." *Qeber* occurs five times in Job; it is translated "grave" four times and "tomb" once. *Gadiysh* occurs twice: as a stack of grain and as a tomb. Obviously, such interchanging of words has caused much difficulty in understanding the concept of *Sheol* and death from the book of Job.

Those speaking in Job knew the difference between the place of *Sheol* in general and the grave specifically. Job said that some yearn for death and the "grave" (*qeber*) (3:21, 22); the body is carried to the "grave" (*qeber*) (10:19); when his days end, the "grave" (*qeber*) comes next (17:1). "Yet shall he be brought to the "grave" (*qeber*), and shall remain in the "tomb" (*gadiysh*) (21:32).

While the grave (*qeber*) specifically received the body, *Sheol* was known as the place-name of both bodies and souls in death. Job said "my flesh is clothed with worms" (7:5), "my life is but breath" (7:7) and man vanishes into *Sheol* at death (7:9). Zophar said that the "depths of God" and the "limits of the Almighty" are "as high as the heavens" and "deeper than *Sheol* (11:7, 8).

Job 14:10-22 should be viewed as Job's unenlightened complaint rather than as theological doctrinal truth about death. Job did not understand doctrines of progressive revelation such as Christ, His judgment, and the resurrection. Job ignorantly wished that he could be like a tree which is cut down and springs to life again when its *still-existing* roots find water (14:7-9). He did not know that this was also true of those who believe in Christ (John 4:14). Job wanted to be hidden in *Sheol* and hope for a future resurrection (14:13).

While expecting the grave (17:1), *Sheol* (17:13) and the pit (17:14), Job's unenlightened hope was to go down into *Sheol* with him (17:15, 16).

Job said that the "*rephaim*," or "departed spirits," consciously "tremble under the waters and their inhabitants" because *Sheol* is naked before God who sees all (26:5, 6).

GENESIS AND *SHEOL*

Gen. 37:35 Then all his sons and all his daughters arose to comfort him, but he refused to be comforted. And he said, "Surely I will go down to *Sheol* in mourning for my son." So his father wept for him.
Gen. 42:38 But Jacob said, "My son shall not go down with you; for his brother is dead and he alone is left. If harm should befall him on the journey you are taking, then you will bring my gray hair down to *Sheol* in sorrow."

Gen. 44:29 And if you take this one also from me, and harm befalls him, you will bring my gray hair down to *Sheol* in sorrow.

Gen. 44:31 It will come about when he sees that the lad is not {with us} that he will die. Thus your servants will bring the gray hair of your servant our father down to *Sheol* in sorrow.

It is very important to notice that, like Job, the Hebrew of Genesis makes a clear distinction between the "grave" and *Sheol*. Q*eber* and *qeburah*, the usual words for "grave," "tomb," "sepulcher" and "burying place," occur thirteen times in Genesis. For example, Abraham called Sarah's burial cave a *qeber* (23:4, 6, 9, 20); Jacob called Rachel's grave a *qeburah* (35:20); Jacob's grave was a *qeburah* (47:30) and a *qeber* (49:30); Joseph called his grave a *qeber* (50:5, 13, 14).

Significantly, though, like Job, the word, *Sheol*, not *qeber*, or *qeburah*, was chosen by Jacob when he complained about not seeing Joseph or Benjamin again. Certainly Jacob carefully chose his words because he knew the difference! Jacob did not believe that his sorrow would end in the grave, but that it would continue into *Sheol*, the conscious realm of the departed souls after death. Jacob expected to go "down to *Sheol* in sorrow."

OTHER *SHEOL* STATEMENTS REFLECT ANCIENT BELIEFS

1 Sam. 2:6 [Hannah's prayer] The LORD kills and makes alive; He brings down to *Sheol* and raises up.

2 Sam. 22:6 [David] The cords of *Sheol* surrounded me; the snares of death confronted me.

I Kings 2:6,9 [David to Solomon concerning Joab] "So act according to your wisdom, and do not let his gray hair go down to *Sheol* in peace…. "Now therefore, do not let him go unpunished, for you are a wise man; and you will know what you ought to do to him, and you will bring his gray hair down to *Sheol* with blood."

Although *Sheol* can also mean "death," "death" should only be an acceptable translation when it is inclusive of both *Sheol* for the soul and the grave for the body. *Sheol* is the "whole" and its "parts" are places for both souls and graves for bodies. "Grave," a part of *Sheol*, should not be used for the whole. Hannah's statement in First Samuel 2:6 that "the LORD brings down to *Sheol*" can, therefore, include "death," but it also goes beyond our idea of "grave."

From Joshua to Second Chronicles, God's Word focuses on the history of Israel. These books only contain *Sheol* four times (1 Sam. 2:6; 2 Sam. 22:6 and 1 Kg. 2:6, 9). On the other hand, *qeber/qeburah* for "grave, tomb, sepulcher" occur thirty times. Over and over again Scripture describes the judges, important leaders and kings as being placed in their graves, or sepulchers (*qeber*), at death. However, Scripture does not state that any person died and the "body" was placed by man into *Sheol* at death!!! Again this demonstrates that "grave" and *Sheol* are not interchangeable terms!

6. *SHEOL* DESCENDS MUCH DEEPER THAN THE GRAVE

Job 11:7-9 Can you discover the *depths* of God? Can you discover the limits of the Almighty? {They are} high as the heavens, what can you do? Deeper than *Sheol*, what can you know? Its measure is longer than the earth, and broader than the sea.

Numb. 16:30 But if the LORD brings about an entirely new thing and the ground opens its mouth and swallows them up with all that is theirs, and they descend alive into *Sheol*, then you will understand that these men have spurned the LORD.

Deut. 32:22 For a fire is kindled in My anger, and burns to the lowest part of *Sheol*, and consumes the earth with its yield, and sets on fire the foundations of the mountains.

Ps. 86:13 For Thy loving-kindness toward me is great, and Thou hast delivered my soul from the depths of *Sheol* .

Ps. 139:8 If I ascend to heaven, Thou art there; if I make my bed in *Sheol*, behold, Thou art there.

Prov. 9:18 But he does not know that the dead are there, {that} her guests are in the depths of *Sheol*.

Isa. 7:11 Ask a sign for yourself from the LORD your God; make {it} deep as *Sheol* or high as heaven.

Isa. 14:14,15 'I will ascend above the heights of the clouds; I will make myself like the Most High.' Nevertheless you will be thrust down to *Sheol*, to the recesses of the pit.

Ezek. 31:16 I made the nations quake at the sound of its fall when I made it go down to *Sheol* with those who go down to the pit; and all the well-watered trees of Eden, the choicest and best of Lebanon, were comforted in the earth beneath [nether world].

Jonah 2:2 And he said, "I called out of my distress to the LORD, and He answered me. I cried for help from the depth of *Sheol*; Thou didst hear my voice.

Jonah 2:6 I descended to the roots of the mountains. The earth with its bars {was} around me forever, but Thou hast brought up my life from the pit, O LORD my God.

Amos 9:2 Though they dig into *Sheol*, from there shall My hand take them; and though they ascend to heaven, from there will I bring them down.

Where is the place called *Sheol* located? It is very obvious from these texts that at least part of *Sheol* is much deeper than the grave! Several texts are comparisons of extremes. When asked to name the lowest places one could imagine, none of us would stop at the grave; instead, we would name the lowest, or deepest, places on earth. Inspired Bible writers believed that *Sheol* was located far below the earth's surface.

Even the King James translators translated *Sheol* in the above texts as "Hell" instead of their usual "grave." However, the New International Version only admits to "depths" in Psalm 139:8. The word "grave" simply does not fit the description given in these texts. Translating *Sheol* as "grave" confuses sincere Bible students and questions the logic of those claiming to disperse God's Word in an understandable format to the entire world.

Common sense also argues against *Sheol* meaning a "place" where the soul is "non-existent."

7. *SHEOL* AND DEATH ARE COMPANIONS

Job 17:13 If I look for *Sheol* as my home, I make my bed in the darkness;
Job 17:14 If I call to the pit [*shachat*], 'You are my father'; to the worm, 'my mother and my sister';
Job 17:15 Where now is my hope? And who regards my hope?
Job 17:16 "Will it go down with me to *Sheol*? Shall we together go down into the dust?
Job 24:19,20 Drought and heat consume the snow waters, {so does} *Sheol* {those who} have sinned. A mother will forget him; the worm feeds sweetly till he is remembered no more. And wickedness will be broken like a tree.
Prov. 5:5 Her feet go down to death, her steps lay hold of *Sheol*.
Prov. 7:27 Her house is the way to *Sheol*, descending to the chambers [*chader*: 2315] of death.
Ps. 55:15 Let death come deceitfully upon them; let them go down alive to *Sheol*, for evil is in their dwelling, in their midst.
Isa. 28:15,18 Because you have said, "We have made a covenant with death, and with *Sheol* we have made a pact. The overwhelming scourge will not reach us when it passes by, for we have made falsehood our refuge and we have concealed ourselves with deception.... And your covenant with death shall be canceled, and your pact with *Sheol* shall not stand; when the overwhelming scourge passes through, then you become its trampling {place.}
Hab. 2:5 Furthermore, wine betrays the haughty man, so that he does not stay at home. He enlarges his appetite like *Sheol*, and he is like death, never satisfied. He also gathers to himself all nations and collects to himself all peoples.

Job 17:13-16; 21:13,32 and 24:10,20 can give an incorrect conclusion if not compared to Job 11:7,8 and other texts which make *Sheol* much more than and much deeper than the grave.

Sheol, "death," and "pit" are not limited to only "grave" in the Bible and equating them merely confuses theology. Although "death" often focuses on the grave, death and *Sheol* are described as traveling companions, or very close friends. Since *Sheol*, death" and "the pit" all include "grave," all three have more than one inner "chamber" and all three include both the destiny of the body and the destiny of the soul.

Old Testament man, like modern man, used the term "death" to refer to the destiny of the body, the soul, either, or both! Compare the following with the Bible equivalents. How often do we hear phrases such as: "God is going to bring that man down to the grave" (1 Sam. 2:6). "I feel like Hell; I think I'm going to die" (2 Sam. 22:6). "I'll be with the Lord soon, and you'll be putting flowers on my grave" (Job 17:13-16). "Hitler is probably in Hell; he's not coming back from the grave" (Job 21:13, 32). "They are probably rotting in Hell" (Job 24:19, 20). "He is so evil; I wish he would die and go to Hell" (Ps. 55:15). "Prostitution will lead you straight to Hell" (Prov. 5:5; 7:27). "Greedy as Hell" (Hab. 2:5). "My grandparents are buried there!"

The point is that our everyday language does not always distinguish between what we believe happens to someone's body and their soul! That does not mean that we do not understand the difference! When we compare Scripture with Scripture, the truth that is clear and undeniable must override that which is unclear. The "house" of "death" is named *Sheol*; that house has rooms which contain souls and bodies; the house looks like a deep pit.

Rev. 6:8 And I looked, and behold, an ashen horse; and he who sat on it had the name Death; and *Hades* was following with him. And authority was given to them over a fourth of the earth, to kill with sword and with famine and with pestilence and by the wild beasts of the earth.
Rev. 20:13, 14 And the sea gave up the dead which were in it, and death and *Hades* gave up the dead which were in them; and they were judged, every one {of them} according to their deeds. And death and *Hades* were thrown into the lake of fire. This is the second death, the lake of fire.

The New Testament sheds further light on the relationship between death and *Sheol*, or *Hades*, especially Revelation 6:8 and 20:13, 14. In these texts "death" AND *Hades* are distinct companions. In Revelation 6:8 death claims the bodies, while *Hades* claims the souls. In Revelation 20:13, 14, in accordance with Old Testament *Sheol*, the depths of the "sea" contain both bodies and souls. However, since most do not perish at sea, the general description will be that "death" will give up the bodies, while *Hades* will give up the "souls"! Although this differs somewhat from Old Testament usage, the dual residence for departed bodies and souls is still clear. Annihilation is not seen.

In summary, although the full revelation of the meaning of death, *Sheol*, and judgment awaited "the truth" in Jesus Christ, Old Testament writers often, though not always, carefully distinguished between the body and soul by the words they chose. The dualism was clear—while the body went to the grave in *Sheol* at death, the souls went to another chamber of *Sheol*. One could speak of both events as one in reference to time. Both were in the pit, but *Sheol* extended much deeper than the tomb and was a place of conscious awareness.

When death and *Sheol/Hades* are cast into the lake of fire (*Gehenna*), the second death, or final separation from God occurs. No longer will any enter THE death, or separation from God (Rev. 21:4). However, those conscious souls from *Sheol* will either continue in God's care, or in *Gehenna* (Rev. 14:11; 21:1-4, 10, 11).

8. *SHEOL* AND UNCONSCIOUSNESS

Job 7:9-11 When a cloud vanishes, it is gone, so he who goes down to *Sheol* does not come up. He will not return again to his house, nor will his place know him anymore. *Therefore*, I will not restrain my mouth; I will speak in the anguish of my spirit, I will complain in the bitterness of my soul.
Job 14:12, 13 So man lies down and does not rise. Until the heavens be no more, He will not awake nor be aroused out of his *sleep.* "Oh that Thou wouldst hide me in *Sheol,* that Thou wouldst conceal me until Thy wrath returns {to Thee,} that Thou wouldst set a limit for me and remember me!
Ps. 6:5 For there is no mention of Thee in death; in *Sheol* who will give Thee thanks?
Ps. 31:17 Let me not be put to shame, O LORD, for I call upon Thee; let the wicked be put to shame, let them be silent in *Sheol.*
Eccl. 9:10, 11 Whatever your hand finds to do, verily, do {it} with all your might; for there is no activity or planning or knowledge or wisdom in *Sheol* where you are going. I again saw under the sun...

Of the 64 *Sheol* texts, the preceding 5 "proof-texts" seem to teach that *Sheol* is empty of conscious thought or expression. They are favorites with those who teach that the soul ceases to exist at death. They are also favorites with some who believe that the soul only goes to unconscious sleep awaiting the resurrection. However, reaching such conclusions ignores the clearer teaching of many other *Sheol* texts and all of them as a unified doctrine.

Context clears up much of the confusion concerning these previous texts. Their *purpose* is to teach that there is no return to the "land of the living" after death *to communicate* with loved ones or others who are still alive. On the one hand, from the *perspective* of those still alive, they cannot hope to have their departed loved ones return, or be conjured up, in a seance, to impart truth to them. However, on the other hand, *from the perspective of those about to die,* they should quickly say what they can while they still have the time and opportunity!

Job 7:9, 10 is explained in 7:11. *"Therefore I will not refrain my mouth, I will speak."* He would speak while he was still alive and had the chance to say something to others who are still alive.

Job 14:12, 13 is partially explained in 14:14, 15. While suffering excruciating pain, Job wished that God would "hide" him in *Sheol* until His wrath had passed, until the end of the world if necessary. He does not state that he would be non-existent or unconscious in *Sheol*, but only that he would not return to the living until God allowed it. Man will physically "live again" on earth, body and soul, when his body is resurrected and his "change comes" (verse 14). Also note the comments in section 5.

In Psalm 6:5 David was physically and emotionally beaten, tired, depressed, and in despair. He called on God in 6:4 to "Return, O LORD, deliver my soul: oh save me for thy mercies' sake." After David had been delivered, he "remembered" God and praised Him before all Israel! However, those in *Sheol* could not return (*through a seance or otherwise) and remind others of the goodness and greatness of God. *Note: There were notable exceptions such as resurrection.

Psalm 31:17, again, from the perspective of the living, the wicked are silenced in *Sheol*. [Note: The discussion of consciousness and suffering in *Sheol* will follow.]

Ecclesiastes 9:10 deserves special attention. In practical language, it says that one should do what one can do while one is alive. Once dead, we cannot do anything to help those still alive. The dead cannot return to perform work or to impart knowledge or wisdom. Neither are they going to be able to finish such work or impart such knowledge in *Sheol*. Jesus Himself made a similar statement in Luke 16:27-31. Though the rich man was certainly conscious and knowledgeable in *Hades*, he was unable to pass that knowledge back to his relatives who were still alive.

Most of Ecclesiastes, like 9:10, is surrounded by texts like 9:9 and 9:11 which refer to "under the sun." With few exceptions, Solomon was describing how *unenlightened vain men* see life without God's guidance. The conclusion of Ecclesiastes is found in 12:13, 14 "Fear God and keep His commandments. For God will bring every act to judgment" (12:14). Without future punishment of the wicked and rewards for the righteous, life makes no sense, and God is not fair. Divine justice will be delivered in the next life, whether it be in *Sheol, Hades,* Paradise, or *Gehenna,* the lake of fire!

Isa. 38:10 I said, "In the middle of my life I am to enter the gates of *Sheol*; I am to be deprived of the rest of my years."
Isa. 38:11 I said, "I shall not see the LORD, the LORD in the land of the living; I shall look on man no more among the inhabitants of the world."
....
Isa. 38:15 What shall I say? For He has spoken to me, and He himself has done it; I shall wander about all my years because of the bitterness of my soul.
Isa. 38:16 O Lord, by {these} things {men} live; and in all these is the life of my spirit; O restore me to health, and let me live!

Isa. 38:17 Lo, for {my own} welfare I had great bitterness; it is Thou who hast kept my soul from the pit of nothingness [corruption], for Thou hast cast all my sins behind Thy back.

Isa. 38:18 For *Sheol* cannot thank Thee, *death* cannot praise Thee; those who go down to the *pit* cannot hope for Thy faithfulness. [Note: this text contains all three equals.]

Isa. 38:19 "It is the living who give thanks to Thee, as I do today; a father tells his sons about Thy faithfulness.

Isaiah 38:9-20 reveals how Old Testament man thought. King Hezekiah of Judah is the speaker on his death-bed (38:9). He said "I shall go to the gates of *Sheol*" at death (38:10). Since he will be in *Sheol*, he will not "see the LORD or man any more in the land of the living" (38:11). Hezekiah asked God for healing (38:16). Afterwards, having been forgiven and healed, he said that God "has in love to my soul [*nephesh*] delivered it from the pit [*bor*: 1097] of corruption [7845: *shachat*]" (38:17).

King Hezekiah continued, "For *Sheol* cannot thank Thee, death cannot praise Thee; those who go down to the pit cannot hope for Thy faithfulness." The key text follows immediately, "It is the living who give thanks to Thee, as I do today; a father tells his sons about Thy faithfulness." The dead in *Sheol* cannot praise God *to the living* on earth, because they cannot return to the land of the living from *Sheol* before the resurrection of the body! Hezekiah could not praise God to his children from *Sheol*, neither could he teach them God's truth.

It is not the purpose of these texts to teach that souls in *Sheol* are either non-existent or unconscious to God or unconscious to each other. *They teach that they are unconscious in relation to those still living on earth. They cannot praise God in front of their children to teach the truth of God.*

9. *SHEOL*: A PLACE FOR SOULS AND BODIES

Ps. 16:10 For Thou wilt not abandon my soul to *Sheol* ; neither wilt Thou allow Thy Holy One to undergo decay [*shachat*].

Ps. 30:3 O LORD, Thou hast brought up my soul from *Sheol*; ' Thou hast kept me alive, that I should not go down to the pit [*bor*].

Ps. 49:14, 15 As sheep they are appointed for *Sheol*; death shall be their shepherd; and the upright shall rule over them in the morning; and their form [strength, rock] shall be for *Sheol* to consume, so that they have no habitation. But God will redeem my soul from the power of *Sheol*; for He will receive me.

Ps. 86:13 For Thy loving-kindness toward me is great, and Thou hast delivered my soul from the depths of *Sheol*.

Ps. 88:3 For my soul has had enough troubles, and my life has drawn near to *Sheol*.

Ps. 89:48 What man can live and not see death? Can he deliver his soul from the power of *Sheol*?

Prov. 23:14 You shall beat him with the rod, and deliver his soul from *Sheol*.

These texts contain a very important fact about the relationship between the "soul" and *Sheol* at death. They also provide a remarkable demonstration of Bible inspiration. Consider the questions, "Does the Bible teach that "souls" go to *Sheol* at death?" "Does the Bible teach that souls go to the grave, that is, '*qeber/qeburah*,' at death?" "Does the Bible teach that souls cease to exist at death awaiting the resurrection?"

Comparative research was made trying to link "soul" (Strong's 5315) with *qeber* and *qeburah* (6913 and 6900), the usual Hebrew words translated as "grave." Although *nephesh* (soul) has many other meanings, one will discover an amazing conclusion. In the Hebrew of the above texts, the "soul" *always* goes to *Sheol* or the "pit" at death!!! The list includes every text that combines "soul" and *Sheol*. The "soul" is never said to enter *qeber* or *qeburah* at death!!! Again, the words, *bor* and *shachat* for "pit" refer to both *Sheol* for souls and the grave for bodies. However, *Sheol* is never translated as "tomb" or "sepulcher."

Once again, it is very unfortunate that Bible translators have often translated all three words (*Sheol, qeber,* and *qeburah*) as "grave." They correctly *refuse* to translate *Sheol* as "tomb," or "*qeber/qeburah*" as "*Sheol*/Hell." Since *Sheol* does not mean "tomb," and "*qeber/qeburah*" do not mean *Sheol/Hades*, then why should these words all mean "grave"? Simple logic states that, if 'A' does not equal 'B,' and 'B' does not equal 'C,' then 'A' cannot equal 'C'.

Inspired writers were convinced that, at death, the soul faced *Sheol*, not extinction. Not once did they link the soul going into the grave at death, or becoming non-existent.

10. *SHEOL* FOR THE RIGHTEOUS

Job 14:13 Oh that Thou wouldst hide me in *Sheol*, that Thou wouldst conceal me until Thy wrath returns {to Thee,} that Thou wouldst set a limit for me and remember me!

Ps. 16:10 For Thou wilt not abandon my soul to *Sheol*; neither wilt Thou allow Thy Holy One to undergo decay.

Ps. 49:14, 15 As sheep they are appointed for *Sheol*; death shall be their shepherd; and the upright shall rule over them in the morning; and their form shall be for *Sheol* to consume, so that they have no habitation. But God will redeem my soul from the power of *Sheol*; for He will receive me.

Prov. 15:24 The path of life {leads} upward for the wise, that he may keep away from *Sheol* below.

Isa. 57:2 He [the righteous] enters into peace; they rest in their beds, {each one} who walked in his upright way.

The Old Testament concept of death was that both righteous and wicked souls went into the various chambers of *Sheol* at death (1 Sam. 2:6; Job 21:13; Ps. 6:5; 18:5). Concerning the righteous in *Sheol*, the preceding texts describe it as a place where "peace" is acquired and where Job wanted God to "hide" his soul from His wrath until the resurrection. Also, there is indication of at least some mourning and sorrow over the loss of loved ones in *Sheol* (Gen. 37:35; 42:38; 44:29; 44:31).

What does Proverb 15:24 mean? Does it mean that the righteous will not die, or that they would live longer because they are righteous? Or is it a hint that Old Testament man hoped for something even better than *Sheol*, perhaps above with God?

Although Psalm 16:10 has reference to Christ in the New Testament, could it also have given hope to Old Testament man that God would somehow eventually "redeem" man even from *Sheol* and not abandon him there (Ps. 49:15)? Unfortunately, this aspect of *Sheol* is vague, though partially clarified by Jesus and through the gospel in the New Testament's further revelation.

11. *SHEOL* FOR THE WICKED

One: Job and Moses believed that *Sheol* was a place for punishment after the death of the body.

Job 21:13 They [the wicked] spend their days in prosperity, and suddenly they go down to *Sheol*.

Job 24:19 Drought and heat consume the snow waters, {so does} *Sheol* {those who} have sinned.

Job 26:5, 6 The departed spirits tremble under the waters and their inhabitants. Naked is *Sheol* before Him And *Abaddon* has no covering.

Numb. 16:29 If these men die the death of all men, or if they suffer the fate of all men, {then} the LORD has not sent me.

Numb. 16:30 But if the LORD brings about an entirely new thing and the ground opens its mouth and swallows them up with all that is theirs, and they descend alive into *Sheol*, then you will understand that these men have spurned the LORD.

Numb. 16:31 Then it came about as he finished speaking all these words, that the ground that was under them split open;

Numb. 16:32 and the earth opened its mouth and swallowed them up, and their households, and all the men who belonged to Korah, with {their} possessions.

Numb. 16:33 So they and all that belonged to them went down alive to *Sheol*; and the earth closed over them, and they perished from the midst of the assembly.

Deut. 32:22 For a fire is kindled in My anger, and burns to the lowest part of *Sheol*, and consumes the earth with its yield, and sets on fire the foundations of the mountains.

Numbers 16:29-33 says something interesting about the location of lowest *Sheol*. When Korah challenged Moses' authority, Moses said in verses 29, 30 "If these men die the death of all men, or if they suffer the fate of all men, {then} the LORD has not sent me. But if the LORD brings about an entirely new thing and the ground opens its mouth and swallows them up with all that is theirs, and they descend alive into *Sheol*, then you will understand that these men have spurned the LORD."

Death was not an "entirely new thing"; neither were men dying in earthquakes. The "entirely new thing" was going "alive" directly into the depths of *Sheol*, both body and soul! And so it happened. Verse 33 states that they "went down alive to *Sheol*."

These Bible verses are meaningless if *Sheol* only means "grave"! While most graves were shallow and could be touched, because of the earthquake, the "graves" for the body were extraordinarily deep inside the earth in *Sheol* with their souls. This was the "entirely new thing." It is very difficult to understand how the NIV can translate *Sheol* as "grave" here.

In Deuteronomy 32:22 a "fire is kindled in God's anger" towards disobedient Israel that will punish them unto the "lowest *Sheol*" and "set on fire the foundations of the mountains." Just as Jacob's sorrow for Joseph would not stop at the grave, neither does God's anger stop at the grave. Deuteronomy distinguishes between *Sheol* and *qeber*, because, in 34:6 it states that Moses was buried in his grave (*qeber*). Deuteronomy 32:22 is also the only verse in which the NIV translators ventured beyond "grave," "death" and "depth" to translate *Sheol* as "the realm of death below."

Two: David, Solomon and the other writers of Psalms believed that souls were punished in *Sheol* after death.

2 Sam. 22:6 The cords [sorrows] of *Sheol* surrounded me; the snares of death confronted me.
Ps. 9:17 The wicked will return to *Sheol*, {even} all the nations who forget God.
Ps. 86:13 For Thy loving-kindness toward me is great, and Thou hast delivered my soul from the depths of *Sheol*.
Ps. 88:3 For my soul has had enough troubles, and my life has drawn near to *Sheol*.
Ps. 88:4 I am reckoned among those who go down to the pit [*bor*]; I have become like a man without strength,
Ps. 88:5 Forsaken among the dead, like the slain who lie in the grave [*qeber*], whom Thou dost remember no more, and they are cut off from Thy hand.
Ps. 88:6 Thou hast put me in the lowest pit, in dark places, in the depths.

Ps. 116:3 The cords [sorrows] of death encompassed me, and the terrors of *Sheol* came upon me; I found distress and sorrow.

Prov. 23:14 You shall beat him with the rod, and deliver his soul from *Sheol*.

Song of Solomon 8:6 Put me like a seal over your heart, like a seal on your arm. For love is as strong as death, jealousy is as severe as *Sheol*; its flashes are flashes of fire, the {very} flame of the LORD.

When out of God's will, David identified with the wicked, and compared his pain with that of *Sheol*. David said his "sorrows" were those of *Sheol* (2 Sam. 22:6) and his soul was delivered from the "lowest *Sheol*" (Ps. 86:13). Psalm 116:3 may be the strongest verse in the Bible describing the suffering in *Sheol* with "terrors," "distress," and "sorrow."

Texts such as Psalm 9:17 and Proverb 23:14 should be translated as *Sheol* rather than the NIV's "grave." Since all go to the same grave, the statement that "the wicked shall be turned into *Sheol*" does not make sense unless some kind of justice is indicated (Psalm 9:17). Likewise, Proverb 23:14, says that the child "will not die," but his "soul" will be delivered "from *Sheol*" makes no sense if only the grave were meant.

Three: Isaiah believed that suffering would continue in *Sheol* after death.

Isa. 14:9 *Sheol* from beneath is excited over you to meet you when you come; it arouses for you the spirits of the dead [*rephaim*], all the leaders of the earth; it raises all the kings of the nations from their thrones.

Isa. 14:10 They will all respond and say to you, "Even you have been made weak as we, you have become like us.

Isa. 14:11 Your pomp {and} the music of your harps have been brought down to *Sheol*; maggots are spread out {as your bed} beneath you, and worms are your covering.

Isa. 14:12 How you have fallen from heaven, O star of the morning, son of the dawn! You have been cut down to the earth, you who have weakened the nations!

Isa. 14:13 But you said in your heart, "I will ascend to heaven; I will raise my throne above the stars of God, and I will sit on the mount of assembly in the recesses of the north.

Isa. 14:14 I will ascend above the heights of the clouds; I will make myself like the Most High."

Isa. 14:15 Nevertheless you will be thrust down to *Sheol*, to the recesses of the pit.

Isa. 14:16 Those who see you will gaze at you, they will ponder over you, {saying,} "Is this the man who made the earth tremble, who shook kingdoms,

Isa. 14:17 Who made the world like a wilderness and overthrew its cities, who did not allow his prisoners to {go} home?"

Isa. 14:18 All the kings of the nations lie in glory, each in his own tomb [house: *bayit*].
Isa. 14:19 But you have been cast out of your tomb [grave: *qeber*] like a rejected branch, clothed with the slain who are pierced with a sword, who go down to the stones of the pit, like a trampled corpse.
Isa. 14:20 You will not be united with them in burial, because you have ruined your country, you have slain your people. May the offspring of evildoers not be mentioned forever.

While discussing the future of the king of Babylon, Isaiah 14 is a very vivid description of conscious existence after death in the lower world of *Sheol*. Verses 10, 11, 16 and 17 are actually spoken by the souls in *Sheol*. It seriously challenges the assertion of those who deny the continued conscious survival of the soul after death prior to the resurrection of the body.

In 14:9 the "**spirits of the dead**" are "**excited,**" "**aroused,**" and "**raised**" to **meet** the dead king of Babylon. In 14:10 they "**all respond**" and speak. In 14:11 they remind the king that his body will be eaten by worms in the grave-part of *Sheol*. While some part of the king is conscious in *Sheol*, his body will be eaten by worms in another part.

In 14:15 God promised the King of Babylon that he would be brought down to *Sheol* which is located in the "recesses of the pit"—here contrasted with *qeber*, the grave. The word for "recesses" in the NAS is *yerekah*. *Yerekah* is translated as "sides" in the KJV, "depths" in the NIV and RSV, "lowest depths" in the NKJV and "uttermost parts" in the ASV. *Brown-Driver-Briggs' Old Testament Lexicon* also includes "extreme parts." It is very unlikely that these descriptions only refer to the first six feet of the grave.

Those that "see" and "speak" in verses 10-18 are the departed spirits, the "rephaim" already in *Sheol*. Next, verse 19 declares that his body will be cast out of the grave [*qeber*]. These texts make no sense if the soul has ceased to exist. They clearly indicate conscious activity in *Sheol*. They also carefully point out that the king's body will be cast out of *qeber*, not *Sheol*. Two different places in the pit are being described here, not one.

Four: Ezekiel believed that the dead would continue to be conscious in *Sheol*.

Ezek. 31:16, 17 I made the nations quake at the sound of its fall when I made it go down to *Sheol* with those who go down to the pit; and all the well-watered trees of Eden, the choicest and best of Lebanon, were comforted in the earth beneath. They also went down with it to *Sheol* to those who were slain by the sword; and those who were its strength lived under its shade among the nations.

Ezek. 32:21 The strong among the mighty ones shall speak of him {and} his helpers from the midst of *Sheol*, "They have gone down, they lie still, the uncircumcised, slain by the sword."
Ezek. 32:27 Nor do they lie beside the fallen heroes of the uncircumcised, who went down to *Sheol* with their weapons of war, and whose swords were laid under their heads; but the punishment for their iniquity rested on their bones, though the terror of {these} heroes {was} once in the land of the living.
Ezek. 32:31 These Pharaoh will see, and he will be comforted for all his multitude slain by the sword, {even} Pharaoh and all his army, declares the Lord GOD.

In Ezekiel 31:16 God promised to cast Pharaoh "down to *Sheol*" with those who "descend" "into the pit," or into the "nether parts of the earth." The other heathen nations also went "down into *Sheol*" (31:17). The wicked speak to Pharaoh out of *Sheol*, not out of *qeber*, the grave (32:21). The wicked nations are "there," meaning *Sheol* (32:22, 24, 26, 29). They are all in the "nether parts of the earth" (32:24). The numerous texts describing the location of the wicked in *Sheol* consistently indicate someplace other than a shallow tomb. God Himself declares that Pharaoh will "see" the other slain nations in *Sheol* (32:31).

Five: Jonah believed that the wicked would continue to suffer in *Sheol* after death.

Jonah 2:1 Then Jonah prayed to the LORD his God from the stomach of the fish,
Jonah 2:2 and he said, "I called out of my distress to the LORD, and He answered me. I cried for help from the depth of *Sheol*; Thou didst hear my voice.
Jonah 2:3 "For Thou hadst cast me into the deep, into the heart of the seas, and the current engulfed me. All Thy breakers and billows passed over me.
Jonah 2:4 "So I said, 'I have been expelled from Thy sight. Nevertheless I will look again toward Thy holy temple.'
Jonah 2:5 "Water encompassed me to the point of death. The great deep engulfed me, weeds were wrapped around my head.
Jonah 2:6 "I descended to the roots of the mountains. The earth with its bars {was} around me forever, but Thou hast brought up my life from the pit, O LORD my God.

While out of God's will, Jonah, like David, identified with the wicked, and compared his pain with that of *Sheol*. Jonah described himself as being in the "belly of *Sheol*" (Jonah 2:2), in the "deep" (2:3), "out of Thy sight" (2:4), and "at the roots [bottoms] of the mountains" (2:6).

Jonah and David both used *Sheol* and "pit" to describe the location of the conscious soul after the death of the body. Their word selection reflected their belief that *Sheol* extends much deeper than an ordinary grave, like a prison pit with bars and cords in the very deepest part of the earth and sea.

In conclusion, one cannot ignore the fact that Job, Moses, David, Solomon, Isaiah, Ezekiel, and Jonah all used the word, *Sheol,* to describe a place of suffering after death. Admittedly, many of the texts are surrounded by poetic imagery which places tangible descriptions on the hopes and fears of Old Testament man. However, while taking this imagery into consideration, the vocabulary reflects what Old Testament man "believed" happened after death.

For the wicked, *Sheol* was a dark place of consciousness deep inside the earth or in the deepest parts of the sea. God punished sinners there (Numb. 16:29-33; Deut. 32:22; Job 24:19). It was a place of sorrow, distress, terror, trembling and jealousy (2 Sam. 22:6; Job 26:5; Ps. 88:3-6; 116:3; Song of Solomon 8:6; Jonah 2:6). And it was a place where the wicked were expelled from God's presence (Jonah 2:4).

Although souls in *Sheol* appear to be in a state of weakness and stillness (Isa. 14:10; Eze. 32:21), they are neither non-existent nor unconscious. The souls are fully capable of becoming aroused and becoming excited (Isa. 14:9). Once fully aroused, the wicked in *Sheol* could see, hear, and speak (Isa. 14:10; Eze. 32:21, 31).

12. *SHEOL* AND THE PIT

Ps. 30:3 O LORD, Thou hast brought up my soul from *Sheol*; Thou hast kept me alive, that I should not go down to the pit [*bor*].

Ps. 88:3 For my soul has had enough troubles, and my life has drawn near to *Sheol* .

Ps. 88:4 I am reckoned among those who go down to the pit [*bor*]; I have become like a man without strength,

Ps. 88:5 Forsaken among the dead, like the slain who lie in the grave [*qeber*], whom Thou dost remember no more, and they are cut off from Thy hand.

Ps 88:6 Thou hast put me in the lowest pit [*bor*], in dark places, in the depths.

Ps. 141:7 As when one plows and breaks open the earth, our bones have been scattered at the mouth of *Sheol*.

Prov. 1:12 [Sinners say] Let us swallow them [our victims] alive like *Sheol*, even whole, as those who go down to the pit [*bor*].

Prov. 7:27 Her house is the way to *Sheol*, descending to the chambers of death.

Isa. 5:14 Therefore *Sheol* has enlarged its throat and opened its mouth without measure; and Jerusalem's splendor, her multitude, her din {of revelry,} and the jubilant within her, descend {into it.}

Isa. 26:19 Your dead will live; their corpses [*nebelah*] will rise. You who lie in the dust, awake and shout for joy, for your dew is as the dew of the dawn, and the earth will give birth to the departed spirits.

Ezek. 31:16, 17 I made the nations quake at the sound of its fall when I made it go down to *Sheol* with those who go down to the pit [*bor*]; and all the well-watered trees of Eden, the choicest and best of Lebanon, were comforted in the earth beneath [nether parts]. They also went down with it to *Sheol* to those who were slain by the sword; and those who were its strength lived under its shade among the nations.

Ezek. 32:21 The strong among the mighty ones shall speak of him {and} his helpers from the midst of *Sheol*, "They have gone down, they lie still, the uncircumcised, slain by the sword."

Ezek. 32:22 Assyria is there [in *Sheol*] and all her company; her graves [*qeburah*] are round about her. All of them are slain, fallen by the sword,

Ezek. 32:23 whose graves [*qeburah*] are set in the remotest parts of the pit [*bor*], and her company is round about her grave [*qeburah*]. All of them are slain, fallen by the sword, who spread terror in the land of the living.

Ezek. 32:24 Elam is there [in *Sheol*] and all her multitude around her grave [*qeburah*]; all of them slain, fallen by the sword, who went down uncircumcised to the lower parts [nether parts] of the earth, who instilled their terror in the land of the living, and bore their disgrace with those who went down to the pit [*bor*].

Ezek. 32:25 They have made a bed for her among the slain with all her multitude. Her graves [*qeburah*] are around it, they are all uncircumcised, slain by the sword (although their terror was instilled in the land of the living), and they bore their disgrace with those who go down to the pit [*bor*]; they were put in the midst of the slain.

Ezek. 32:26 Meshech, Tubal and all their multitude are there [in *Sheol*]; their graves [*qeburah*] surround them. All of them were slain by the sword uncircumcised, though they instilled their terror in the land of the living.

Ezek. 32:27 Nor do they lie beside the fallen heroes of the uncircumcised, who went down to *Sheol* with their weapons of war, and whose swords were laid under their heads; but the punishment for their iniquity rested on their bones, though the terror of {these} heroes {was} once in the land of the living.

Ezek. 32:28 But in the midst of the uncircumcised you will be broken and lie with those slain by the sword.

Ezek. 32:29 There also is Edom [in *Sheol*], its kings, and all its princes, who for {all} their might are laid with those slain by the sword; they will lie with the uncircumcised, and with those who go down to the pit [*bor*].

Ezek. 32:30 There also are the chiefs of the north, all of them, and all the Sidonians, who in spite of the terror resulting from their might, in shame went down with the slain. So they lay down uncircumcised with those slain by the sword, and bore their disgrace with those who go down to the pit [*bor*].

Ezek. 32:31 These Pharaoh will see, and he will be comforted for all his multitude slain by the sword, {even} Pharaoh and all his army, declares the Lord GOD.

Without a proper definition of *Sheol* these passages in Ezekiel become extremely confusing. *Sheol*, the pit, and the grave are all mentioned. Again, *Sheol* is the specific "name" of the place where souls and corpses go at death. "Death" is the "general description" of the souls and corpses in *Sheol*. "The pit" is the "geographical description" of the place of death named *Sheol*. To use another metaphor, in Sheol "death" and "the pit" are the "house" while "souls" and "corpses" are the residents of its "chambers."

The pit is best described as containing the graves of bones and corpses scattered around its mouth and sides. The souls of the wicked occupy the pit's lowest regions at the bottoms of the mountains either in the heart of the earth or the bottom of the sea. While "souls" are located in one part of *Sheol*, death and the pit—"graves" occupy another part of *Sheol*, death and the pit. *Sheol* and the pit "swallow whole" its inhabitants, both body and soul (Prov. 1:12).

It is important to note that, while *Sheol* and *bor* are always singular, *qeber,* and the feminine form *qeburah,* are often plural.

13. *SHEOL* AND THE *REPHAIM* (SPIRITS OF THE DEAD)

Job 26:5, 6 The *departed spirits* [RSV: shades] tremble under the waters and their inhabitants. Naked is *Sheol* before Him and *Abaddon* has no covering.
Ps. 88:3, 10 For my soul has had enough troubles, and my life has drawn near to *Sheol*.... Wilt Thou perform wonders for the dead? Will the *departed spirits* rise {and} praise Thee?
Prov. 2:18 For her house sinks down to death, and her tracks {lead} to the *dead* [*rephaim*].
Prov. 9:18 But he does not know that the *dead* [*rephaim*] are there, {that} her guests are in the depths of *Sheol*.
Prov. 21:16 A man who wanders from the way of understanding will rest in the assembly of the *dead* [*rephaim*].
Isaiah 14:9 *Sheol* from beneath is excited over you to meet you when you come; it arouses for you the *spirits of the dead*, all the leaders of the earth; it raises all the kings of the nations from their thrones.
Isa. 26:14 The dead [of our other masters] will not live, the *departed spirits* will not rise; therefore Thou hast punished and destroyed them, and Thou hast wiped out all remembrance of them.
Isa. 26:19 Your dead [of your nation] will live; their corpses will rise. You who lie in the dust, awake and shout for joy, for your dew is as the dew of the dawn, and the earth will give birth to the *departed spirits*.

Like *Sheol* and *Abaddon*, *rephaim* (Strong's #7496) is another word that remains unrevealed in many versions. It only occurs in the eight texts quoted. The KJV usually translates it as "the dead" and the RSV prefers "shades." The NIV does, however, read "spirits of the departed" and "departed spirits" in Isaiah 14:9 and 26:14 respectively. *Brown-Driver-Briggs Hebrew Lexicon* calls the *rephaim* "ghosts of the dead," "shades" and "spirits."

The *rephaim* are not dead bodies in a tomb. Job 26:5 says they "tremble." Proverbs 21:16 mentions the "assembly," or "congregation of departed spirits." In Isaiah 14:9, *Sheol* is excited and arouses the "spirits of the dead."

Isaiah 26:19 is the most interesting *rephaim* text. First it says that the "dead" [*mut:* 4191] will live and "their" "dead bodies" or "corpses" [*nebelah:* 5038] will rise. Secondly it says that the "departed spirits," or *rephaim* will awake and shout. By defining *Sheol* as the place of both souls and bodies, this passage makes sense. None of the *rephaim* texts remotely suggest that they are either unconscious or non-existent.

14. *SHEOL* AND NECROMANCY

Lev. 19:26 You shall not eat {anything} with the blood, nor practice divination or soothsaying.
Lev. 19:31 Do not turn to mediums or spiritists; do not seek them out to be defiled by them. I am the LORD your God.
Lev. 20:6 As for the person who turns to mediums and to spiritists, to play the harlot after them, I will also set My face against that person and will cut him off from among his people.
Deut. 18:10 There shall not be found among you anyone who makes his son or his daughter pass through the fire, one who uses divination, one who practices witchcraft, or one who interprets omens, or a sorcerer.
1 Chron. 10:13, 14 So Saul died for his trespass which he committed against the LORD, because of the word of the LORD which he did not keep; and also because he asked counsel of a medium, making inquiry {of it} and did not inquire of the LORD. Therefore He killed him, and turned the kingdom to David the son of Jesse. [See 1 Samuel 28.]
Isa. 8:19 And when they say to you, "Consult the mediums and the spiritists who whisper and mutter," should not a people consult their God? {Should they} {consult} the dead on behalf of the living?
Isa. 29:4 Then you shall be brought low; from the earth you shall speak, and from the dust {where} you are prostrate, your words {shall come.} Your voice shall also be like that of a spirit from the ground, and your speech shall whisper from the dust.

"Necromancy" was (and still is) an almost universal practice of consulting "familiar spirits" through seances using witches, wizards or spiritual mediums. "Familiar spirits" occurs sixteen times in the Old Testament, and its companion, "unclean spirits," occurs twenty-five times in the New Testament. Although the "spirits" (if actually conjured up) are fallen angels, or demons, unenlightened mankind believes that they are the departed souls of their loved ones. Our actions reveal our belief system. Our actions demonstrate that we reject the idea of an unconscious, or non-existent, soul at death.

Although the Old Testament teaches that souls are conscious in *Sheol*, Scripture also teaches that God does not normally allow communication between them and the living. King Saul attempted to seek counsel from one who consulted with the dead. Whether one believes that King Saul actually spoke with a familiar spirit, or Samuel himself, is irrelevant. Either conclusion is an admission that King Saul *believed* that some part of mankind survives death in another realm. The point is that the prohibitions against the practice prove that Old Testament man believed that consciousness survived death.

15. *SHEOL* AND *ABADDON*

Job 26:6 Naked is *Sheol* before Him, and *Abaddon* has no covering.
Job 28:22 *Abaddon* and death say, "With our ears we have heard a report of it."
Job 31:12 For it would be fire that consumes to *Abaddon*, and would uproot all my increase.
Prov. 15:11 *Sheol* and *Abaddon* {lie open} before the LORD, how much more the hearts of men!
Prov. 27:20 *Sheol* and *Abaddon* are never satisfied, nor are the eyes of man ever satisfied.

Sheol and *Abaddon* are paired in Job 26:6; Proverb 15:11, and 27:20. While the King James translates it as "destruction" all five times, the New King James, and the New International Version, often capitalize the word, thus indicating that it is either a place-name or personification. *Sheol* and *Abaddon*, like *Sheol* and death, appear to be inseparable. Since "destruction" is translated from twenty-four different words in the KJV, here again, the NAS's *Abaddon* is best left untranslated in order to avoid doctrinal error in God's Word.

Even more mysterious than *Sheol*, *Abaddon* may be the deepest part of *Sheol*, even deeper than the place for the departed wicked souls of mankind. God is constantly viewing two places—*Sheol* and *Abaddon* (Job 26:6). This would not be necessary if they only contained dead bodies!!! Both those in *Abaddon* and those in the death of *Sheol* consciously "hear" (Job 28:22). If God knows what is happening in *Sheol* and *Abaddon*, then He certainly knows what is happening in men's hearts (Prov. 15:11).

Matt. 25:41 Then He will also say to those on His left, "Depart from Me, accursed ones, into the eternal fire which has been prepared for the devil and his angels."

2 Pet. 2:4 For if God did not spare angels when they sinned, but cast them into Hell [*tartaros*] and committed them to pits of darkness [gloomy dungeons: NIV; gloomy caves: TLB], reserved for judgment.

Rev. 9:11 They have as king over them, the angel of the abyss; his name in Hebrew is *Abaddon*, and in the Greek he has the name *Apollyon*.

Rev. 20:1-3 And I saw an angel coming down from heaven, having the key of the abyss and a great chain in his hand. And he laid hold of the dragon, the serpent of old, who is the devil and Satan, and bound him for a thousand years, and threw him into the abyss, and shut {it} and sealed {it} over him, so that he should not deceive the nations any longer, until the thousand years were completed; after these things he must be released for a short time.

It is very likely that *Abaddon*, *Tartaros* and the "bottomless pit" are identical. *Abaddon*'s description also fits the "pit" of deepest *Sheol*. *Abaddon* may be the same place where some of the fallen angels are kept and thus corresponds to *Tartaros*. In Revelation 9:11, *Abaddon* is the angel of the abyss, or bottomless pit, thus connecting *Abaddon* with the pit. Since Satan, "Death and *Hades* (or *Sheol)*" will all be cast into "the lake of fire" (Rev. 20:10, 14), one may conclude that *Abaddon* and its inhabitants will meet the same fate as the wicked in *Sheol*.

16. *SHEOL*: JESUS AND PSALM 16:10

Ps. 16:10 For Thou wilt not abandon my soul to *Sheol*; neither wilt Thou allow Thy Holy One to undergo decay [*qeburah*: pit, corruption].

Acts 2:27 Because Thou wilt not abandon my soul to *Hades*, nor allow Thy Holy One to undergo decay [corruption].

Acts 2:31 he looked ahead and spoke of the resurrection of the Christ, that He was neither abandoned to *Hades*, nor did His flesh suffer decay.

Eph. 4:9 (Now this {expression,} "He ascended," what does it mean except that He also had descended into the lower parts of the earth?

1 Pet. 3:18, 19 For Christ also died for sins once for all, {the} just for {the} unjust, in order that He might bring us to God, having been put to death in the flesh, but made alive in the spirit; in which also He went and made proclamation to the spirits {now} in prison.

Psalm 16:10 is quoted in Acts 2:27, 31; 13:35 and alluded to in Acts 13:34, 36, 37. It is applied to Jesus Christ.

One: The texts prove that the New Testament meaning of *Hades* and the Hebrew *Sheol* are interchangeable.

Two: The texts reveal that Jesus' "soul" [*psuche*] did not cease to exist at death.

Three: Jesus' "soul" went to *Sheol/Hades* at death. It did not cease to exist.

Four: Jesus' body, or flesh, did not see corruption or decay in the pit [*qeburah*]. Although "pit" includes all of the "death" concept, the words for "grave," "tomb," and "sepulcher" are not used here. The Greek word of "corruption" is *diaphthora* (Strong's 1312) and is defined as the bodily decay after death. The word occurs six times in the New Testament and always refers to Psalm 16:10.

Five: According to Ephesians 4:9, Jesus "descended into the lower parts of the earth." This is another clear connection between *Sheol* and *Hades*, and not to the grave. Jesus' grave, tomb, or sepulcher was a cave *above* ground (Mt. 27:61, 64, 66; 28:1). Although the Greek word for grave occurs forty times in the New Testament, it is clearly not the "lower parts of the earth" which has a distinctly *Sheol* or *Hades* implication.

The *Jamieson, Fausset and Brown Commentary* says, "[This is] not the place of torment; nor, on the other hand, merely the grave, which is not referred to until the next clause; but the unseen world of disembodied souls: the Hebrew *Sheol*, the Greek *Hades*." [Acts 2:27]

Barnes Notes says, "The language used here implies, of course, that what is here called the soul would be in the abode to which the name Hell [*Sheol*] is given, but "how long" it would be there is not intimated. The thought simply is, that it would not be "left" there; it would not be suffered to "remain" there." [Acts 2:27]

The *Keil & Delitzsch Commentary* says, "There is no passage of Scripture that so closely resembles this as 1 Thess. 5:23.... David here expresses as a confident expectation; for 'ap (Heb. 639)] implies that he also hopes for his body that which he hopes for his spirit-life centered in the heart, and for his soul raised to dignity both by the work of creation and of grace." [Acts 2:27]

Luke 16:22, 23, 26 Now it came about that the poor man died and he was carried away by the angels to Abraham's bosom; and the rich man also died and was buried. And in *Hades* he lifted up his eyes, being in torment, and saw Abraham far away, and Lazarus in his bosom.... "And besides all this, between us and you there is a great chasm fixed, in order that those who wish to come over from here to you may not be able, and {that} none may cross over from there to us."

Luke 23:43 And He said to him, "Truly I say to you, today you shall be with Me in Paradise."

2 Cor. 12:4 [He] was caught up into Paradise, and heard inexpressible words, which a man is not permitted to speak.

Rev. 2:7 He who has an ear, let him hear what the Spirit says to the churches. To him who overcomes, I will grant to eat of the tree of life, which is in the Paradise of God.

Before the resurrection of Christ, "Paradise" is first seen corresponding to the upper division of *Sheol/Hades*, the habitation of the righteous souls. In Luke 16:19-31 Lazarus is conscious and at rest with Abraham and the rich man is conscious and in torment in the lower region of *Hades*. Jesus promised the dying thief on the cross, "Today you shall be with Me in Paradise." There is a great gulf separating the two regions.

After Christ's resurrection, "Paradise" seems to have been transferred to heaven. When did the change occur? At the time of Christ's crucifixion, Paradise, or upper *Sheol*, was still part of *Hades*. Jesus did not "ascend" that day, but "descended" (John 20:17)! Ephesians 4:8, 9 states that "When he [Christ] ascended up on high, he led captivity captive," because He had "descended first into the lower parts of the earth." Years later, the Apostle Paul described "Paradise" as being "in the third heaven" (2 Cor. 12:2-4). Even later, the Apostle John on Patmos also placed Paradise in heaven (Rev. 2:7). The change of Paradise from *Sheol/Hades* into Heaven must have occurred between Christ's resurrection and ascension. This change may also explain the events of Matthew 27:52, 53 as "firstfruits" to God. Compare also Colossians 2:15, First Corinthians 15:20-23, and possibly First Peter 3:18-22. The souls of the departed righteous had not ceased to exist and lost consciousness. David knew that God would not leave the righteous in *Sheol* (Ps. 16:10 and especially 49:15).

Those who believe that souls cease to exist at death and await re-creation along with the resurrected body must ask themselves, "Where did Jesus' soul go when He died? Did Jesus the God-man cease to exist from Friday evening until Sunday morning? Was His "soul" "nothing-ness," or was His "soul" a "something" which continued to exist?"

17. *SHEOL* AND THE JUDGMENT

Job 14:10 But man dies and lies prostrate. Man expires, and where is he?

Job pondered the question that we are still trying to answer many centuries later. The NAS says "man expires," the KJV says "gives up the ghost," and the NIV and RSV say "breathes his last." The Today's Living Bible reads "But when a man dies and is buried, where does his spirit go?"

Job 10:11 {As} water evaporates from the sea, and a river becomes parched and dried up,
Job 10:12 So man lies down and does not rise. Until the heavens be no more, He will not awake nor be aroused out of his sleep.
Job 10:13 Oh that Thou wouldst hide me in *Sheol*, that Thou wouldst conceal me until Thy wrath returns {to Thee,} that Thou wouldst set a limit for me and remember me!

Job 10:14 If a man dies, will he live {again?} All the days of my struggle I will wait, until my change comes.
Job 10:15 Thou wilt call, and I will answer Thee; Thou wilt long for the work of Thy hands.

When the body dies, where does the soul go? Job asked God to "hide me in *Sheol*" until His wrath is finished and wait "until my change comes" when God calls. This is not God's statement of the facts of death; it is Job's hope.

Isa. 28:15 Because you have said, "We have made a covenant with death, and with *Sheol* we have made a pact. The overwhelming scourge will not reach us when it passes by, for we have made falsehood our refuge and we have concealed ourselves with deception.
Isa. 28:16 Therefore thus says the Lord GOD, "Behold, I am laying in Zion a stone, a tested stone, a costly cornerstone {for} the foundation, firmly placed. He who believes {in it} will not be disturbed.
Isa. 28:17 And I will make justice the measuring line, and righteousness the level; then hail shall sweep away the refuge of lies, and the waters shall overflow the secret place.
Isa. 28:18 And your covenant with death shall be canceled, and your pact with *Sheol* shall not stand; when the overwhelming scourge passes through, then you become its trampling {place.}
Hosea 13:14 Shall I ransom them from the power of *Sheol*? Shall I redeem them from death? O death, where are your thorns? O *Sheol,* where is your sting? Compassion will be hidden from My sight.

One's pre-conceived view of the judgment influences what one believes happens to the soul at death. Note the two views presented below.

Nelson's Bible Dictionary: "Judgment": "The final judgment will be comprehensive in scope; it will include all people and nations from the beginning of the world to the end of history, as well as fallen angels. Those who trust in the Lord, repent of sin, and walk in His ways will not be condemned but will enter into eternal life. The purpose of the final judgment is the glory of God through the salvation of the ELECT and the condemnation of the ungodly."

Nelson's view: (1) fits the idea of "soul-sleep" or "soul non-existence" at death; (2) it makes *Sheol* an unconscious grave for the body only; (3) it also fits the view that God has not yet decided who will be finally saved before the judgment; (4) it implies that the believer only has forgiveness of past sins at the moment of justification, because future sins can cause him to fall from grace. (5) Therefore those in *Sheol* have not been pre-determined by God to be either righteous or wicked before the judgment.

The New Unger's Bible Dictionary: "Intermediate State": "From what is revealed in the Scriptures it may reasonably be concluded (a) that the intermediate state is not for the wicked that of their final misery, nor for the righteous that of their completed and final blessedness. They await the resurrection and the judgment of the great day. (b) The state of those "who die in the Lord" is, even for this period, pronounced "blessed." It is so, for the reason that though they wait for the final consummation, they are "with Christ."

The New Unger's Bible Dictionary: Judgment Seat of Christ": 2 Cor. 5:10 "The manifestation of the believer's works is in question in this judgment. It is most emphatically not a judgment of the believer's sins. These have been fully atoned for in the vicarious and substitutionary death of Christ, and remembered no more. It is quite necessary, however, that the service of every child of God be definitely scrutinized and evaluated (Matt. 12:36; Rom. 14:10; Gal. 6:7; Eph. 6:8; Col. 3:24-25). As a result of this judgment of the believer's works, there will be reward or loss of reward. *In any event, the truly born-again believer will be saved* (1 Cor. 3:11-15). The judgment seat, literally *bema*, evidently is set up in heaven previous to Christ's glorious second advent to establish His earth rule in the millennial kingdom. The out-taking of the church must first be fulfilled. The Judgment Seat of Christ is necessary for the appointment of places of rulership and authority with Christ in His role of 'King of kings and Lord of lords' at His revelation in power and glory."

Unger's view: (1) fits the idea that the souls continue in conscious existence after death either in *Sheol/Hades* or Heaven; (2) it separates *Sheol* into separate chambers for bodies, the souls of the righteous and the souls of the wicked; (3) it fits the view that God already knows who will be eternally saved before the judgment; (4) it holds that the believer is free from the condemnation of even his future sins at the moment of justification and can only fall from fellowship, but not from relationship with God. (6) Therefore, the righteous in *Sheol*, do not face a judgment of condemnation because they have already been given the judgment sentence of eternal life before death.

Unger's view holds that there are two future key judgments after death. First, at the Judgment Seat of Christ, the righteous will be judged and their faithfulness of service will determine, not salvation, but the degrees of their rewards. Second, at the Great White Throne Judgment, the wicked will be judged, *not to determine salvation,* but to determine the degrees of punishment they will receive in *Gehenna*, the lake of fire. However, there are many other views which are accepted and are between these two opposites.

The "soul-sleep" (more accurate "annihilationist") position rests primarily on a pre-supposition that the "soul" does not exist separate from the body and that there is no consciousness after death. A secondary pre-supposition equates *Sheol* with "the grave." Since it has become very clear that *Sheol* is never solely the grave, the "soul-sleep" position must be abandoned.

Then what does happen at death? That the "soul becomes non-existent at death" position is simply unscriptural. This can only be used as an explanation of a handful of the *Sheol* texts. It ignores the definition of *Sheol*, the location of *Sheol*, and the conscious status of souls in *Sheol*.

The view that souls enter a very active full reward or punishment immediately at death is also far from adequate. First, if one places the Bema, or Judgment Seat of Christ, in the future, then one implies that Christ has not yet determined the "degrees" of reward for the saints whose souls are already with God in heaven. Likewise, if the Great White Throne Judgment will decide the "degrees" of punishment for the wicked, then they must not already be suffering to their full extent in *Hades*.

In other words, the joy of souls in the presence of God without their immortal bodies must be *less than* the joy experienced after the Bema and after the time when they will receive their immortal bodies. Likewise, the suffering of the wicked in *Hades* must be *less than* when they receive varying degrees of punishment and are cast into the lake of fire.

18. AFTER-LIFE JUDGMENT

The following is this author's suggested solution. It accounts for the *Sheol* texts and the status of souls both before and after death.

Eccl. 12:14 For God shall bring every work into judgment, with every secret thing, whether it be good, or whether it be evil.

One: After-death "judgments," whether the "Judgment Seat of Christ" for the righteous or the "Great White Throne Judgment" for the wicked, do not determine whether or nor one is "righteous" or "unrighteous"! Judgment is the time when God "evens things out." The wicked who have prospered will suffer loss. The righteous who have suffered will be blessed. Only **degrees** of reward or punishment are determined in the after-death judgments.

Heb. 9:26 Otherwise, He would have needed to suffer often since the foundation of the world; but now once at the consummation of the ages He has been manifested to put away sin by the sacrifice of Himself.
Heb. 9:27 And inasmuch as it is appointed for men to die once and after this {comes} judgment,
Heb. 9:28 so Christ also, having been offered once to bear the sins of many, shall appear a second time for salvation without {reference to} sin, to those who eagerly await Him.

Two: Although the declaration in Hebrews 9:27 that "it is appointed for men to die once and after this {comes} judgment" is used by many to prove that God will not determine anybody's salvation until after death, it actually does not say, or mean, that at all.

Verse 26 has just stated that Christ died once for all time for all sins. At Calvary he brought together "all of the ends" (Greek: *sun-te-lei-a*) of all ages and paid one sacrifice for all sin (past, present, and future). All of the guilt and condemnation of judgment for all sins fell on Christ when he offered himself a perfect sacrifice (Rom. 5:18, 19; Heb. 7:27; 9:12; 10:10; 1 Jn. 2:2).

The key word in Hebrews 9:26-28 is "once," not "judgment." Christ died "once" for all sin (verse 26); man is appointed to die "once" for his sins (verse 27); Christ's sacrifice, having been offered "once," is sufficient to guarantee salvation to believers (verse 28). It is linguistically and theologically improper to separate verse 27 from verses 26 and 28. Verse 27 begins with "and inasmuch as…" and verse 28 continues the thought with "so also…." Those who "eagerly await Him" have already had Christ's judgment imputed, or placed into their account. Those who have accepted Christ do not face a judgment of condemnation but look forward to His appearing "a second time for salvation," for the final redemption of the body (Jn. 5:24; Rom. 8:1, 14-23; 2 Cor. 5:21).

Three: God is omniscient, that is, He knows all things. God does not require an after-death judgment to determine who shall be saved (Hebrews 4:13; 1 John 3:20; Isa. 46:10). Revelation 6:9 describes the righteous as already under the altar—God recognizes them as His own. In 9:4 and 14:1 God knows who have His seal, or name.

Four: The names of the redeemed are written in the book of life before the Great White Throne Judgment (Rev. 20:15).

Five: While yet alive, mankind's faith response to God's truth and calling determines his ultimate standing before God. Although man's destiny is to die and enter some kind of judgment before God, God's judgment on Christ at Calvary moved up the judgment which determines salvation to decisions made while alive (Heb. 9:27, 28).

John 3:18 He who believes in Him is not judged; he who does not believe has been judged already, because he has not believed in the name of the only begotten Son of God.
John 5:24 Truly, truly, I say to you, he who hears My word, and believes Him who sent Me, has eternal life, and—does not come into judgment, but has passed out of death into life.

Rom. 8:1 There is therefore now no condemnation for those who are in Christ Jesus.
[Note: "no condemnation" literally means "no contrary judgment sentence or verdict"]
Gal. 3:9 So then those who are of faith are blessed with Abraham, the believer.
Tit. 2:11 For the grace of God has appeared, bringing salvation to all men.

Six: The "righteous" are called "righteous" even BEFORE they enter *Sheol*. As one of the righteous, Job expected his part of *Sheol* to be a place of safety until God's wrath was past, until the end of time if necessary (Job 14:13; 17:13-16). Other righteous persons looked to *Sheol* without fear (Ps. 16:10; 49:15; 88:13; Prov. 15:24; 23:14).

Seven: In addition to the preceding texts, the following texts also teach that believers already possess God's judgment verdict of eternal life, access into His presence, adoption as His children, deliverance, an eternal guaranteed seal, forgiveness of all sin guilt, judgment-guilt immunity, justification, ownership by God, peace, perfection, presence as sinless in Christ, sanctification, a seating with him in heaven, and holy standing in His presence. Matt. 28:20; John 3:16; 14:16, 27; Rom. 3:24; 4:3; 5:1, 2; 8:15, 33; 1 Cor. 1:30; 6:19, 20; Eph. 1:7, 13; 2:8; 3:12; 4:30; Phil. 4:7; Col. 1:13; 2:13; 3:1, 3; Titus 3:5; Heb. 9:26; 10:14, 19, 22.

Eight: The souls of the righteous are already safe and secure at peace in the custody of God. This was upper *Sheol*, or upper *Hades*, and is now called "Paradise" in the presence of God. Although their ultimate salvation is secure, and they are in God's presence, their bodies have not been resurrected and they have not been "judged" to determine the "degrees" of their final reward. Their present reward is much more than an unconscious sleep, but less than with the resurrected body (Rom. 8:14-23).

Nine: The "wicked" are also "wicked" BEFORE they enter *Sheol* and judgment (Job 21:13, 29, 30; Numb. 16:30; Ps. 9:17; 31:17; 49:14; 55:15; Prov. 5:5; 7:27; 9:16; Isa. 5:14; 14:9-15; Ezek. 31:15-17). They are designated as such before death. Most of the book of Revelation describes God's wrath falling on them before the judgment *because* they were *already* determined to be wicked (Rev. 6:17; 8:4; 11:18; 12:12; 14:8, 10, 19; 15:1, 7; 16:1, 19; 18:3; 19:15). Therefore the Great White Throne Judgment does not determine whether or not the wicked are guilty. This final Judgment demonstrates to the entire creation that God's judgments are "true and righteous" because the wicked steadfastly continued to "blaspheme" God and refused to repent (Rev. 16:7, 11).

Ten: The souls of the wicked are still in the lower regions of *Sheol*, or *Hades*, expelled from the presence of God, but not His sight. Their ultimate damnation was decided when they rejected God while alive. However, their bodies have not been resurrected and they have not yet been "judged" to determine the "degrees" of their final punishment in the lake of fire, or *Gehenna*. Although they are already suffering some kind of punishment for rejecting God, their current consciousness is also more than sleep, but less than their full punishment.

Eleven: The Great White Throne Judgment will totally, finally, and eternally separate the wicked from the righteous and, especially, from God. Whatever punishment is received in lower *Sheol*, or *Hades*, will be infinitely greater in the "lake of fire."

Twelve: Due to the nature of progressive revelation, one should not expect to find a complete understanding of what happens at death in the Old Testament. Even Job admitted that he had declared wonderful things that he did not understand (42:3).

19. CONCLUDING REMARKS

Sheol is a "place" and not a "state of mind" or non-existence. The inspired Bible writers used terminology such as "going down to *Sheol*," "into *Sheol*," "lowest *Sheol*," "deeper than *Sheol*," " *Sheol* is my house," "gates of *Sheol*" and many other physical terms to describe *Sheol*. They give no evidence that it simply means a total cessation of existence at death. God unleashes his anger against the wicked in *Sheol* even before the judgment of the last day.

Man's vocabulary, especially his slang, reveals beliefs that his society has long accepted. When we hear phrases such as "hot as Hell," "tired as Hell," "go to Hell," "lowdown as Hell," "vicious as Hell," "scared as Hell," "mean as Hell," and "crazy as Hell," exactly what do we mean? We would not substitute the words "grave" or "tomb" because we know the difference between Hell and the grave. Our society has accepted Hell as a concept for comparing reality; otherwise the term and phrases which employ it are meaningless.

Old Testament man was no different. Even more so than us, because God inspired Bible writers to deliberately choose *Sheol* because of its specific inclusion beyond the grave to the place of the soul. *Sheol* is the name of the multi-chambered place where all souls and bodies went prior to the resurrection of Christ. The word "soul" is most often connected to *Sheol* and the "grave" is that part of *Sheol* where the bodies reside. Both souls and bodies are in the pit of death.

Just as *Sheol* or Hell are never translated *from* the common Hebrew words for "grave," neither should *Sheol* be translated as "grave." First, translating *Sheol* as "grave" diminishes its all-inclusive meaning and assigns it to a mere six-foot deep hole in the earth. Second, translating *Sheol* as "grave" robs it of its meaning as the place-name where both souls and bodies reside after death. Third, translating *Sheol* as "grave" breaks its vital connection with the "soul."

It is also incorrect to translate *Sheol* as Hell. For many, this incorrectly makes it identical to *Gehenna*, or the "lake of fire" instead of merely *Hades*. Since Jesus Himself distinguished between *Hades* and *Gehenna*, it is difficult to understand why so many reference books also equate these two terms. Just as our language would not permit us to use Hell when we meant the grave, Bible writers would not use *Hades* when they meant *Gehenna*.

In order for the truth of God's Word to make us free, we must be allowed to grasp that truth in any reputable translation. Confusion should never be associated with God's Word. The highest integrity should be applied to translations of the greatest book ever written, The Holy Bible!

SHEOL TEXTS IN THE OLD TESTAMENT

Genesis 37:35; 42:38; 44:29,31; Numbers 16:30,33; Deuteronomy 32:22; 1st Samuel 2:6; 2nd Samuel 22:6; 1st Kings 2:6,9; Job 7:9; 11:8; 14:13; 17:13,16; 21:13; 24:19; 26:6; Psalm 6:5; 9:17; 16:10; 18:5; 30:3; 31:17; 49:14,15; 55:15; 86:13; 88:3; 89:48; 116:3; 139:8; 141:7; Proverb 1:12; 5:5; 7:27; 9:18; 15:11,24; 23:14; 27:20; 30:16; Ecclesiastes 9:10; Song of Solomon 8:6; Isaiah 5:14; 14:9,11,15; 28:15,18; 38:10,18; 57:9; Ezekiel 31:15,16,17; 32:21,27; Hosea 13:14,14; Amos 9:2; Jonah 2:2; Habakkuk 2:5

64 *SHEOL* TEXTS IN THE OLD TESTAMENT (Strong's 7585)

	KJV	NKJV	NIV	NAS/RSV
				WHERE TEXTS DIFFER FROM KJV
Genesis 37:35	grave	.	.	*Sheol*
Genesis 42:38	grave	.	.	*Sheol*
Genesis 44:29	grave	.	.	*Sheol*
Genesis 44:31	grave	.	.	*Sheol*
Numbers 16:30	pit	.	grave	*Sheol*
Numbers 16:33	pit	.	grave	*Sheol*
Deu 32:22	lowest Hell	.	realm of death below	lowest *Sheol*/depths of *Sheol*
1st Sam 2:6	grave	.	.	*Sheol*
2nd Sam 22:6	Hell	*Sheol*	grave	*Sheol*
1st Kings 2:6	grave	.	.	*Sheol*
1st Kings 2:9	grave	.	.	*Sheol*
Job 7:9	grave	.	.	*Sheol*
Job 11:8	Hell	*Sheol*	grave	*Sheol*
Job 14:13	grave	.	.	*Sheol*
Job 17:13	grave	.	.	*Sheol*
Job 17:16	pit	*Sheol*	death	*Sheol*
Job 21:13	grave	.	.	*Sheol*

Job 24:19	grave	.	.	*Sheol*
Job 26:6	Hell	*Sheol*	death	*Sheol*
Psalm 6:5	grave	.	.	*Sheol*
Psalm 9:17	Hell	.	grave	*Sheol*
Psalm 16:10	Hell	*Sheol*	grave	*Sheol*
Psalm 18:5	Hell	*Sheol*	grave	*Sheol*
Psalm 30:3	grave	.	.	*Sheol*
Psalm 31:17	grave	.	.	*Sheol*
Psalm 49:14(2)	grave	.	.	*Sheol*
Psalm 49:15	grave	.	.	*Sheol*
Psalm 55:15	Hell	.	grave	*Sheol*
Psalm 86:13	Hell	*Sheol*	grave	*Sheol*
Psalm 88:3	grave	.	.	*Sheol*
Psalm 89:48	grave	.	.	*Sheol*
Psalm 116:3	Hell	*Sheol*	grave	*Sheol*
Psalm 139:8	Hell	.	depths	*Sheol*
Psalm 141:7	grave	.	.	*Sheol*
Proverb 1:12	grave	*Sheol*	.	*Sheol*
Proverb 5:5	Hell	.	grave	*Sheol*
Proverb 7:27	Hell	.	grave	*Sheol*
Proverb 9:18	Hell	.	grave	*Sheol*
Proverb 15:11	Hell	.	death	*Sheol*
Proverb 15:24	Hell	.	grave	*Sheol*
Proverb 23:14	Hell	.	death	*Sheol*
Proverb 27:20	Hell	.	death	*Sheol*
Proverb 30:16	grave	.	.	*Sheol*
Eccl 9:10	grave	.	.	*Sheol*
Song 8:6	grave	.	.	*Sheol*
Isaiah 5:14	Hell	*Sheol*	grave	*Sheol*
Isaiah 14:9	Hell	.	grave	*Sheol*
Isaiah 14:11	grave	*Sheol*	.	*Sheol*
Isaiah 14:15	Hell	*Sheol*	grave	*Sheol*
Isaiah 28:15	Hell	*Sheol*	grave	*Sheol*
Isaiah 28:18	Hell	*Sheol*	grave	*Sheol*
Isaiah 38:10	grave	*Sheol*	death	*Sheol*
Isaiah 38:18	grave	*Sheol*	.	*Sheol*
Isaiah 57:9	Hell	*Sheol*	grave	*Sheol*
Ezekiel 31:15	grave	Hell	grave	*Sheol*
Ezekiel 31:16	Hell	.	grave	*Sheol*
Ezekiel 31:17	Hell	.	grave	*Sheol*

Ezekiel 32:21	Hell	.	grave	*Sheol*
Ezekiel 32:27	Hell	.	grave	*Sheol*
Hosea 13:14	grave	.	.	*Sheol*
Amos 9:2	Hell	.	grave	*Sheol*
Jonah 2:2	Hell	*Sheol*	grave	*Sheol*
Habakkuk 2:5	Hell	.	grave	*Sheol*

APPENDIX 2

Hades AND THE SOUL

This is a continuation of the article on Old Testament *Sheol*. From the previous study it is clear that the Old Testament Hebrew word, *Sheol*, is equivalent to the New Testament Greek, *Hades*. These are all-inclusive terms for "death," or the "realm of the dead." While they include the grave, in strong disagreement with SDA theology, they are by no means exclusive terms for the grave. *Sheol/Hades* also includes the abode of conscious souls, or spirits, of the dead.

Seventh-Day Adventists teach that, at death that which returns to God is only the breath of life, and not a conscious eternal part of man. They reject the idea that some part of mankind is inherently immortal and can continue a conscious existence outside of the body at the moment of death. Like Jehovah's Witnesses, SDAs teach that *Hades* is only the "grave" for the body and all conscious existence ceases at death until recreation at the resurrection.

Since there are scores of very good books in circulation which adequately refute the SDA theology of conditional immortality, I will not repeat most of those arguments. In conjunction with my chapter on Old Testament *Sheol*, I will limit my discussion to the use of Hell in the New Testament.

It is the purpose of this study to demonstrate that *Hades* is not exclusively the same as the "grave" or "tomb," and that all "souls" and bodies went to *Hades* before Calvary. It will also be demonstrated that inspired writers deliberately chose *Hades* instead of "sepulcher" in order to teach that conscious existence survives death and the grave before the resurrection of the body.

It is unfortunate that the various Bible versions give so many different meanings to the same Greek words. Only the *New American Standard* is consistent. For example, in the *King James Version* of the New Testament, the English word "Hell" occurs 33 times from 3 different Greek words: *Gehenna* (22 times), *Hades* (10 times), and *Tartaros* (1 time). The RSV and NASV, plus margin notes in many King James' Versions, distinguish between these three words. *Gehenna* is the "lake of fire," into which Death and *Hades* are cast in Revelation 20:14. Although *Sheol* is *Hades*, for some unknown reason, the KJV often incorrectly translates *Sheol* as "grave," but only translates Hades as "grave" once.

Like the previous study of *Sheol* in the Old Testament, the following information provides the Greek words used and available for expressing truth in the New Testament:

One: *Thanatos* (Strong's 2288), in the King James, is translated **"death"** 120 times and "grave" once in Ist Cor. 15:56.

Two: *Mneimion* (Strong's 3419) is derived from "memory" and is a visible remembrance, memorial, or monument. It occurs 41 times: as **"sepulcher"** 29 times, **"grave"** 8 times and **"tomb"** 4 times.

Three: *Gehenna* (Strong's 1067) is **"Hell"** of the "lake of fire" and occurs 22 times as "Hell." Except for James 3:6, only Jesus used the word. It is the Hebrew word for "valley of Hinnon" transliterated into Greek.

Four: *Hades* (Strong's 86) occurs 10 times, and is always **"Hell"** in the KJV. Many versions clarify by using *Hades* instead of "Hell."

Five: *Abussos* (Strong's #12) is the English "abyss." It occurs 9 times: **"bottomless pit"** 7 times and "deep" twice.

Six: *Phrear* (Strong's 5421) occurs 7 times: **"pit"** 5 times and "well" twice.

Seven: *Bothunos* (Strong's 999) occurs 3 times: **"ditch"** twice and "pit" once.

Eight: *Tartaros* (Strong's 5020) occurs once in 2 Peter 2:4.

What is *Hades*? While the KJV translated *Sheol* as "grave" in 31 of its 64 O. T. occurrences, the KJV only translated *Hades* as "grave" once in its 11 N. T. occurrences—yet *Sheol* and *Hades* are the same in Acts 2:27 and 2:31.

However, like *Sheol*, *Hades* is neither the "grave" nor the "lake of fire." **The most fundamental error of those who teach conditional immortality is their mistranslation of *Hades* as "grave."**

Mark 12:26 And as touching the dead, that they rise: have you not read in the book of Moses, how in the bush God spoke to him, saying, I am the God of Abraham, and the God of Isaac, and the God of Jacob?
Mark 12:27 *He is not the God of the dead,* but the God of the living: you therefore do greatly err.

Most Jews who heard Christ's sermons believed that, at death, their spirits either went to Eden, to the throne of God, or into Abraham's bosom (*Matthew Henry Commentary*, Luke 16). Jesus' statements in Mark 12: 26, 27 went beyond the resurrection to the continued consciousness of the spirit (see verses 18-27). When the Sadducee asked a mocking question about the resurrection, Jesus' answer implied that the Sadducee was also wrong about the nature of the immortal spirit. Not only did he "err" about the resurrection, but he "greatly erred" about death itself. Yahweh told

Moses "I am the God of Abraham, and the God of Isaac, and the God of Jacob." He did not say "I **was** their God and I will be their God again at the resurrection." Jesus' commentary on His own statement as Yahweh to Moses in Exodus 3:6, 14-16 was "**He is not the God of the dead, but the God of the living.**" Jesus did not say that God "will be" the "God of the living" after the resurrection. Instead, He said that God **is presently** the "God of the living" because the spirits of Abraham, Isaac and Jacob were still alive! God is the God of the "living" because there is no death of the immortal spirit.

The reality of conscious existence of the spirit expressed by the Greek word, *Hades,* merely continued the Hebrew understanding of *Sheol.* Just as we have seen that the Hebrew word, *Sheol,* had an upper area for the righteous and a lower region for the wicked, so did the Greek word, *Hades* in the New Testament before the resurrection of Christ.

Matt. 11:23 (Luke 10:15) And you, Capernaum, which is exalted unto heaven, shalt be brought down to Hell [*Hades*]; for if the mighty works, which have been done in you, had been done in Sodom, it would have remained until this day.

Jesus prophesied that Capernaum would "be brought down to **Hades** for rejecting the Gospel. If *Hades* were only the grave, then this statement would be meaningless because all die and go to the grave. Obviously, all those living in Capernaum in Jesus' time have long ago physically met death and physically been buried in the grave. Therefore, the meaning of *Hades* here must go beyond that of a mere grave at death. Capernaum still survives as a city today.

Therefore, since all die, **Jesus' promise would have been meaningless if He were merely saying that they would die and go to the grave!** Jesus used *Hades* instead of *mneimion* (grave) to teach that they would continue conscious punishment when they died, because they had rejected His gospel.

Matt. 16:18 And I say also to you, That you are Peter [*petros*: little rock], and upon this rock [*petra*; giant rock] I will build my church; and the gates of Hell [*Hades*] shall not prevail against it.

In this verse *Hades* is not the grave, but a kingdom, or city, with fortified "gates." Jesus was teaching that Satan's plots, schemes, and strategy to overthrow the church would fail. If the church is here portrayed attacking the gates of its enemy, it would prevail and retrieve the spirits of the saints from *Sheol/Hades* at the soon ascension of Christ (Eph. 4:8-10; 2 Cor. 12:1-4). On the other hand, if the enemy is portrayed here attacking believers, *Hades* would similarly be unable to retain or grasp the spirits of believers.

The phrase, "**gates of *Sheol*,**" occurs only once in the Old Testament, in Isaiah 38:10. While King Hezekiah declared in verse 18 that *Sheol* cannot praise thee," verse 19 explains that he meant the spirits in *Sheol* shall not praise you "in front of the living." "The living, the living, he shall praise thee, as I do this day, the father to the children shall make known thy truth." Therefore, the context of this statement does not teach that those in *Sheol* are unconscious, but that they cannot return to earth to praise God before the living (also Luke 16:26).

Again we must ask, if Jesus meant "grave" (*mneimion*) or "death" (*thanatos*), then, why did He not use those words instead of *Hades*? Neither did David believe that his body and spirit would eternally reside in their respective pars of *Sheol*: "But God will redeem my soul from the power of **the grave (*Sheol*),** for he shall receive me" (Ps. 49:15). Solomon also declared that the righteous would overcome *Sheol*: "The way of life is above to the wise, that he may depart from **Hell (*Sheol*)** beneath" (Prov. 15:24).

Luke 16:22 And it came to pass, that the beggar died, and was carried by the angels into Abraham's bosom: the rich man also died, and was buried;
Luke 16:23 And in Hell (*Hades*) he lifted up his eyes, being in torments, and saw Abraham afar off, and Lazarus in his bosom.
Luke 16:25 .. now he is comforted, and you are tormented.
Luke 16:26 And beside all this, between us and you there is a great gulf fixed: so that they which would pass from hence to you cannot; neither can they pass to us, that would come from thence.

Seventh-day Adventists and Jehovah's Witnesses teach that *Hades* is only the grave. They teach that Jesus' story of Lazarus and the rich man is only a parable and does not teach truth about conscious suffering in *Hades*.

In response to the "parable only" claim, first, this story is surrounded in Luke by other statements which are *not* called parables by Jesus (lost coin, 15:8-10; prodigal son, 15:11-32; unjust steward, 16:1-12; serving two masters, 16:13-18; *Hades*; forgiveness, 17:1-6; service, 17:7-10). Although Jesus' parables probably came from His own eye-witness accounts, the biblical evidence suggests that Jesus had shifted from parables to plain teaching. However, whether these are parables, or not, is irrelevant, because **Jesus used real incidents for illustrations as parables.** Since no parable actually names people, Jesus' audience might have actually known this Lazarus.

A second area of disagreement involves the use of the word, *Hades*. Greek religion and language had already been used in Israel for over 300 years when Jesus told this parable. ***Hades* was not the grave in the Greek language!** The Greek view of *Hades* was that of consciousness after death and a river of separation.

However, since Jesus' teachings were usually taken from everyday common knowledge, it is inconceivable to think that He would reach back into a pagan Greek understanding of *Hades* to teach any lesson! **Jesus used known, recognized, truth to illustrate further truth. He reached back beyond the Greek definition of *Hades* into the Old Testament concept of *Sheol*, or the realm of both dead bodies and conscious spirits.**

The rich man looked "up" from the lower part of *Hades* and saw Abraham and Lazarus "afar off" across a "great gulf" in the upper part of *Hades*. This corresponds to the Old Testament idea of *Sheol* which is much older than the Greek idea of *Hades*. In *Sheol* the wicked would have to look "up" from the "lowest part," the "recesses of the pit," the "lower parts of the earth," and the "depth of *Sheol*" (Deut. 32:22; Isa. 14:15; Eze. 32:24; Jonah 2:2).

"Abraham's bosom" and "paradise" are both ideas from the Hebrew *Talmud*. Before Christ's ascension, "Abraham's bosom" was located in the upper region of *Sheol*, corresponding to the "paradise" portion of *Hades*. Old Testament writers understood this to be a temporary place for conscious souls nearer the "gates," or entrance to *Sheol*. Compare Gen. 37:35; Ps. 49:15; 86:13; 139:8; 141:7; Prov. 15:24; Isa. 5:14; 38:10.

Jesus said that the rich man was BEING "in torments." Once again, **Jesus would not possibly use a lie to teach a truth; such was against His divine character. He could have, and did, illustrate the truth of this parable without resorting to a pagan Greek mythological lie.** Again, the Old Testament teaching of conscious torment in lower *Sheol* agrees with Jesus' teaching here. Compare Job 26:5; Psalm 116:3; Song of Solomon 8:6; Isaiah 14:9,10; Ezekiel 32:21, 31.

Since the events of Luke 16 correlate with the Old Testament teaching of *Sheol*, there is absolutely no reason to conclude that Jesus used the Greek mythological prototype of *Hades* to teach truth. The truth is that, after Christ's ascension, conscious existence survives death in the Heavenly Paradise for the souls of the righteous and in *Hades* for the wicked. Those souls in *Sheol/Hades* cannot return from there to earth to praise God (Isa. 38:18, 19).

Acts 2:24 Whom [Christ] God has raised up, having loosed the pains of death; because it was not possible that he should be held by it.
Acts 2:27 Because you will not leave my soul in Hell (*Hades*), neither will you allow your Holy One to see corruption.
Acts 2:31 He [David] seeing this before spoke of the resurrection of Christ, that his soul was not left in Hell (*Hades*), neither did his flesh see corruption.

Seventh-day Adventists teach that the "body" plus the "breath from God" produces a "living soul." They use Genesis 2:7 as if it were the only text in the entire Bible. This is fully discussed in many other books. Next, they reason, death reverses this: the "body" returns to dust and the "spirit," or life principle, returns to God and the **"soul" ceases to exist** until the resurrection. Although SDAs call this "soul sleep," they really mean "annihilation," because the soul ceases to exist at death.

However, Acts 2:27 quotes Psalm 16:10 and clearly teaches that the "soul" continues to exist after the body dies. At Christ's death, His Divine Immortal "soul" went to one part of *Hades* while His human body, or flesh, risked decay, or "corruption," in the grave section of *Sheol/Hades.*

Acts 2:27 Greek: soul, *psuche* (5590) was not left in Hell, *Hades* (86)
Ps. 16:10 Hebrew: soul, *nephesh* (5315) was not left in Hell, *Sheol* (7585)
Acts 2:27 KJV body "neither His flesh did see corruption"
Ps. 16:10 KJV body: "neither wilt Thou suffer thine Holy One to see corruption"

The Old Testament clearly teaches that, at death, the "soul" goes into *Sheol* (Psalm 16:10; 30:3; 49:15; 86:13; 88:3; 89:48; Prov 29:14). It does not cease to exist; neither does it go to the grave. *Sheol* is also called the deep "pit" (*bor:* 953) (Ps 30:3; 88:6; Prov. 28:17).

Contrary to the KJV and NIV translations, but in agreement with the NAS and RSV translations, *Qeber* (Strong's 6913), not *Sheol*, is the Hebrew word for "grave, "tomb," or "sepulcher" and is equivalent to the New Testament Greek *mneimion. Qeber* occurs 84 times; the "soul" is NEVER said to go there, only the body. Neither does the "soul" go to the shallow "pit" (*pachath:* 6354).

The Old Testament writers were divinely inspired and carefully chose the correct words to convey truth. While *Sheol/Hades* includes the entire realm of the dead, including the grave, it is proof of inspiration that the body always goes to the grave/memorial (*qeber/mneimion*) part of *Sheol/Hades* while the soul/spirit (*nephesh/psuche*) always deeper into *Sheol* before Christ's ascension.

Was Jesus Christ a different kind of man than we are in his humanity? Seventh-day Adventists build their argument of death on Genesis 2:7 and teach that man ceases to exist at death when the body dies and only the life-principle (not the immortal soul) returns to God. What about Jesus? Did Jesus cease to exist when His body died and His breath was exhaled? How do SDAs explain that? Where did the eternal omniscient omnipotent divine part of Jesus go between Friday evening and Sunday morning?

Gen. 3:24 So he drove out the man; and he placed at the east of the garden of Eden cherubim, and a flaming sword which turned every way, to keep the way of *the tree of life.*

Luke 23:43 And Jesus said to him, Verily I say to you, To day you shall be with me in *paradise.*

Ephesians 4:8-10 "..When he ascended up on high, he led captivity captive, and gave gifts to men. (Now that he ascended, what is it but that he also *descended first into the*

lower parts of the earth? He that descended is the same also that ascended up above all heavens, that he might fill all things).

2 Cor. 12:4 How that he was caught up into *paradise* and heard unspeakable words which it is not lawful for a man to utter.

Rev. 2:7 He that has an ear, let him hear what the Spirit says unto the churches. To him that overcomes will I give to eat of the *tree of life,* which is in the midst of the *paradise* of God.

In disagreement with SDA theology about death, the soul of Christ did not cease to exist while His body was in the tomb. The tree of life from Genesis 3:24 is seen in heavenly paradise in Revelation 2:7. This change of location may have occurred between the time of Jesus' parable in Luke 16 and Paul's vision in Second Corinthians 12:1-4. Many interpret Ephesians 4:8-10 as the explanation of when this change in location took place. Since it is unlikely that an above-ground sepulcher would be called a "lower part of the earth," Ephesians 4:9 must refer to the abode of the soul in the depths of *Sheol/Hades.* Once again the familiar Old Testament contrast between heaven being "far above all heavens" and *Sheol/Hades* extending far beneath the earth is clear. The abode of the body in the tomb is not discussed in these texts.

The point here is that Jesus' soul did not cease to exist at his death. While his body was in the tomb, some part of Jesus moved Paradise to heaven. SDAs cannot say that Jesus' soul survives death, but the souls of others do not.

Rev. 1:18 I am He that lives and was dead; and, behold, I am alive for evermore, Amen; and have the keys of Hell (*Hades*) and of death.

Revelation 6:8 And I looked, and behold a pale horse: and his name that sat on him was Death, and Hell (*Hades*) followed with him. And power was given unto them over the fourth part of the earth, to kill with the sword, and with hunger, and with death, and with the beasts of the earth.

Rev. 20:13-14 And the sea gave up the dead which were in it; and death and Hell (*Hades*) delivered up the dead which were in them: and they were judged every man according to their works. And death and Hell (*Hades*) were cast into the lake of fire. This is the second death.

Once again, from the list at the beginning of the article, *mneimion,* the Greek word for "grave," "tomb" and "sepulcher" occurs 41 times in the New Testament. Since the "grave" is only part of *Hades* and "death," the *New American Standard* correctly retains

Hades as *Hades* and does interpret it as the "grave." *Hades* and "death," like *Sheol* and the "pit," are all-inclusive terms which include both "graves" for the body and various lower regions for departed souls.

Although there is some kind of parallelism involved between Death and *Hades* in Revelation 1:18; 6:8 and 20:13-14, it is also obvious that some subtle differences are also implied in these three sets of texts. In 1:18 Christ has the "keys," plural, of places named *Hades* and Death." In 6:8 they are personifications: Death sits on a pale horse and *Hades* is following closely behind. In 20:13,14 Death and *Hades* are two different places. In order to be consistent with the Old Testament texts already studied, the sea gives up both the bodies and the souls of the dead deposited therein while the land gives up the bodies and souls deposited in Death and *Hades*. The souls of the wicked dead were consigned to conscious punishment in the deepest parts of the pit or the sea (Jonah 2:2-6; Eze. 32:24). Those cremated, burned at the stake and consumed by animals would similarly also be included, because of the second resurrection of the wicked (John 5:29; Rev. 20:1-5). A review of the Old Testament use of *Sheol* is necessary in order to understand these texts. When 20:14 says that Death and *Hades* were cast into *Gehenna*, the lake of fire, after judgment, it must include both the bodies and the souls found within Death and *Hades*. While the Apostle John, the possible inspired writer of Revelation used the common Greek word for "grave" and "sepulcher," *mneimion*, 16 times in the book of John, it does not occur even once in the Revelation. Therefore, since both Death and *Hades* include more than merely the "grave," the absence of *mneimion* in Revelation is a strong argument against the SDA belief that conscious souls do not continue in *Hades* after the death of the body.

SDAs counter this argument by teaching that the judgment in Revelation 20:13, 14 follows the end of their "Investigate Judgment" which began in 1844 and will end immediately before Christ returns to earth. Therefore, since nobody's eternal fate could have been sealed before 1844, no dead unbeliever is suffering yet. Also (they say), it makes no sense for those who had already been suffering in *Hades* to be raised, judged for the first time, and then cast again into *Gehenna*'s lake of fire.

Actually, the judgment that determines eternity fell on Christ at Calvary (Heb. 9:26, 27). The Gospel itself is a judgment message and those who reject it are judged already (John 3:16-19; 5:24). When a person believes the Gospel, the judgment, death and resurrection of Christ become the believer's. Therefore, the believer does not face a future judgment to determine guilt (Rom. 8:1; Heb. 9:28). By rejecting the Gospel, the unbeliever does not require another future judgment which will determine guilt or innocence (John 3:18, 19). The Great White Throne Judgment in Revelation 20 merely proves to all creation once-for-all that God is just and has always been just, even in respect to the suffering unbelievers in *Sheol/Hades*.

Russell Earl Kelly, Ph. D.   221

Rev. 14:10,11 The same shall drink of the wine of the wrath of God, which is poured out without mixture into the cup of his indignation; and he shall be tormented with fire and brimstone in the presence of the holy angels, and in the presence of the Lamb: And the smoke of their torment ascendeth up for ever and ever: and they have no rest day nor night, who worship the beast and his image, and whosoever receives the mark of his name.
Rev 14:12 Here is the patience of the saints: here are they that keep the commandments of God, and the faith of Jesus.

Rev 21:8 But the fearful, and unbelieving, and the abominable, and murderers, and whore-monger, and sorcerers, and idolaters, and all liars, shall have their part in the lake which burns with fire and brimstone: which is the second death.

Seventh-day Adventists get their marching orders from the three angels' messages of Revelation 14:1-12. They teach that the 144,000 of 14:1-15 are from their church, God's exhibit to the world that His Law can be perfectly obeyed. The three angels' messages describe their mission, and verse 12 is a summary description of themselves as Sabbath-keepers who have the prophetic guidance of Ellen G. White (compare with 19:10).

Therefore, common sense should tell us that SDAs would teach that unbelievers will suffer "for ever" "day and night" because of verses 10 and 11 located in the very heart of their own mission statement. Yet, amazingly, they actually teach that unbelievers will soon burn up after being cast into the lake of fire! It seems ironic for God to place the Bible's strongest description of continuing torment of the soul in verses 10 and 11.

Do unbelievers cease to exist when their non-immortal bodies are cast into the lake of fire—as SDAs teach happens at death? No, otherwise the present tense verbs of 14: 10, 11 and 21:8 are meaningless and the fire would soon burn out. Therefore, and this is important, that which is being punished must be the conscious souls, or spirits, of the unbelievers.

APPENDIX 3

JEWELRY, DRESS CODE AND DECEIT

Seventh-day Adventists in the United States are told not to wear jewelry. Their women should only wear dresses. They are not to drink caffeine or eat "unclean" foods. Although part of these rules stem from their interpretation of Scripture, most get their real strength from Ellen G. White quotations. It is not the "texts" that make it "plain," but Ellen G. White! A prolific writer on these subjects, she is much more forceful and clearer about not wearing jewelry and what not to eat than the Scriptures, and must be obeyed.

JEWELRY AND DRESS CODE

First Timothy 2:9 "In like manner also, that the women adorn themselves in modest apparel, with propriety and moderation, not with braided hair or gold or pearls or costly clothing (NKJ)." Although this key text only teaches moderation and reflects first century prohibitions, it is the favorite text used by SDAs to support clothing, hair and jewelry reform. For example, J. L. Shuler says concerning this verse, "We are to adorn ourselves in modest apparel, and not to adorn ourselves with gold or pearls as ornaments (*Helps to Bible Study*, 3CD, page 54). "The Scripture **rule** laid down in 1 Timothy 2:9 makes it plain that God's people are **not** to wear jewelry for the purpose of ornamenting their bodies" (ibid, 6CD, page 54). However, if the text meant "no jewelry," then it should also mean "no clothing"!

Genesis 3:21 is the account of God covering Adam and Eve with animal skins. Shuler concludes from these two verses, "Christian women should dress modestly. They should not appear in public with sleeveless dress, or dresses that are too short, or any other form of dress that does not properly cover the body" (ibid, 4CD, page 54).

Exodus 33:5,6 "Take off your ornaments, that I may know what to do to you." Shuler merely says, "God commanded His people to take off all their ornaments" (10CD, page 56). He completely ignores the context of these verses. Exodus 33:4 says, "And when the people heard this bad news, they mourned, and no one put on his ornaments." This is the aftermath of the golden calf incident which brought God's wrath. In deep mourning, many of the people removed their ornaments. Such removal was a common custom. In mourning, King Saul, in First Samuel 19:24 and Micah, in

Micah 1:8, stripped to nakedness. There is no indication that this was a permanent situation that continued when the mourning was over.

Exodus 35:22 says that the Israelites came "as many as had a willing heart, and brought earrings and nose rings, rings and necklaces, all jewelry of gold, that is, every man who made an offering of gold to the LORD." Shuler says, "These texts make it **plain** that God's people should **not** wear rings, earrings, necklaces, beads, or any other kind of jewelry **that serves only as** an ornament" (ibid,' 11CD, page 55). Again, the context says otherwise. Evidently, the mourning of 33:4-6 had ended and the people had resumed wearing their jewelry. God had accepted their repentance and replaced the broken Ten Commandments (34:1-35). The context of 35:22 is that of collecting material to build the sanctuary (35:1-35). These "sinful" ornaments were converted into God's dwelling place! They were a small part of free-will gifts. There was absolutely nothing said or implied that such ornament-wearing was sinful.

Judges 8:24 "Then Gideon said to them, "I would like to make a request of you, that each of you would give me the earrings from his plunder. For they had gold earrings, because they were Ishmaelites." Shuler says, "The Ishmaelites were distinguished as heathen people by the fact that they wore gold earrings" (ibid, 7CD, page 56). This simply is not the truth! All Semitic peoples, Ishmaelite and Israelite, men and women, then and now, wore jewelry! Wearing earrings does not brand the wearers as "heathen." Gideon knew that Ishmaelites were fond of wearing gold earrings and he wanted the gold. However, Gideon then turned the gold earrings into something even worse, as recorded in verse 27.

"We are to adopt the most healthful diet possible and abstain from the unclean foods identified in the Scriptures. Since alcoholic beverages, tobacco, and the irresponsible use of drugs and narcotics are harmful to our bodies, we are to abstain from them as well," Fundamental Belief #21, *Who Are The Seventh-day Adventists?*, John Seaman, 1997, pages 55,56.

To most of us, the preceding Seventh-day Adventist logic is somewhat ridiculous and unimportant. Even most Adventists ignore the prohibitions concerning short sleeves, women wearing pants, and cola drinks with caffeine. If the Adventists did not make this such an important issue, it would not have been included in this book.

Fundamental Belief #21 begins a sentence with "While recognizing cultural differences..." While married ministers and believers in the United States do not wear wedding rings, their counterparts in other countries do, sometimes because of the imposition of local laws and customs. This has caused some conflict within Seventh-day Adventism, since Ellen White is insistent about the jewelry.

SDAs have even changed their own often quoted "Thou shalt not wear jewelry" to "Thou shalt not—unless it is *'functional.'*" For example, the "forbidden" become acceptable if it is an expensive golden diamond-laden watch, which has been exchanged at weddings instead of rings. Once again, SDAs do not wear rings because Ellen G. White forbids it, not the Bible.

WHAT THE BIBLE SAYS ABOUT ADORNMENT

First Timothy 2:9 "In like manner also, that the women adorn themselves in modest apparel, with propriety [modesty] and moderation [discreetly], not with braided hair or gold or pearls or costly clothing." (NKJ)

First Peter 3:3,4 "Do not let your adornment be merely outward—arranging the hair, wearing gold, or putting on fine apparel—rather let it be the hidden person of the heart, with the incorruptible beauty of a gentle and quiet spirit, which is very precious in the sight of God." (NKJ)

First Timothy 2:9 and First Peter 3:3, 4 simply teach moderation, and not total abstinence. It is humorous that SDAs place such an exaggeration on First Timothy 2:9, while they are forced to downplay 3:10, 11, "Let a woman learn in silence with all submission. And I do not permit a woman to teach or to have authority over a man, but to be in silence" (NKJ). Just in case they missed it, Ellen White was a woman, leader, and keynote speaker at many SDA meetings. Yet they do not have women elders.

Genesis 24:22 "So it was, when the camels had finished drinking, that the man took a golden nose ring weighing half a shekel, and two bracelets for her wrists weighing ten shekels of gold (NKJ)." God's people have always possessed and worn jewelry. In Genesis 24:22, 30, 47, 53 Abraham gave Rebekah a "golden nose ring and two bracelets of gold" and other jewelry of silver and gold.

Exodus 32:2, 3 "And Aaron said to them, "Break off the golden earrings which are in the ears of your wives, your sons, and your daughters, and bring them to me. So all the people broke off the golden earrings which were in their ears, and brought them to Aaron (NKJ)." These texts prove conclusively that, even after the Ten Commandments had been received, and after the Old Covenant had been ratified, ALL of the Israelites, male and female, were *still wearing golden earrings*! God, through Moses, had not told them to remove those earrings. Neither were they described as symbols of pagan worship—such would not have been tolerated.

Isaiah 3:16-24 records God's promise to remove the Israelite women's jewelry because they were haughty and sinned with seductive eyes. "Therefore the Lord will strike with a scab the crown of the head of the daughters of Zion, and the LORD will uncover their secret parts (3:17)." *The context implies that they had been blessed with much jewelry and would be punished by its removal.*

The list of jewelry and other items is extensive: jingling anklets, scarves, crescents, pendants, bracelets, veils, headdresses, leg ornaments, headbands, perfume boxes, charms, rings, nose jewels, festal apparel, mantles, outer garments, purses, mirrors, fine linen, turbans, and robes (3:18-23). "And so it shall be: instead of a sweet smell there will be a stench; instead of a sash, a rope; instead of well-set hair, baldness; instead of a rich robe, a girding of sackcloth; and branding instead of beauty" (NKJ).

Isaiah 61:10 "I will greatly rejoice in the LORD, my soul shall be joyful in my God; for He has clothed me with the garments of salvation, he has covered me with the robe of righteousness, *as a bridegroom decks himself with ornaments, and as a bride adorns herself with her jewels* (NKJ)." Again, there is no implication here that the jewels were themselves sinful; instead they were symbols of blessing!

Jeremiah 2:32 "Can a virgin forget her *ornaments*, or a bride her attire? Yet My people have forgotten Me days without number." (NKJ)

Ezekiel 16 is an extremely interesting story when seen in the context of personal adornment. The parable of the good Samaritan is very similar to the original context from Ezekiel. God told Ezekiel to tell Jerusalem that they had been unclean and defiled when He found them (16:1-3). After describing Israel as a discarded newborn, He then washed and swaddled them (16:4-6). Israel became beautiful, God loved her and entered into a marriage covenant with her (16:7-8).

As God's bride, Ezekiel 16:9-44 is *an extremely detailed description of God's blessings in terms of adornment.* He washed and anointed Israel (16:9), and clothed her in fine linen and silk (16:10). "I adorned you with **ornaments**, put **bracelets** on your wrists, and a **chain** on your neck; and I put a **jewel in your nose, earrings** in your ears, and a beautiful **crown** on your head (16:11-12). "Thus you were adorned with gold and silver...You were exceedingly beautiful, and succeeded to royalty (16:13)." Your beauty "was *perfect through My splendor which I had bestowed on you* (16:14)."

Israel's sin was not the adornment itself which was actually a blessing from God, but trusting in her own beauty. "But you trusted in your own beauty, played the harlot because of your fame, and poured out your harlotry on everyone passing by who would have it (16:15)."

Israel took the blessing which God had given her and became a harlot. "You took some of your garments and adorned multicolored high places for yourself, and played the harlot on them. Such things should not happen. You have also taken *your beautiful jewelry from My gold and My silver, which I had given you*, and made for yourself male images and played the harlot with them (16:16-17)." Verses 18-34 detail the further degradation of God's bride, Israel.

"Now then" (16:35), God promised, "**because** your filthiness was poured out and your nakedness uncovered in your harlotry with your lovers, and with all your **abominable** idols, and **because** of the blood of your children which you gave to them (16:35), "I will judge you" (16:38-39). Your lovers will "strip you of your clothes, take your beautiful jewelry, and leave you naked and bare (16:39)." "Because you did not remember the days of your youth, but agitated Me with all these things, surely I will also recompense your deeds on your own head (16:44)."

Clearly, the Bible is not anti-adornment, or anti-jewelry. It is only anti-extravagance and anti-vanity, pride and self-centeredness. In ancient times, where money could not be invested as it is with us, precious stones and elaborate jewelry formed one of the safest and most convenient ways of preserving great wealth in small bulk—easy to transport and to conceal. Therefore, while SDAs teach that jewelry is sinful, the Bible teaches that *lack of jewelry signifies a lack of God's blessings.*

Jesus Christ Himself made numerous references to jewelry, but not in an "abstinence" sense. He called the kingdom of heaven "**one pearl of great price**" (Mt. 13:45-46). Many believe that the "**ten silver coins**" of Luke 15:8 were worn as jewelry, possibly as a marriage dowry. Matthew 6:29 "I say to you that even Solomon in all his glory was not arrayed [adorned in jewelry and fine clothes] like one of these." Throughout all eternity the saints will be surrounded by the most beautiful jewels that God has created (Revelation 21:11-21).

DECEITFUL EVANGELISM PRACTICES

When SDAs hold evangelistic meetings outside of their own churches, they try their very best to disguise their identity until AFTER they have preached a sermon on the Sabbath (which comes later in the crusade). They often describe their evangelists as "world travelers just back from Israel." Even when using their own churches (from personal experience) they tell visitors that they are only using the SDA church because it was available.

Waiting rooms in doctors offices and dentist offices often have the innocent-looking Bible story books by Arthur Maxwell which contain cards inside. Neither the cards nor the books identify themselves as Seventh-day Adventists. The books offered on the cards are usually the five Conflict of the Ages Series by Ellen G. White. When the cards are mailed, a person from the Home Health Education Service will knock at your door and try to sell you the heretical cult books of Ellen G. White. The sales person will not identify himself as a Seventh-day Adventist.

Even worse, SDAs are joining ministerial associations and their medical facilities are merging with non-SDA facilities. They endeavor to present themselves as normal conservative evangelical Christians who just happen to worship on Saturday. However, they dare not openly admit that their "second and third angel's messages" condemn all other churches as "false Babylon" who will be destroyed when Jesus returns because they are not worshiping on Saturday and do not adhere to the other "special truths" of Seventh-day Adventism.

978-0-595-36342-1
0-595-36342-3

.

Printed in the United States
121302LV00004B/85/A

9 780595 363421